P9-EGM-226

Hiking through History
Washington

HELP US KEEP THIS GUIDE UP TO DATE

Every effort has been made by the authors and editors to make this guide as accurate and useful as possible. However, many things can change after a guide is published—trails are rerouted, regulations change, techniques evolve, facilities come under new management, and so on.

We would appreciate hearing from you concerning your experiences with this guide and how you feel it could be improved and kept up to date. While we may not be able to respond to all comments and suggestions, we'll take them to heart, and we'll also make certain to share them with the authors. Please send your comments and suggestions to the following address:

Globe Pequot Press
Reader Response/Editorial Department
PO Box 480
Guilford, CT 06437

Or you may e-mail us at: editorial@GlobePequot.com

Thanks for your input, and happy trails!

Hiking through History
Washington

Exploring the Evergreen State's
Past by Trail

Nathan and Jeremy Barnes

FALCONGUIDES

GUILFORD, CONNECTICUT
HELENA, MONTANA
AN IMPRINT OF GLOBE PEQUOT PRESS

To buy books in quantity for corporate use
or incentives, call **(800) 962-0973**
or e-mail **premiums@GlobePequot.com.**

FALCONGUIDES®

Copyright © 2014 Morris Book Publishing, LLC

ALL RIGHTS RESERVED. No part of this book may be reproduced or transmitted in any form by any means, electronic or mechanical, including photocopying and recording, or by any information storage and retrieval system, except as may be expressly permitted in writing from the publisher. Requests for permission should be addressed to Globe Pequot Press, Attn: Rights and Permissions Department, PO Box 480, Guilford, CT 06437.

FalconGuides is an imprint of Globe Pequot Press.
Falcon, FalconGuides, and Outfit Your Mind are registered trademarks of Morris Book Publishing, LLC.

Photos by Nathan and Jeremy Barnes
Maps: Tim Kissel/Trailhead Graphics, Inc. © Morris Book Publishing, LLC
Text design: Sheryl P. Kober
Project editor: Julie Marsh
Layout: Sue Murray

Library of Congress Cataloging-in-Publication Data
Barnes, Nathan.
    Hiking through history, Washington : exploring the Evergreen State's
past by trail / Nathan Barnes, Jeremy Barnes.
        pages cm. – (Hiking through history)
    Summary: "The 40 hike profiles in Hiking through History Washington go
beyond miles and directions and GPS coordinates for each hike to include
 rich descriptions of the history underfoot. This book is the perfect
companion for any hiker with an interest in history, complete with beautiful
photos, detailed maps, and sidebars outlining enough historical information
to satisfy every curiosity along the way." – Provided by publisher.
    ISBN 978-0-7627-9225-2 (pbk.)
        1. Hiking–Washington (State)–Guidebooks. 2. Washington (State)–
History–Guidebooks. I. Barnes, Jeremy. II. Title.
    GV199.44.W22B37 2014
    917.9704–dc23
                                        2013034600

Printed in the United States of America

The authors and Globe Pequot Press assume no liability for accidents happening to, or injuries sustained by, readers who engage in the activities described in this book.

For everyone who has supported hikingwithmybrother.com over the years, especially our friends and family for believing in us.

A magnolia on the shore of Lake Crescent (hike 1).

Contents

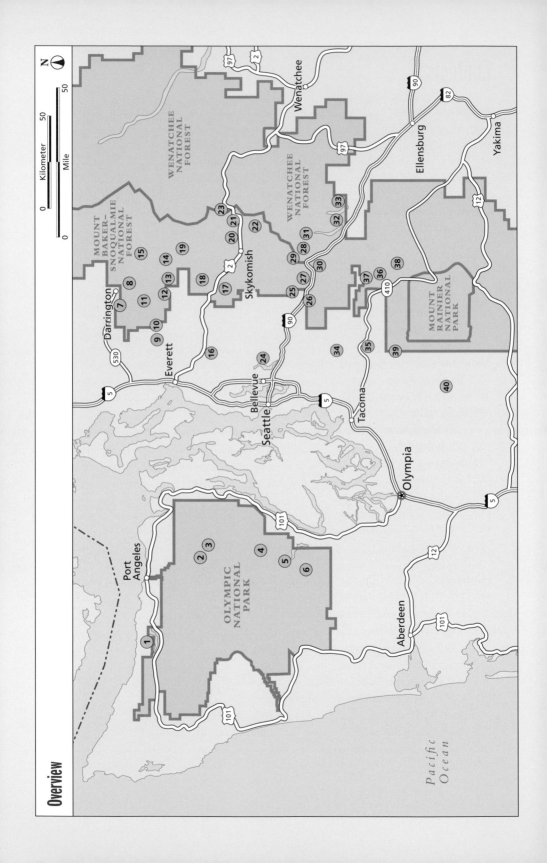

Overview

ACKNOWLEDGMENTS

This guidebook would not be possible without the unwavering support and encouragement of the whole community that has grown around hikingwithmybrother.com. We are indebted to countless users who contributed their insights to particular hikes, corrected our mistakes, and motivated us to keep hiking week after week.

Many, many people have helped get us to this point, but a few have been there from the beginning or took a chance on a then-obscure hiking blog. In particular we'd like to thank Kim Phillips at *Backpacker Magazine* as well as Nina Pardo and Bob Payne at the *Seattle Times* for partnering with us to get our hikes out to a larger audience. All of our friends and family continue to be endlessly supportive and encouraging, and a few have put in the extra time to help us make the blog that much better: Diane Barnes, Emily Barnes, Margaret Barnes, Deborah Hoyer, Megan Manthos, April Von Allmen, and Alysha Yagoda. We can't thank you enough.

And of course we'd like to thank all the volunteers and stewards of the outdoors for maintaining the trails we love.

Finally, we thank Tim Berners-Lee, the inventor of the World Wide Web: Without the Internet, we would never have had the opportunity to put together this guidebook.

◀ *Twin Lakes (hike 30)*

Map Legend

Transportation

≡🛡90🛡≡   Interstate Highway

═(2)═   US Highway

═(410)═   State Highway

═[4065]═   Local/ County/Forest Road

= = = =   Unimproved Road

------   Featured Trail

- - - - -   Trail

+—+—+   Railroad

Water Features

   Body of Water

   Glacier

   Marsh/Wetland

   River/Creek

   Waterfall

Land Management

   National Park/
Forest Boundary

   State/Local/
Open Space Park

   Wilderness Boundary

Symbols

✕   Airport

⛰   Campground

▲   Campsite

→   Direction Arrow

⛱   Gate

▭   Lodging

🅿   Parking

)(Pass/Gap

▲   Peak/Summit

🛆   Picnic Area

■   Point of Interest/Structure

   Ranger Station

   Restroom/Privy

   Ski Area

   Tower

○   Town

①   Trailhead

   Viewpoint/Overlook

?   Visitor Center

INTRODUCTION

Thousands of miles of hiking trails have been carved into Washington State. They switchback up glacier-carved mountains, wander through quiet forests, and follow rivers to their sources. With a relatively mild climate and diverse landscapes, Washington is a playground for anyone who loves the outdoors.

Each year Washington's trails welcome millions of boot steps of hikers and backpackers looking to escape the daily grind of urban life, just as they have for well over a hundred years. With so much to take in and see, it is easy to forget that there is a story behind the creation of every trail. There is a reason that a trail exists—whether it be a repurposed railroad line, an access trail to an airplane beacon, a fire road blazed to fight a wildfire, or simply a path leading to a lofty summit. Often, a trail's story is wrapped up in the history of the area. Learning about that history provides a little context and helps connect the hiker with the trail's past.

In this guidebook we tell the stories of forty-plus trails around Washington State while lending a little historical background to these hikes. Yet this is not a book of history. It is a guidebook designed to give hikers everything they need to explore and enjoy these trails. The historical background provides a glimpse into the past, a flavor of the local history to enhance the experience. We selected hikes with particularly interesting backgrounds and that have a wide variety of popularity, difficulty, landscapes, and locations. The book is organized by region, roughly defined by the major highways that provide access to the trailheads. Every hike in this volume is within a two-hour drive of Seattle, though we hope future volumes will eventually reach every corner of the state.

Weather

Washington's climate is dominated by a rain shadow that creates two dramatically different weather patterns on either side of the Cascade Mountain Range. Western Washington is generally wetter and milder than eastern Washington. This guidebook directs you to hikes in both of these areas.

Although Washington's generally mild climate allows for hiking year-round, the best months for hiking are late May through late September. In a typical year, snow has melted from most elevations by late May and what remains is usually navigable with ease. Temperatures in western Washington during the hiking season tend to be between 60° and 70°F without a dramatic variance between day and evening temperatures. Eastern Washington will get hotter, typically ranging between 70° and 80°F and have a larger variance between night and day.

Rain, fog, and cloudy weather are always a possibility, though clear skies are much more likely in eastern Washington. Weather can also change very quickly, and hikers should always be prepared for rain and cool temperatures. Make a habit of checking the weather for the area where you plan to hike before heading out to the trailhead.

The Weather Channel, Weather Underground, weather.gov, and Accuweather are all good online resources that allow searches by zip code. See hikingwithmybrother .com/p/hiking-resources.html for more details.

Flora and Fauna

Washington's weather patterns also influence the vegetation and wildlife you'll encounter. This guidebook contains hikes in three distinct ecological areas of the state: the Olympic Peninsula, the western Cascades, and the eastern Cascades.

The Olympic Peninsula contains one of the few temperate rain forests on the planet and is home to a number of unique species, including Jeremy's favorite, the Olympic marmot. The Olympic Mountains get the most precipitation of any region in Washington, and as a consequence the forests tend to be lush with moss and undergrowth. The forests are populated with Douglas fir, western hemlock, and Sitka spruce and are well known for an abundance of wild rhododendrons. Hikers could encounter a variety of wildlife, including brown bears, mountain goats, elk, and deer.

The western Cascades are drier than the Olympics, with forests of alder and vine maple at lower elevations and Douglas fir, western hemlock, and western red cedar at higher elevations. Deer, bears, and cougars and are all present in this region, as are bald eagles, pikas, marmots, and martens.

When crossing to the east side of the Cascades, the landscape changes dramatically. Much drier and dustier than the western portion of the state, the forests are still full of Douglas fir, but here they are accompanied by ponderosa pine, lodgepole pine, and western larch. The wildlife is similar to that of the western Cascades, although you are more likely to encounter snakes and other sun-loving animals here.

Wilderness Restrictions and Regulations

Washington State contains six national forests, thirteen national parks, twenty-three national wildlife refuges, thirty-one national wilderness areas, 138 state parks, 143 State Department of Natural Resources recreation areas, and hundreds of city and county parks and recreation areas. These lands are managed by a patchwork of federal, state, and local agencies, each with slightly different requirements for hiking in these areas. In wilderness areas in particular, be sure to review the restrictions on campfires, garbage, and pets.

The majority of the hikes in this guidebook will take you through national forests and national wilderness areas, though occasionally a hike will explore a state or county regional park. Generally, hiking in a national forest will require a Northwest Forest Pass, and many state lands will require a Discover Pass. Information on whether a pass is required is provided for each hike in the book.

◀ *Mule deer (hike 2)*

How to Use This Guide

This guide is meant to provide accurate and concise information on some of the best hiking in Washington. Our goal is to answer the question: "Where should I go hiking this weekend?" The overview map plots hiking destinations in relation to geographic regions and major roads.

The guide groups hikes into the following five geographic regions: the Olympic Peninsula, Mountain Loop Highway Corridor, Highway 2 Corridor, Interstate 90 Corridor, and Highway 410 Corridor. With the exception of the Interstate 90 Corridor, hikes within a region are similar in ecology, habitat, flora, fauna, and geology. The Interstate 90 Corridor contains hikes in both eastern and western Washington, which have differing ecologies.

Use the map to decide on a hike in the part of the state you would like to visit, then read the appropriate entry to begin more detailed planning of your trip. Each entry contains the following information:

Start: This is the trailhead where the hike begins.

Distance: The total distance in miles that the hike travels is listed here.

Hiking time: This is an estimate of how long it will take to hike the trail. (This is just an estimate and can vary widely according to hiking pace, weather, trail conditions, and stops along the way.)

Difficulty: Our subjective opinion of the difficulty of the hike. Hikes are classified as easy, moderate, or difficult.

Best season: A suggested best time of year in which to hike the trail.

Traffic: This section tells you if you should expect to see other trail users during your hike, such as hunters, mountain bikers, horseback riders, etc.

Maps: This section provides a listing of park maps and USGS 1:24,000 quad maps available for the hike. (Within the guidebook entry for each hike, we provide a detailed map showing trailheads, parking, trails, peaks, and other landmarks. These maps are not, however, meant for orienteering or compass work.)

Trail contacts: The address, phone number, and website for acquiring up-to-date local information are included here.

Special considerations: Specific trail hazards or warnings, such as when hunting season takes place, when there might be ice on the trail, or a lack of water, are indicated here.

Finding the trailhead: Directions to the trailhead are provided. Often, two or more sets of directions are listed to get you to different trailheads or to guide you from different starting points. This information should be used in conjunction with the maps in this guide, USGS maps, and state road maps. Abbreviations used in this section include:

- I—interstate
- US—US highway
- SR—state road
- Highway—state road
- CR—county road
- FR—forest road

The Hike: Generally, the hike is described to give the reader a flavor of what to expect along the trail. By design, these descriptions seek to capture the most important aspects of the hike while still leaving plenty of room for discovery. Alternate routes or suggestions for other nearby hikes may also be included here.

Miles and Directions: Trail junctions, geographic features, or other important points are listed here.

Historical Background: Every hike has a story, and this section gives the reader a glimpse into the past, whether it is the origins of the trail, background on the surrounding area, or just a little historical context.

Trail Finder

Best Hikes for Great Views
10 Mount Pilchuck
12 Vesper Peak
13 Gothic Basin
20 Beckler Peak
23 Skyline Lake
26 McClellan Butte
27 Mount Defiance and Mason Lake
28 Kendall Peak and Kendall Katwalk
29 Snoqualmie Mountain
30 Silver Peak Loop and Twin Lakes
31 Rachel Lake and Alta Mountain
32 Kachess Ridge Beacon
33 Hex Mountain
37 Kelly Butte

Best Hikes for Lake Lovers
1 Spruce Railroad
2 Royal Basin
4 Lake of the Angels
13 Gothic Basin
15 Goat Lake
17 Lake Serene and Bridal Veil Falls
19 Blanca Lake
22 Surprise and Glacier Lakes
23 Skyline Lake
27 Mount Defiance and Mason Lake
31 Rachel Lake and Alta Mountain
36 Echo and Greenwater Lakes

Best Hikes for Waterfalls
7 Boulder River
15 Goat Lake
17 Lake Serene and Bridal Veil Falls
31 Rachel Lake and Alta Mountain
38 Snoquera Falls
40 Pack Forest

◀   *The town of Easton sits below the ridgeline (hike 32).*

Best Hikes for Families

1 Spruce Railroad
5 Staircase Rapids
6 Lower Skokomish River
7 Boulder River
8 Old Sauk River
9 Lime Kiln
14 Monte Cristo Townsite
16 Lord Hill Regional Park
21 Iron Goat Trail
24 Soaring Eagle Regional Park
34 Franklin Townsite
35 Mud Mountain Rim Trail
36 Echo and Greenwater Lakes
40 Pack Forest

Best Hikes for Backpacking

2 Royal Basin
4 Lake of the Angels
6 Lower Skokomish River
13 Gothic Basin
14 Monte Cristo Townsite
15 Goat Lake
22 Surprise and Glacier Lakes
27 Mount Defiance and Mason Lake
30 Silver Peak Loop and Twin Lakes
31 Rachel Lake and Alta Mountain
36 Echo and Greenwater Lakes

Best Hikes for the Winter

1 Spruce Railroad
6 Lower Skokomish River
7 Boulder River
8 Old Sauk River
9 Lime Kiln
16 Lord Hill Regional Park
18 Index Town Wall
24 Soaring Eagle Regional Park
34 Franklin Townsite
35 Mud Mountain Rim Trail
39 Melmont Townsite
40 Pack Forest

Olympic Peninsula

During the last ice age, as glaciers crept down from Canada to carve Washington's basins and valleys, the Olympic Mountains were an island of land above the ice. For that reason, the Olympic Peninsula is home to a unique ecology that has been largely preserved within the Olympic National Park. Those same rugged peaks of the Olympic Mountains kept the interior of the peninsula a mystery nearly a hundred years after Captain George Vancouver first entered the Strait of Juan de Fuca in 1792. Today, the mountains and river valleys provide some of the best hiking in the state.

A trail winds through old-growth Douglas firs (hike 6).

1 Spruce Railroad

This easy 8.0-mile walk along the shores of Lake Crescent follows the route of a historic railroad line.

Start: Spruce Railroad Trailhead
Distance: 8.0 miles out and back
Hiking time: About 3–4 hours
Elevation gain: 100 feet
High point: 650 feet
Difficulty: Easy with very little elevation
Best season: Hikeable year-round; best May–Oct
Traffic: Equestrian and bike use, heavy foot traffic

Fees and permits: None
Maps: USGS Lake Crescent; *Green Trails Map #101* (Lake Crescent)
Trail contacts: Hood Canal Ranger District—Quilcene, 295142 Highway 101 S., PO Box 280, Quilcene, WA 98376; (360) 765-2200; fs.usda.gov/olympic

Finding the trailhead: From Seattle take the Bainbridge Island Ferry, following SR 305 through Poulsbo to SR 3. Follow SR 3 to the Hood Canal Bridge, taking a left over the bridge onto SR 104. Follow SR 104 as it merges onto US 101 and continue another 36 miles to Port Angeles, taking a left on Lincoln Street to stay on US 101. Continue 17 miles to East Beach Road and take a right. Continue for about 4 miles, crossing the Lyre River to a road signed SPRUCE RAILROAD TRAIL. Take a left and find the parking for the trailhead where the public road ends. Trailhead GPS: N48 05.619' / W123 48.148'

The Hike

Two trailheads serve the Spruce Railroad Trail, allowing hikers to start at either end or to take two cars and shuttle between the trailheads for a shorter hike. From the eastern trailhead, the route begins easily, following the bones of one of the many logging roads built to bring lumber down to the railway in 1918. Firs and hemlocks thicken as you move beyond a few cabins and houses clustered near the trailhead. Before long the trail finds portions of the rail bed as it skirts the lake. The first mile of trail involves a few ups and downs as you make your way around the base of Pyramid Mountain, and the views of the lake begin to widen.

As you progress, the firs begin to give way to madronas and the trail dips down to the lakeshore and crosses over a deep swimming hole known as the Devil's Punchbowl. The bridge offers one of the first of many big views of Lake Crescent and the surrounding mountains. Pick out Mount Storm King almost directly across the water and Mounts Aurora and Sugardough as you look to the south.

As you continue past the bridge, you soon regain the rail bed and may notice a rough path up the mountainside. If you're feeling adventurous, scramble up to find

◄ *Hikers explore the inside of the McFee Tunnel near Devil's Punchbowl.*

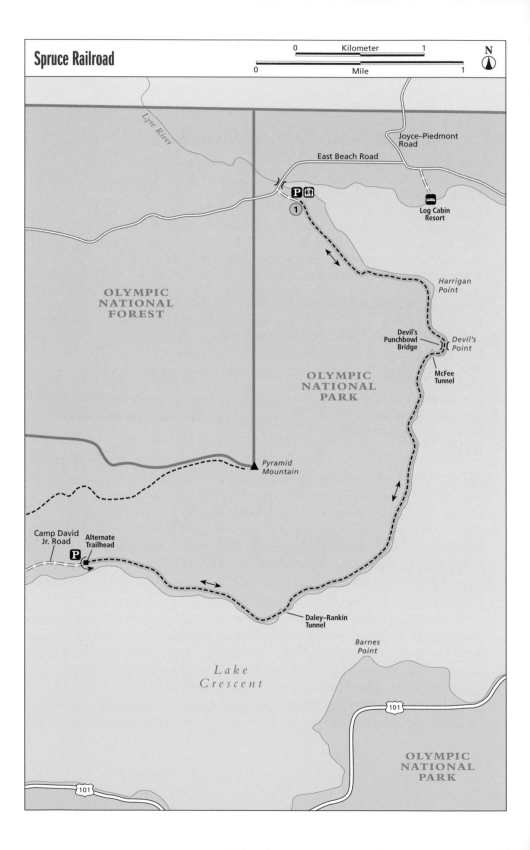

Spruce Railroad

0   Kilometer   1

0   Mile   1

Lyre River

Joyce–Piedmont Road

East Beach Road

P

1

Log Cabin Resort

OLYMPIC NATIONAL FOREST

OLYMPIC NATIONAL PARK

Harrigan Point

Devil's Punchbowl Bridge

Devil's Point

McFee Tunnel

Pyramid Mountain

Camp David Jr. Road

Alternate Trailhead

P

Daley–Rankin Tunnel

Barnes Point

Lake Crescent

101

OLYMPIC NATIONAL PARK

101

Historical Background

In 1856 the deep, 12-mile glacial lake now known as Lake Crescent was dubbed Lake Everett by John Everett and John J. Sutherland, a pair of hunters and trappers who also lent their name to nearby Lake Sutherland. But by 1890, boosters in nearby Port Crescent began referring to it as Lake Crescent in a bid to raise the prominence of the logging boomtown and attract more settlers. The ploy failed, and by the end of 1893, Port Crescent was all but abandoned. Today, the settlement is gone, but Lake Crescent remains, likely named not only for its own vaguely crescent shape but also after the shape of Crescent Bay, where Port Crescent once stood.

In 1917 the United States entered World War I and quickly needed vast supplies of Sitka spruce to produce warplanes. At the time, Sitka spruce was the gold standard in warplane material, and within a year the army formed the Spruce Production Division to help pull as much spruce out of Northwest forests as possible. To that end, the Spruce Production Division Railroad No. 1 began construction in May 1918, eventually stretching 36 miles along Lake Crescent and into the Olympic Forest. The effort involved the blasting of two tunnels and was constructed at breakneck speed, compressing a one- to two-year project into just six months. As impressive as that feat was, it was not fast enough to beat the end of the war, which stopped timber operations before the railroad could haul a single spruce. The railway languished for a few years, until 1925 when Port Angeles Western Railroad operated the line before tapering off in 1951 and officially abandoning it in 1953. The Spruce Railroad again languished, this time for nearly thirty years, until 1981, when portions of the line along the lake were converted to the Spruce Railroad Road Trail.

one of the tunnels built for the railway. These are not particularly safe at the moment, and we don't recommend exploring them unless you have the right experience and gear. After you've taken a look at the tunnel, press onward along the lakeshore for more pristine views of Lake Crescent and sections of quiet forest. There are some great spots to take a break along the way. After 4 miles you'll reach the far trailhead. Turn around and enjoy the walk in reverse.

This trail is a great winter hiking option, as the lake tends to minimize the snow. It is relatively flat, with just a few portions of elevation as the trail deviates

▶ Between November 1917 and October 1918, Washington produced 88,471,594 board feet of spruce to help the war effort.

Hikers walk the railroad grade in stands of second-generation forest.

from the rail bed, making it a good choice for bringing along the whole family or maybe some of your nonhiking friends. This is also a mixed-use trail, and one that allows mountain bikes and stock. So you can expect a variety of company along the way during the warmer months. A project is under way that will reroute and pave portions of the trail, reopen the tunnels, and add new sections to the trail, all with the intent of bringing more traffic to the area. Whatever the effect of this change, the Spruce Railroad Trail will continue to be a decent winter hike well into the future.

Miles and Directions

0.0 At the Spruce Railroad Trailhead, start by crossing the gravel road and head south on the trail. A privy is located at the trailhead.

1.2 Cross over the steel bridge spanning Devil's Punchbowl at Devil Point.

1.3 Shortly after the bridge, turn right and scramble up a loose-gravel hill to the entrance of the McFee Tunnel.

3.0 After rounding a bluff, turn right and backtrack to the Daley-Rankin Tunnel.

4.0 Trail end: Find the alternate parking area at the end of Camp David Jr. Road here.

8.0 Arrive back at the trailhead.

2 Royal Basin

Take on this 16.0-mile hike out to a set of pristine alpine lakes.

Start: Upper Dungeness Trailhead
Distance: 16.0 miles out and back
Hiking time: About 11–12 hours
Elevation gain: 3,000 feet
High point: 5,700 feet
Difficulty: Moderate due to elevation and length
Best season: June–Sept
Traffic: Equestrian use permitted; heavy foot traffic
Fees and permits: Northwest Forest Pass

Maps: USGS Mount Deception; *Green Trails Map #136* (Tyler Peak)
Trail contacts: Hood Canal Ranger District–Quilcene, 295142 Highway 101 S., PO Box 280, Quilcene, WA 98376; (360) 765-2200; fs.usda.gov/olympic
Special considerations: Portions of this trail are in wilderness areas that require additional permits to stay overnight. Contact the ranger station for more information.

Finding the trailhead: From Seattle take the Bainbridge Island Ferry, following SR 305 through Poulsbo to SR 3. Follow SR 3 to the Hood Canal Bridge, taking a left over the bridge onto SR 104. Follow SR 104 as it merges onto US 101, continue another 18 miles, and turn left onto Palo Alto Road. From here take a right onto FR 2880 near the Dungeness River. Continue just under 2 miles to FR 2870. Head left and follow that road for 6.5 miles to the trailhead. Trailhead GPS: N47 52.693'/W123 08.208'

The Hike

The trail begins at Upper Dungeness Trailhead #833.2, a parking area along FR 2870 near the Dungeness River. Climb up the Dungeness River Trail through looming moss-covered firs and thick underbrush for about a mile to a junction pointing you toward Royal Basin. Sheltered under the thick forest canopy, begin the long trek to the lake alongside the constant burbling of Royal Creek, your companion for nearly the entire journey.

As you progress, the forest will occasionally open, revealing glimpses of nearby peaks lining the valley. Streams both small and large cut across the trail, often snaking down narrow grass-filled valleys that invariably seem filled with small herds of deer.

▶ The very cold waters of the Dungeness River are one of a few habitats of the endangered bull trout in Olympic National Park.

The mild grade is occasionally interspersed with a short set of switchbacks, though eventually the trail flattens out into expansive meadows before hitting the last and most strenuous portion of the hike. Push through the final series of switchbacks to reach the lakeshore. Royal Lake sits directly beneath Mount Clark, with Mount Deception looming over the far end of the lake. For those feeling like a little extra adventure, a footpath leads around the lake and gives access to the upper basin at the base of Mount Deception.

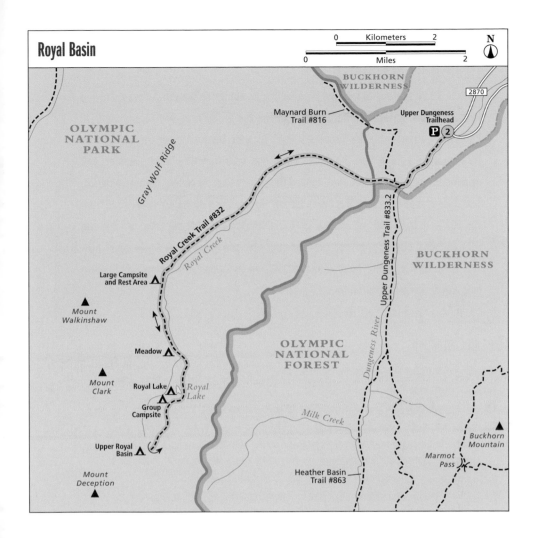

Royal Basin

0 Kilometers 2
0 Miles 2

N

BUCKHORN WILDERNESS

2870

Maynard Burn Trail #816

Upper Dungeness Trailhead

P 2

OLYMPIC NATIONAL PARK

Gray Wolf Ridge

Royal Creek Trail #832

Royal Creek

Upper Dungeness Trail #833.2

BUCKHORN WILDERNESS

Large Campsite and Rest Area

Mount Walkinshaw

Meadow

Mount Clark

Royal Lake

Royal Lake

Group Campsite

Upper Royal Basin

Mount Deception

OLYMPIC NATIONAL FOREST

Dungeness River

Milk Creek

Heather Basin Trail #863

Buckhorn Mountain

Marmot Pass

Whether you are spending the night or are just out on an extended day hike, find a quiet space to settle in and take in the panorama.

This is an excellent hike, one that we recommend you consider for a weekend backpack. The distance from Seattle and the length of the hike make this a very long day if you're not planning on an overnight—though on a sunny day, the Royal Creek Valley is picturesque in and of itself, making a shortened version of this hike well worth the effort. Although definitely a popular and well-known hike, it is entirely possible to encounter more wildlife than people—everything from deer to marmots to the occasional black bear.

◄ *Backpackers trek through the alpine meadows.*

Historical Background

Back in 1917, a group of intrepid backpackers working for the USDA Forest Service hiked into then-unexplored Royal Basin. Among the group were Roy Strom and G. A. Whitehead, a ranger for the Quilcene Ranger District. Upon entering the basin these trail veterans agreed that the alpine basin and lake were the most stunning and pristine they had ever seen. They dubbed the area "royal" to reflect its preeminence. They also named the creek Roy Creek for Roy Strom. Maps of the area produced from the 1920s to the 1940s all show a Roy Creek flowing out of Royal Lake. In 1946 the US Geological Survey produced the first map with the name Royal Creek. The USDA Forest Service followed the lead of the USGS on the maps it produced, and before long Roy Creek disappeared from all maps.

Miles and Directions

0.0 Begin at Upper Dungeness Trailhead #833.2.

1.0 Turn right onto Royal Creek Trail #832.

1.2 At the junction with Maynard Burn Trail #816, continue straight ahead.

5.2 Take a rest at a large campsite under the tree canopy next to Royal Creek.

6.2 Arrive at the lower meadows of Royal Basin, which are filled with huckleberry. There are plenty of campsites here, but keep pushing on to more scenic accommodations.

6.9 Mount Clark reflects in the trout-filled waters of Royal Lake.

7.0 A large group campsite next to a stream offers ideal overnight camping.

8.0 Reach the upper basin. The crags of Mount Deception rise over the small lake and alpine terrain.

16.0 Arrive back at the trailhead.

3 Tubal Cain Mine and Tull Canyon

This hike explores former mining communities and the wreckage of a B-17 Flying Fortress.

Start: Tubal Cain Mine Trailhead
Distance: 8.5 miles out and back
Hiking time: About 4-5 hours
Elevation gain: 1,600 feet
High point: 4,600 feet
Difficulty: Moderate due to some steep sections
Best season: May-Oct
Traffic: Moderate foot traffic

Fees and permits: None
Maps: USGS Mount Townsend; *Green Trails Map #136* (Tyler Peak)
Trail contacts: Hood Canal Ranger District—Quilcene, 295142 Highway 101 S., PO Box 280, Quilcene, WA 98376; (360) 765 2200; fs.usda.gov/olympic

Finding the trailhead: From Seattle take the Bainbridge Island Ferry, following SR 305 through Poulsbo to SR 3. Follow SR 3 to the Hood Canal Bridge, taking a left over the bridge onto SR 104. Follow SR 104 as it merges onto US 101, continue another 18 miles, and turn left onto Palo Alto Road. Continue about 8 miles to Road #2880. Veer right and steeply descend to the Dungeness River, past Dungeness Forks Campground. In about 2 miles head left on Road #2870 and continue about 11 miles to the Tubal Cain Mine Trailhead. Trailhead GPS: N47 53.180'/W123 05.504'

The Hike

The Tubal Cain Mine Trail begins in a young forest of fir, hemlock, and rhododendron. Wide and flat, the trail gently guides you past the Silver Creek shelter and over a log bridge that spans the creek. Soon the trail climbs up into Copper Creek Canyon and the Buckhorn Wilderness, before flattening out along the slopes above Copper Creek. After about 3 miles of smooth trail, you'll reach the Tull Canyon Trail and an exploratory adit dug by the mining companies. The tunnel only goes back 50 feet or so, though we don't recommend you do any exploring here.

From here, head upward along the Tull Canyon Trail for about a mile to find the remnants of the B-17 and the leavings of Tull City. The trail is a sharp contrast to the Tubal Cain Mine Trail—it's steep, rocky, and narrow. Climb for a little less than a mile to the site of the wreckage, scattered among the trees, ponds, and creeks. Linger here, or continue along the trail to the meadows at the far end of the canyon, where Tull City once stood. When you're done exploring, retrace your steps back to the Tubal Cain Mine Trail and continue toward the mine.

Before long you'll pass by the few rusting remains of Copper City and should see a large slope of tailings from the Tubal Cain Mine on the left side of the trail. A short climb up the mountainside leads to the mine and the creek that spills out from its depths. If you're looking to

▶ The Pacific rhododendron was officially designated Washington's state flower in 1959.

B-17 landing gear in Tull Canyon

add some more mileage, you can return to the trail and press on for another 2 miles to a short trail leading down to Buckhorn Lake or continue farther to climb up to Buckhorn Pass for decent views of the surrounding Buckhorn Wilderness.

This hike has a little bit of everything, from lakes and creeks to canyons and mountain passes. With multiple destinations along the trail, you can tailor this hike depending on your time and company. The trail to the mine is a good choice for a late-season hike and should be approachable for almost every hiker. And while Tull Canyon Trail is more challenging, the promise of the B-17 Flying Fortress wreckage provides ample motivation. The trek out to Buckhorn Pass is for those folks looking to put in a 10- or 11-mile day. Whatever you're looking to do, this hike is a great opportunity to head out to the Olympic Mountains and explore the Buckhorn Wilderness.

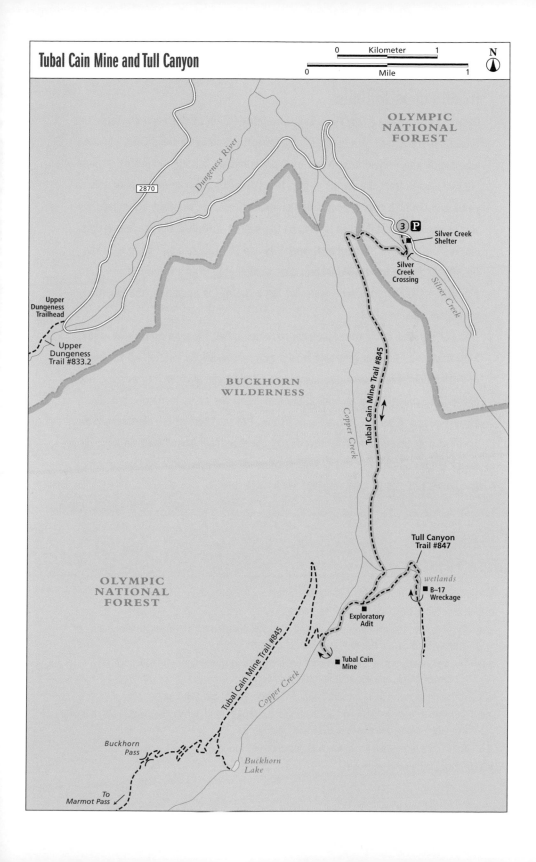

Tubal Cain Mine and Tull Canyon

Kilometer
Mile

N

OLYMPIC
NATIONAL
FOREST

2870

Dungeness River

3 P
Silver Creek
Shelter

Silver
Creek
Crossing

Silver Creek

Upper
Dungeness
Trailhead

Upper
Dungeness
Trail #833.2

BUCKHORN
WILDERNESS

Copper Creek

Tubal Cain Mine Trail #845

Tull Canyon
Trail #847

wetlands

B–17
Wreckage

OLYMPIC
NATIONAL
FOREST

Exploratory
Adit

Tubal Cain
Mine

Tubal Cain Mine Trail #845

Copper Creek

Buckhorn
Pass

Buckhorn
Lake

To
Marmot Pass

Historical Background

Back in 1903, miners led by Victor Tull consolidated their mining claims to form the Tubal Cain Copper and Manganese Mining Company. Named for Tubal-Cain, a biblical blacksmith who worked bronze and iron, the company had high hopes of extracting vast wealth from the depths of Iron Mountain. But between nearly nonexistent yields and the high cost of accessing the remote area, the company struggled. Two small camps were established to support the mining activities, and the foundations and rusting metal left behind by Copper City and Tull City can still be found today. Despite digging nearly 1,500 feet into the mountain, the mine was never able to turn a profit. In 1912 an avalanche destroyed the heart of the operation, and the mines were abandoned by 1920.

For the next thirty years, the area remained quiet. Then, on January 19, 1952, a modified B-17 bomber returning from a search-and-rescue mission off the coast of British Columbia became disoriented in a blizzard and crashed into the ridgeline above Tull Canyon. The plane slid 2,000 feet down the steep mountain, scattering parts across a massive debris field. Somehow, five members of the eight-man crew survived and were rescued the next day by another team from their own unit. The wreck lingers all these years later—parts of massive wheels, large sections of wing, and pieces of the B-17's four engines are easy to find.

Miles and Directions

0.0 Park at the Tubal Cain Mine Trailhead #845.

0.1 Cross Silver Creek on the wooden bridge.

3.0 Turn left onto the Tull Canyon Trail #847. The cave located here is an exploratory adit cut roughly 50 feet into the rock in search of copper.

3.8 The trail opens into a pond and surrounding wetland where the B-17 wreckage is scattered. This is a good turnaround point.

4.5 Arrive back at the trail junction. Continue on the Tubal Cain Mine Trail.

4.9 Turn left onto a well-defined boot path that eventually leads up a steep gravel hill (left over from the mining operation) to the Tubal Cain Mine.

5.0 Reach the Tubal Cain Mine, which is flooded year-round with runoff.

8.5 Arrive back at the trailhead.

4 Lake of the Angels

Challenge yourself on this 7.0-mile hike into a less-traveled portion of the Olympic National Park.

Start: Carl Putvin Trailhead
Distance: 7.0 miles out and back
Hiking time: About 7–8 hours
Elevation gain: 3,400 feet
High point: 4,950 feet
Difficulty: Difficult due to steep elevation and rugged trail
Best season: June–Oct
Traffic: Low foot traffic
Fees and permits: None

Maps: USGS Mount Skykomish; *Green Trails Map #168* (The Brothers), #167 (Mount Steel)
Trail contacts: Hood Canal Ranger District–Quilcene, 295142 Highway 101 S., PO Box 280, Quilcene, WA 98376; (360) 765-2200; fs.usda.gov/olympic
Special considerations: The last 5 miles of the road to the trailhead are unpaved and have seen some washouts. A high-clearance vehicle is recommended.

Finding the trailhead: From Seattle take I-5 south to Olympia to exit 104 toward Aberdeen and Port Angeles. Follow US 101 along Hood Canal almost 49 miles through Shelton and Hoodsport to FR 25, also known as the Hamma Hamma River Road. Take a left and follow the road 12 miles to the trailhead just beyond Boulder Creek. Trailhead GPS: N47 35.005' / W123 14.033'

The Hike

This route, the Carl Putvin Trail #813, is the most direct and frequently used approach to the Lake of the Angels. From the trailhead the route immediately plunges into the trees, following Boulder Creek up past Putvin's grave and winding past ancient moss-covered boulders. Here a forest of pine and hemlock rises out of a thick layer of salal and huckleberry, occasionally thinning to allow glimpses of Mount Pershing and Jefferson Ridge on the far side of the Hamma Hamma Valley. The trail continues to gain elevation at a fairly steady pace, though there are a few ups and downs involved when navigating a couple of large gullies that streams have carved into the mountainside. After about 1.5 miles, you will find yourself on the remains of an abandoned forest road in front of a small registration station. From here the real work begins.

Start your ascent, and be prepared for a workout. The trail is not only steep, it is also rougher than the trail below, adding to the challenge. Soon the trail ushers you into the Mount Skokomish Wilderness and the sounds of Whitehorse Creek. As you switchback ever upward, breaks in the tree line offer views of Mount Skokomish towering over the rocky headwall you will need to clamber up to reach the Valley of Heaven. If you're on the trail when the tree leaves are either still budding or

▶ Often sighted on the hillsides above the Lake of the Angels, the Olympic marmot is found only in the mountains of the Olympic Peninsula and was made a state symbol of Washington in 2009.

Lake of the Angels

starting to fall, your efforts will be rewarded with increasingly better views of the creek tumbling down the headwall into a broad alder-filled plateau before disappearing into the trees below.

After a bit of scrambling, you'll stumble into subalpine meadows, crossing slow creeks and passing the Pond of the False Prophet—a large pond one might mistake for the Lake of the Angels in the fevered hope that the journey is at an end. You're close, so press onward to the Olympic National Park boundary and the last series of steep switchbacks up an avalanche chute to the Valley of Heaven. Here, the Lake of the Angels is gently cupped in a cirque between Mounts Skokomish and Stone, fed by the snowfields that cling to the craggy ridgeline connecting the two mountains. Expect to run into some wildlife up here: Mountain goats and marmots are common. Settle in and enjoy a little slice of heaven.

While we highly recommend this hike, it's definitely not for the unprepared. At the same time, many guidebooks give the impression that this trail requires some serious mountaineering skills to tackle. This is not the case. While there is one very small section that will probably require you to use some handholds to help you climb up the roots and rocks, that's as harrowing as it gets. If you're a strong hiker and are

Lake of the Angels

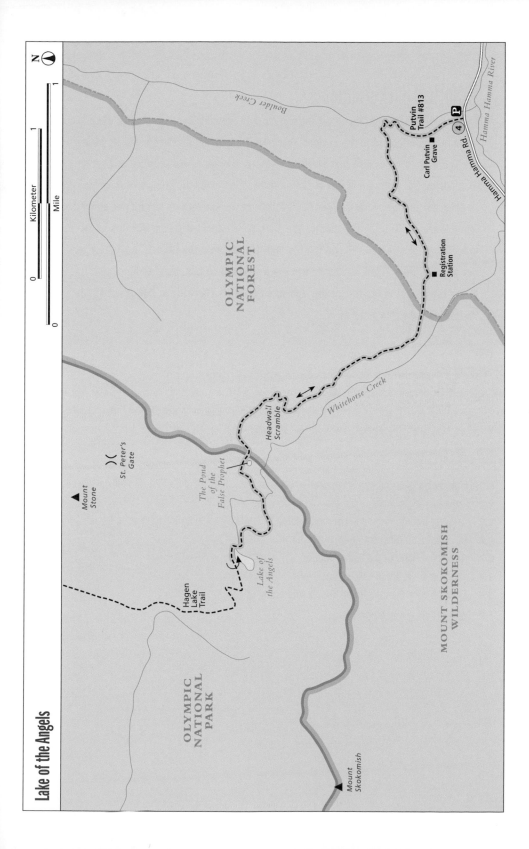

Historical Background

The trail runs right past its namesake's grave, and probably because he died at such a young age, folks are pretty curious about what happened to 21-year-old Carl Putvin. There are a lot of different stories out there, though all seem to agree that he died during the winter, a victim of the elements. Some say the trapper was headed to get medicine for a sick daughter that Putvin never had; others say he was simply found frozen, sitting by the side of the trail. We've decided to go with his great-granddaughter's version: Putvin left the family cabin near the Lake of the Angels to get supplies from Eldon, and along the way a tree fell on him, pinning him under it. Either the impact of the tree or the elements ended his short life in January of 1913. He left behind a wife and son.

looking for something a little out of the ordinary, this is a trail to check out. There are a few wilderness campsites around the lake, making an overnight an easy option. From the lake there is access to a variety of destinations, including Hagen Lake or Mount Stone and the Stone Ponds via a pass known as St. Peter's Gate.

Miles and Directions

0.0 Find a small parking area just past Boulder Creek that marks the Carl Putvin Trailhead #813.

0.2 Arrive at the gravesite of 21-year-old trapper Carl Putvin.

1.2 Arrive at an abandoned forest road and an Olympic National Park Registration Station.

2.2 Begin the steep ascent of the headwall.

2.7 Reach the Pond of the False Prophet.

3.4 Arrive at an outlet of Lake of the Angels.

3.5 Find the best camping on the north side of the lake.

7.0 Arrive back at the trailhead.

5 Staircase Rapids

Explore a short 2.0-mile loop following portions of the route taken by the O'Neil Expedition.

Start: Staircase Ranger Station
Distance: 2.0-mile loop
Hiking time: About 1–2 hours
Elevation gain: 100 feet
High point: 900 feet
Difficulty: Easy and family-friendly
Best season: Hikeable year-round; best Apr–Oct

Traffic: High foot traffic
Fees and permits: National Park Pass
Maps: USGS Mount Skykomish; *Green Trails Map #136* (Mount Steel)
Trail contacts: Hood Canal Ranger District—Quilcene, 295142 Highway 101 S., PO Box 280, Quilcene, WA 98376; (360) 765-2200; fs.usda.gov/olympic

Finding the trailhead: From Seattle take I-5 south to Olympia to exit 104 toward Aberdeen and Port Angeles. Follow US 101 along Hood Canal just over 35 miles through Shelton to Hoodsport. Turn left onto Lake Cushman Road/SR 119 and follow it for a little over 9 miles to a T intersection. Head left onto FR 24. Continue for about 6 miles to the Staircase Ranger Station and the parking lot. Note that FR 24's pavement turns to gravel after the first 2 miles. Trailhead GPS: N47 30.933'/W123 19.774'

The Hike

The trail begins from the Staircase Ranger Station and crosses a causeway over the North Fork Skokomish River. Here the Shady Lane Trail branches off to the left, but keep to the right and follow the Rapids Loop trail into the forest. The wide, flat trail wanders beneath a canopy of fir, hemlock, and cedar. Almost immediately a sign beckons you toward the Big Cedar, which succumbed to age and winter storms in 1999. Still, the fallen giant is 14 feet in diameter and is worth the short side trip to visit it.

Return to the main trail and before long the route bends toward the river and the roar of the rapids. Take time to linger at the many alcoves and viewing points to enjoy the cascading water and large pools. At about 1 mile the trail branches off to the bridge and connects with the North Fork Skokomish Trail. The current suspension bridge replaced a bridge that had been washed out since the 1990s, finally restoring the route to a complete loop. Now hikers are able to easily cross the water and make the loop back to the parking lot.

▶ The 1985 Beaver Fire was the largest fire in the history of Olympic National Park, burning 1,170 acres. It was caused by an illegal campfire.

If you're looking for a little more hike, you can continue onward past the bridge for another mile to Beaver Flats, a wide expanse that offers views of Mount Lincoln

Staircase Rapids on the North Fork Skokomish River in the winter

and the lingering traces of the 1985 Beaver Fire, which was accidentally set by campers in the area. The trail here is a little rougher and less traveled, but it is still navigable out to the 2-mile mark, where the trail intersects Four Stream, so named because it's the fourth of nine streams that enter the river between Lake Cushman and the river's source.

This truly is a hike for all seasons. Accessible all year, this loop works for a quick snowshoe or a short summer hike. Because the distance and elevation are fairly minimal, the hike is ideal for young hikers and first-time snowshoers. This is also a very popular hike, with many trails linking to other nearby destinations, so expect a little company as you head out to Staircase. There's less traffic in the winter, so if you're looking for an introductory snowshoe, Staircase Rapids is a good bet.

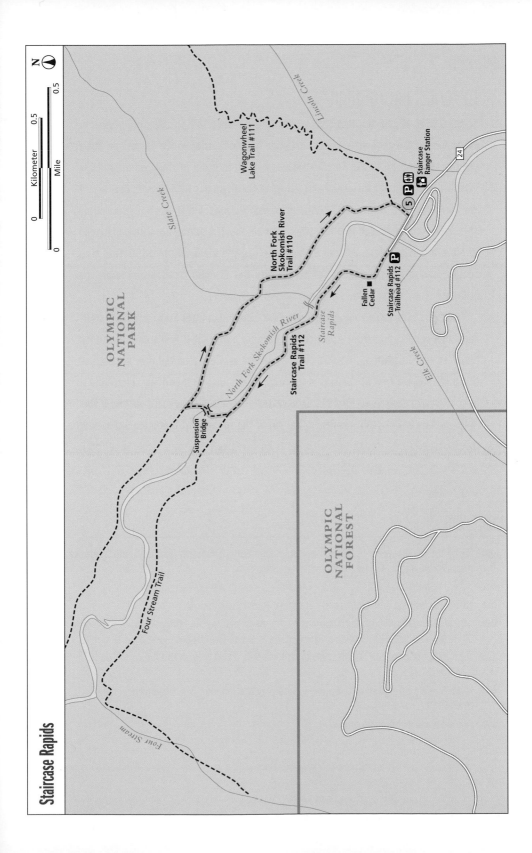

Staircase Rapids

Historical Background

As the 1880s began, the fact that no one had explored the Olympic Mountains, or even crossed the peninsula, was a challenge that industrious men of the age felt a need to respond to. Native American tribes had no interest in the area beyond the foothills, which meant the peaks and valleys of the Olympics held secrets that few, if any, had ever seen. A few parties attempted explorations, but it was ambitious army officer Lieutenant Joseph P. O'Neil who, after an aborted attempt in 1885, managed to blaze a serviceable mule trail 93 miles across the peninsula in 1890. That trail became one of the main points of access into the Olympic interior, and today the Staircase Rapids Trail follows portions of that early route.

Although the rapids along the North Fork Skokomish River look a bit like a staircase, the name comes from a particularly difficult bluff that O'Neil's mule trail took travelers over at one time. A small cedar staircase was constructed over portions of this bluff, and the task of climbing it was unpleasant enough that many referred to it as the "Devil's Staircase." By 1911, money was put toward smoothing out the O'Neil route, and an easier path was dynamited out of the rocky bluff that once stood near the Staircase Campground to make what is now referred to as the Shady Lane Trail.

Miles and Directions

0.0 From the parking area, head west over the North Fork Skokomish River and find Staircase Rapids Trail #112. A privy is located at the trailhead.

0.2 Arrive at a junction with a short spur trail that leads to a large fallen cedar.

0.4 The trail climbs a small cliff as the Staircase Rapids roar below.

0.9 Arrive at a trail junction. To continue the loop, head right to the bridge crossing the North Fork Skokomish River. Continuing straight leads out to Four Stream in another 1.0 mile.

1.0 Turn right onto the North Fork Skokomish River Trail #110 to start the return trip on the loop.

1.9 Continue right to return to the parking area past the junction with Wagonwheel Lake Trail #111.

2.0 Arrive back at the parking area.

A Honorable Mention: Mount Rose

Enjoy a 6.5-mile partial-loop hike on one of the few trails through the Mount Skokomish Wilderness.

Start: Mount Rose Trailhead
Distance: 6.5-mile lollipop
Hiking time: About 5–6 hours
Elevation gain: 3,500 feet
High point: 4,300 feet
Difficulty: Difficult due to some steep sections
Best season: June–Sept
Traffic: Moderate foot traffic

Fees and permits: None
Maps: USGS Mount Skykomish; *Green Trails Map #136* (Mount Steel)
Trail contacts: Hood Canal Ranger District—Quilcene, 295142 Highway 101 S., PO Box 280, Quilcene, WA 98376; (360) 765-2200; fs.usda.gov/olympic

Finding the trailhead: From Seattle take I-5 south to Olympia to exit 104 toward Aberdeen and Port Angeles. Follow US 101 along Hood Canal just over 35 miles through Shelton to Hoodsport. Turn left onto Lake Cushman Road/SR 119 and follow it for a little over 9 miles to a T intersection. Head left onto FR 24. Continue for just under 3 miles to the signed driveway of the trailhead parking lot.

Lingering traces of the 2006 fire

Historical Background

Mount Rose is named for Mr. and Mrs. Aldred Rose, who traveled to the Pacific Northwest in 1885. They traded their life in California for a 150-acre claim on the shores of Lake Cushman. Sadly, Aldred died of smallpox in January 1889, and the mountain is likely named in his honor after his untimely death.

The Mount Skokomish Wilderness was established by Congress through the Washington State Wilderness Act of 1984. Today, the 13,015-acre wilderness remains wild; only four trails provide access to the area—the Mildred Lakes Trail, Mount Ellinor Trail, Mount Rose Trail, and the Carl Putvin Trail—all with a combined length of less than 14 miles. Still, the area is not so remote as to avoid the touch of man. In 2006 a man-made forest fire that began on the shores of Lake Cushman quickly spread toward Mount Rose, charring large sections of the mountain and searing most of the vegetation off the summit.

The Hike

Mount Rose #814 begins along a reclaimed road, through lush mixed forest that teems with stands of fir. The hike climbs into the Mount Skokomish Wilderness, catching glimpses of Mount Ellinor and Copper Mountain through the trees. Once you reach the top, settle in to take in Lake Cushman and the mountains spreading out before you. Directly across the water are Lightening Peak and Timber Mountain. In the distance behind them, you can pick out Capital Peak, Wonder Mountain, and Church Peak.

This is not an easy hike. Like most of the hikes in the Mount Skokomish Wilderness, the grade is steep and offers little respite along the way. Mount Rose also makes an excellent alternative to Mount Ellinor, as it receives a fraction of the traffic and offers a nearly identical experience. This hike is perfect for those looking for a challenge with rewarding views, searching for a new conditioning route, or heading to Mount Ellinor and deciding they want something a little different.

6 Lower Skokomish River

Follow trade paths first cut by the Skokomish Indians on this 8.5-mile hike along the Skokomish River.

Start: Lower South Fork Skokomish Trailhead
Distance: 8.5 miles out and back
Hiking time: About 4–5 hours
Elevation gain: 800 feet (500 feet in; 300 feet out)
High point: 900 feet
Difficulty: Easy, without much elevation gain
Best season: Hikeable year-round; best May–Sept

Traffic: Open to biking; moderate equestrian use; moderate foot traffic
Fees and permits: Northwest Forest Pass
Maps: USGS Mount Tebo; *Green Trails Map #199* (Mount Tebo)
Trail contacts: Hood Canal Ranger District–Quilcene, 295142 Highway 101 S., PO Box 280, Quilcene, WA 98376; (360) 765-2200; fs.usda.gov/olympic

Finding the trailhead: From Seattle take I-5 south to Olympia to exit 104 toward Aberdeen and Port Angeles. Follow US 101 along Hood Canal just over 27 miles through Shelton to Skokomish Valley Road. Take a left and follow the road 5.5 miles to FR 23. Head right and continue a little over 9 miles to FR 2353. Turn right and cross over the South Fork Skokomish River in less than 1 mile. Turn left at the four-way intersection and find the trailhead within a few tenths of a mile. Trailhead GPS: N47 25.127'/W123 19.749'

The Hike

Although logging has been banned in the Olympic National Forest since the late 1980s, the river here continues to feel the lingering effects of the clear-cuts. The Skokomish continues to be extremely flood-prone, most recently on December 3, 2007, when storm water caused the river to swell to more than twenty times its mean flow, discharging almost 30,000 cubic feet per second. The flood destroyed Camp Comfort, an open section of riverbank that had been a stopping point for hikers of the Lower South Fork Skokomish Trail for generations.

The trail begins with a series of switchbacks, quickly climbing a few hundred feet past sword fern and salal before leveling out high above the river in a section of old-growth firs. The wide, well-maintained trail breezes past trees hundreds of years old and then abruptly descends back down to the riverside. From here the trail becomes tame, with only minor elevation changes and small creeks to tiptoe across. As you wander along, enjoy the sounds of the river and watch as the

▶ In 1909 President Theodore Roosevelt established the Mount Olympus National Monument in an effort to preserve the elk population. Today Olympic National Park is host to the largest unmanaged herd of Olympic elk in the world. Somewhat unsurprisingly, Olympic elk are also known as Roosevelt elk.

A small creeklet flows over the trail.

forest shifts easily between stands of maple and alder to hemlock and fir. Also keep an eye out for wildlife, especially the herds of Olympic elk that frequent the area.

There are a number of decent stopping points along the trail. Some like to call it a day at a bridge and waterfall 0.25 mile short of Camp Comfort. At almost exactly 4 miles, Camp Comfort was an ideal destination before it was washed away in 2007. Others like to get closer to the 5-mile mark and turn around at a viewpoint at a river bend. We recommend aiming for Camp Comfort and clambering across the rocks and driftwood for a lunch by the river.

This popular hike has some of the best of the Olympics' flora and fauna and is well worth a visit. Not surprisingly, the trail attracts hikers year-round as well as mountain bikers and equestrians, so expect some company. The hike is approachable for hikers of every skill level, and while the initial 300-foot hurdle might be challenging for some youngsters, most of the route is a decent trek for kids.

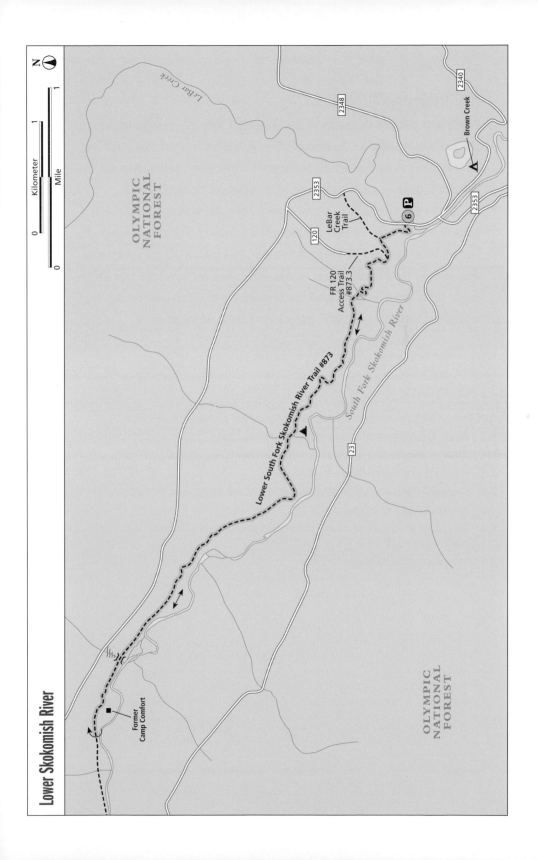

Lower Skokomish River

OLYMPIC
NATIONAL
FOREST

OLYMPIC
NATIONAL
FOREST

LeBar Creek

Brown Creek

2340

2348

2353

2353

120

LeBar Creek Trail

FR 120 Access Trail #873.3

6 P

Lower South Fork Skokomish River Trail #873

South Fork Skokomish River

23

Former Camp Comfort

N

0 — Kilometer — 1

0 — Mile — 1

Historical Background

People have relied on the waters of the Skokomish River for hundreds of years. A Salishan people known as the Twana Indians maintained at least nine permanent settlements along the river system. The largest of these village communities was the Skokomish, which means "big river people" or "people of the river" in Salish.

Before European settlers arrived around 1860, the Skokomish established a network of trails along the river to trade with the Quinault Indians to the east. As settlers slowly displaced the Skokomish Indians, they cut a wider and more permanent route to the Quinault Indians to help move resources out of the river valley. In the 1950s timber interests used this permanent route when clear-cutting large areas along the river. Today's trail largely follows these old timber roads.

Miles and Directions

0.0 Park at the lower trailhead and find Lower South Fork Skokomish River Trail #873.

0.3 Continue straight ahead at the LeBar Creek Trail junction.

0.4 Continue straight ahead at the FR 120 Access Trail #873.3 junction.

1.8 Pass an unmarked campsite near the river.

3.8 Stop on the large wooden bridge to enjoy the waterfall sliding down the rocks.

4.0 Arrive at former Camp Comfort.

4.2 Take a hard left and follow a faint boot path toward the wide-open rocky shore, perfect for enjoying lunch by the river.

8.5 Arrive back at the trailhead.

Mountain Loop Highway

The thirst for gold and mineral wealth fueled the creation of the Mountain Loop Highway. The highway was constructed between 1936 and 1941, largely following the railroads and wagon ruts cut by miners and prospectors to reach Monte Cristo and other nearby claims. Today the mining is almost entirely gone, and the area sees more recreational use than anything else. Several rivers permeate this area—the Stillaguamish, Sauk, and Boulder—each of which provides some great hiking opportunities, while lofty peaks complete with wide vistas draw peakbaggers from all over the state.

Snow-dusted Bald Mountain (hike 11)

7 Boulder River

Follow the Boulder River on the most popular trail in the Boulder River Wilderness.

Start: Boulder River Trailhead
Distance: 8.2 miles out and back
Hiking time: About 3–4 hours
Elevation gain: 700 feet
High point: 1,560 feet
Difficulty: Easy due to gentle grade
Best season: Mar–Oct
Traffic: Heavy foot traffic

Fees and permits: None
Maps: USGS Meadow Mountain; *Green Trails Map #77* (Oso), *#109* (Granite Falls)
Trail contacts: Verlot Public Service Center, 33515 Mountain Loop Hwy., Granite Falls, WA 98252; (360) 691-7791; fs.usda.gov/mbs
Special considerations: Parking at the trailhead is limited.

Finding the trailhead: From Seattle take I-5 north to exit 208 and drive east on SR 530 for about 19 miles to milepost 41. Immediately after the milepost, turn right onto FR 2010—some maps call this French Creek Road, but it's not well signed. Follow the unpaved road almost 4 miles to its end and the trailhead. Trailhead GPS: N48 15.048' / W121 49.031'

The Hike

The trail begins by following a 1909 railroad grade above the river for about 0.5 mile before crossing the Boulder River Wilderness boundary. The rushing sound of Boulder River Falls can be heard in this first section of the trail, but the waterfall itself is obscured by thick underbrush. While it is tempting to try to bushwhack down to them, we suggest you skip it, because referring to this set of boulder-strewn set of rapids as a waterfall is a bit overgenerous. Instead, continue onward to

▶ The water ouzel has an extra eyelid that allows it to see underwater.

what some folks refer to as Pre-Show Falls, a small horsetail waterfall tumbling down the rock walls opposite the trail. A trail leads down to the rocky riverside for a closer view and a glimpse of the next set of falls, unofficially known as Feature Show Falls, 0.25 mile upriver.

Feature Show Falls are perhaps the most dramatic stopping point along the trail—a large outcropping splits the falls in half as the water spills down the moss-covered rock face. For some this is destination enough, and you can settle in on the trailside bench or clamber down the riverbank to find a picnic spot. Others continue on for another mile through a thickening forest of fir and hemlock to the final falls, sometimes called Meditation Falls. If you're up for a longer day, continue past Meditation Falls to hike the full 4 miles to the end of the trail at Boulder Ford. At one time hikers

Feature Show Falls

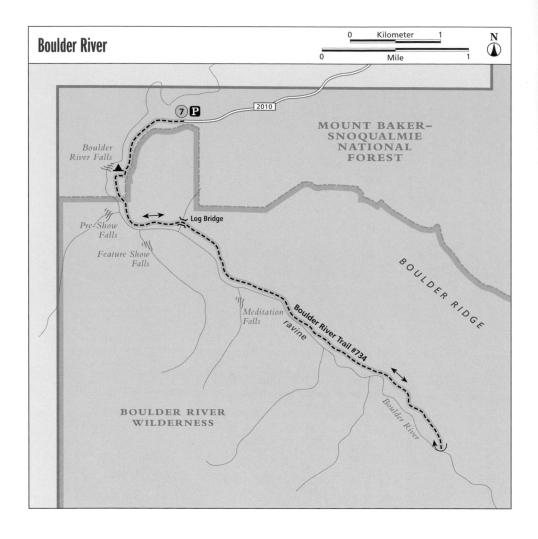

could cross the river here and continue onward and upward to the Three Fingers Fire Lookout, but the route has long been abandoned in favor of other approaches.

It's unsurprising that the Boulder River Trail is a popular hike. This trail gently takes you through a dramatic and impressive landscape. Once beyond Feature Show Falls, the forest becomes moss-laden and heavy, losing much of the undergrowth prominent in the early portions of the trail. The river remains a nearly constant companion, always within hearing distance even as it slips from view. Creeks cut across the trail, winding down to the river in contrast to the more dramatic cascades on the opposite bank. Even the wildlife is unexpected: Water ouzels, wood ducks, and hummingbirds all make an appearance. With only a few hundred feet of elevation gain and worthy destinations early on, this trail is an excellent way to give children or the reluctant hiker a taste of the wilderness.

Historical Background

Around the turn of the twentieth century, logging companies in Washington began eyeing valuable stands of timber that had been protected by the Forest Reserve Act of 1891. These National Forest Reserves were meant to protect forests for future generations and were the beginning of today's system of National Forests. However, by 1907 the timber industry convinced Congress to allow limited harvests in the Reserves. One of the earliest sales under this program was made to the Hazel Lumber Company in 1908, allowing the company to harvest 7.8 million board feet of mature cedar, fir, and hemlock from 320 acres around the French Creek area. The next year, the company began building a railway along the Boulder River to transport men and equipment to logging camps and to haul trees back toward Darrington to be milled.

Today the Boulder River Trail follows portions of that abandoned railroad grade and the Boulder River runs through the Boulder River Wilderness. The wilderness encompasses nearly 50,000 acres of wildlands that have been protected since 1984 and boast the only virgin timber in the Mount Baker–Snoqualmie National Forest. The vast majority of the wilderness is untouched—there are only 25 miles of maintained trail in the area, leaving the rest to black bears, mountain goats, and elk.

Miles and Directions

0.0 Start at the Boulder River Trailhead #734.

0.7 Pass a campsite that's located down an embankment.

1.2 Follow a side trail to the river and Feature Show Falls.

1.5 Cross a log bridge.

2.2 Arrive at Meditation Falls.

2.6 Look for a path leading to the top of a ravine cut by the river. Use caution, as the cliffs are steep and abruptly drop into the river.

4.1 Arrive at Boulder River Ford and the end of the trail.

8.2 Arrive back at the trailhead.

8 Old Sauk River

This 6.0-mile stroll through an area that was once home to the Sauk–Suiattle tribe follows portions of the wagon road that once connected Darrington and Monte Cristo.

Start: Old Sauk River Trailhead
Distance: 6.0 miles out and back
Hiking time: About 3–4 hours
Elevation gain: 100 feet
High point: 800 feet
Difficulty: Easy with nearly flat, well-maintained trail
Best season: Hikeable year-round; best Mar–Oct

Traffic: Moderate foot traffic
Fees and permits: None
Maps: USGS Helena Ridge; *Green Trails Map #110* (Silverton)
Trail contacts: Verlot Public Service Center, 33515 Mountain Loop Hwy., Granite Falls, WA 98252; (360) 691-7791; fs.usda.gov/mbs

Finding the trailhead: From Seattle take I-5 north to exit 208 and drive east on SR 530 to Darrington. Follow the signs to the Mountain Loop Highway, heading south out of town. After 4 miles find the signed Old Sauk River Trailhead on your left. Trailhead GPS: N48 12.911' / W121 33.576'

The Hike

From the gravel parking lot, the trail quickly cuts toward the Sauk River. Wander through a mixed forest of evergreens and maples nestled beneath looming old-growth firs, thankfully skipped over when the area was last logged in the 1930s. Once you reach the river, keep an eye out for wildlife. It's not uncommon to encounter a few of the many animals attracted to the river. The trailside is thick with moss, berry bushes, and views of the river. Depending on the time of year, there will be something to pause and take a closer look at—whether it's blooming flowers, a handful of huckleberries, or a bald eagle sighting.

▶ In 1978, 158.5 miles of the Skagit River system, including the Sauk River, were brought into the National Wild and Scenic Rivers System, which seeks to preserve the free flow of rivers. It is one of only three in Washington State.

While the trail is ideal for hikers of all ages, it does not have the big reward of broad vistas or a remote alpine lake. Instead, the Old Sauk Trail is a chance to slow down, take a closer look at the landscape, and enjoy the sounds of

Bridge along the river shore ▶

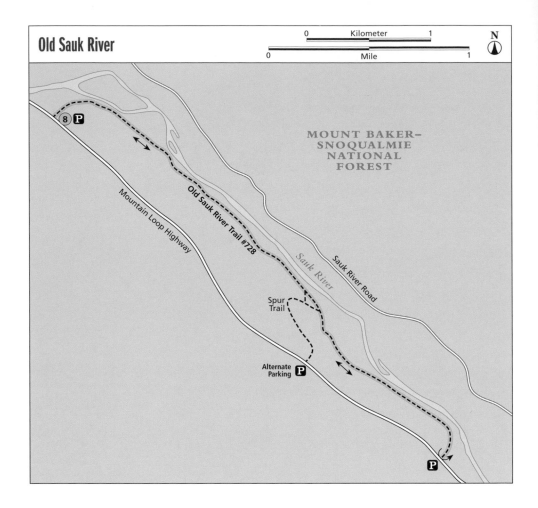

the rushing Sauk River. With almost no elevation to speak of and year-round access, this trail is a great little escape during the winter or a last-minute walk with the family during the summer months.

The Washington Trails Association has been doing a lot of work on the Old Sauk Trail, updating the main trailhead and repairing trail damage from recent floods. In 2011 a new trailhead was added roughly halfway between the two ends of the current trail, and a new trail was cut from the Mountain Loop Highway to the river. Increased access should mean that the Old Sauk Trail will see more use in the future.

Historical Background

While short, the Old Sauk Trail wanders through land thick with history. The Sauk-Suiattle tribe spent generations plying the Sauk, Suiattle, Cascade, Stillaguamish, and Skagit Rivers before signing a treaty with the US government in 1855. In 1867 settlers surveyed Darrington and nearby parcels, and the 1889 discovery of gold at Monte Cristo drew more settlers to the rapidly developing area. Parts of the Old Sauk Trail follow the route of the wagon road that connected Darrington to Monte Cristo. As time passed and settlement expanded, the Sauk-Suiattle were pushed out. By 1924 the tribe had shrunk to eighteen members. Ultimately, however, the tribe managed to rebound, reorganizing and attaining federal tribal recognition in 1973. Today a small reservation just outside Darrington is home to a handful of the tribe's 200 members.

Miles and Directions

0.0   Park in the small gravel lot. Find Old Sauk River Trail #728 at the end of the lot.

0.3   The Sauk River comes into view.

1.7   Arrive at a trail junction. Continue left, paralleling the river. The path to the right leads to the alternate parking area.

1.8   Continue straight past another trail junction to the alternate parking area.

3.0   The trail turns away from the river and follows Murphy Creek back to the Mountain Loop Highway.

6.0   Arrive back at the trailhead.

9 Lime Kiln

This 7.0-mile hike wanders down former logging roads and railroad grades to the remnants of a limekiln that long ago anchored a railway community.

Start: Lime Kiln Trailhead
Distance: 7.0 miles out and back
Hiking time: About 3-4 hours
Elevation gain: 500 feet
High point: 750 feet
Difficulty: Easy, marginal elevation gains
Best season: Hikeable year-round; best Mar-Oct

Traffic: Moderate foot traffic
Fees and permits: None
Maps: USGS Granite Falls; *Green Trails Map #109* (Granite Falls)
Trail contacts: Verlot Public Service Center, 33515 Mountain Loop Hwy., Granite Falls, WA 98252; (360) 691-7791; fs.usda.gov/mbs

Finding the trailhead: From Seattle take I-5 north to exit 194. Follow Highway 2 for about 2 miles. Stay in the left lane and merge onto Lake Stevens Highway 204. Follow it for 2 miles to SR 9. Take the left onto SR 9 toward Lake Stevens. In just under 2 miles, reach SR 92 to Granite Falls. Take a right and continue for about 8 miles to a four-way stop in Granite Falls. Take a right onto Granite Avenue, and in 3 blocks take a left onto Pioneer Street. Continue for a little over 1 mile as the road changes to Menzel Lake Road, and veer left onto Waite Mill Road. Continue for 0.5 mile to the school bus turnaround, and take the left-branching gravel road to the trailhead. Trailhead GPS: N48 04.653' / W121 55.952'

The Hike

From the trailhead, the route snakes through second-growth Douglas fir onto a logging road and into Robe Valley. The road is still in use and privately owned, but after 0.75 mile through managed forest, you are plunged onto wilder trail. Pass marshy Hubbard Lake, and follow the trail down into the valley, arriving on the grade high above the river. The forest feels more remote and untamed here. The thick, moss-heavy undergrowth occasionally encroaches on the trail, while endless streamlets constantly trickle across the path. Soon, artifacts will appear—buckets, dishes, equipment, and unidentifiable rusting metal—leading like breadcrumbs to the limekiln. Beyond the kiln nearly 1 mile of trail awaits. Follow the path out to a small sandy beach, or climb up to a massive cement foundation—all that remains of the bridge that once spanned the river.

Although the Lime Kiln Trail is a little light on sprawling vistas and pristine alpine lakes, the Robe Valley lends an air of ruggedness and feels more remote than it is. The trail is somewhat popular, so expect some company year-round, but at about 7.0

▶ Quicklime (calcium oxide) is thought to have been a component of Greek fire because of its reactivity with water that can release enough heat to ignite combustible materials.

Limekiln

miles round-trip and 500 feet of elevation, this little hike is a good winter hiking option. And with a fairly mild grade and lots of artifacts, the Lime Kiln Trail could be perfect for a young family out for a hike.

Miles and Directions

0.0 Begin the Lime Kiln Trail at the north end of the lot to start the hike.

0.6 The gravel road comes to a junction. Follow the sign and take the road leading down and to the right.

0.9 Depart from the road and onto actual trail. This short trail wanders past Hubbard Lake and reconnects with an old roadbed.

1.3 Arrive at a junction. Turn left off the old gravel road and onto a trail that follows Hubbard Creek down into Robe Canyon.

2.5 Reach the limekiln.

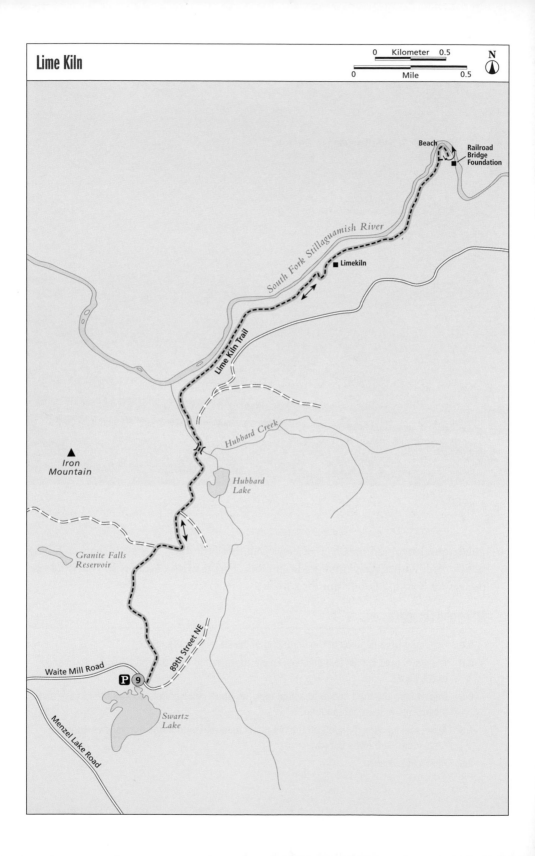

Lime Kiln

0 Kilometer 0.5
0 Mile 0.5

N

Beach
Railroad
Bridge
Foundation

South Fork Stillaguamish River

Limekiln

Lime Kiln Trail

Hubbard Creek

Iron
Mountain

Hubbard
Lake

Granite Falls
Reservoir

89th Street NE

Waite Mill Road

P 9

Swartz
Lake

Menzel Lake Road

Historical Background

Opened in 2004 after years of work by volunteers, much of the Lime Kiln Trail hugs the South Fork Stillaguamish River as it passes through Robe Valley, following the Everett and Monte Cristo Railway grade. Back in 1892, the railroad owners sought to keep construction costs down by ramming a rail line above the Stillaguamish rather than follow a more expensive route proposed by surveyors that considered the Robe Valley unstable. The decision proved costly—flood damage, sometimes severe enough to destroy bridges and collapse tunnels, required annual repair. The railway doggedly pulled minerals and timber out of the area for forty years before finally ceasing regular service in 1932. In 1936 the rails were pulled up to make way for the Mountain Loop Highway.

Remnants of the railway still litter Robe Canyon, though nothing is quite as impressive as the limekiln. Used to produce quicklime by heating limestone to high temperatures, the 20-foot structure was a continuous kiln, fed from the top. The quicklime made here was shipped to Everett to make plaster and mortar. Saw blades and artifacts aplenty can be found nearby, a testament to the fledgling community of Cut-Off Junction that the kiln and railroad supported.

3.3 Arrive at a junction for a short loop trail. Head to the left and continue following the path of the South Fork Stillaguamish River.

3.4 Come to a small beach on the South Fork Stillaguamish River.

3.5 The trail comes to a junction. Continue going 100 feet more to the left to the end of the trail at the site of an old railroad bridge that once spanned the river. On the return trip, take the path to the right for a quicker route back.

7.0 Arrive back at the trailhead.

This 3.0-mile hike follows the route of the Everett and Monte Cristo Railroad into the Robe townsite.

Start: Robe Canyon Trailhead
Distance: 3.0 miles out and back
Hiking time: About 2-3 hours
Elevation gain: 300 feet
High point: 1,080 feet
Difficulty: Easy with well-maintained trails and little elevation
Best season: Hikeable year-round; best Apr–Oct

Traffic: Moderate foot traffic
Fees and permits: None
Maps: USGS Verlot; *Green Trails Map #109* (Granite Falls)
Trail contacts: Verlot Public Service Center, 33515 Mountain Loop Hwy., Granite Falls, WA 98252; (360) 691-7791; fs.usda.gov/mbs

Finding the trailhead: From Seattle take I-5 north to exit 194. Follow Highway 2 for about 2 miles. Stay in the left lane and merge onto Lake Stevens Highway 204. Follow it for 2 miles to SR 9. Take the left onto SR 9 toward Lake Stevens. In just under 2 miles, reach SR 92 to Granite Falls. Take a right and continue for about 8 miles to Granite Falls. Proceed through the town to the Mountain Loop Highway, following it for 6 miles. Keep an eye out for cars parked on the right side of the road and a brick monument marking the trail just across from Green Mountain Road. Park on the shoulder.

Historical Background

Robe Canyon Historic Park covers nearly 1,000 acres along 7 miles of the South Fork Stillaguamish River and includes the historic Robe townsite. The town was established by Truitt K. Robe in 1892 or 1893 as a lumber- and shingle-manufacturing center along the newly constructed Everett and Monte Cristo Railway. Robe quickly prospered and, by 1899, was producing 75,000 shingles a day. As the town expanded, it could no longer support its nearly 200 citizens, forcing leaders to abandon the original townsite and move a few miles downstream to its current location. Although the public has been visiting the Robe townsite for decades, the first portions of Robe Canyon Historic Park weren't purchased until 1995. Over the next six years, the park expanded, and the Old Robe Trail—first built by Boy Scouts in the late 1960s—continued to provide access to the river and remnants of Washington's industrial history.

Old railway bed on the Stillaguamish River

The Hike

Perhaps the trickiest part of this hike is finding the trailhead, which is literally off the side of the Mountain Loop Highway, with parking limited to the highway's shoulders. Beyond that hurdle, the trail is perfect for a short walk in the woods. The trail begins through young forest before quickly dropping to the railroad grade on the valley floor. Wander past marshes and swamps beneath mossy alders as you follow the rushing sounds of the Stillaguamish River to the riverside. Along the way you'll note the lingering traces of Robe: crumbling bricks, twisted pieces of metal, and abandoned pieces of lumber.

We recommend this 3.0-mile jaunt as an after-work hike or just a quick visit to nature. For a short hike, this trail manages to cover a variety of landscapes and is steeped in history. While not at all something you need to break out the compass and gaiters for, it is still a little wilder than Mount Si or Tiger Mountain.

10 Mount Pilchuck

Tackle this 5.2-mile ascent through a former ski resort to a historic fire lookout.

Start: Mount Pilchuck Trailhead
Distance: 5.2-mile summit
Hiking time: About 5-7 hours
Elevation gain: 2,200 feet
High point: 5,324 feet
Difficulty: Difficult due to elevation and grade
Best season: May-Sept; popular snowshoe trail Sept-May

Traffic: Heavy foot traffic
Fees and permits: Northwest Forest Pass
Maps: USGS: Verlot; *Green Trails Map #109* (Granite Falls)
Trail contacts: Verlot Public Service Center, 33515 Mountain Loop Hwy., Granite Falls, WA 98252; (360) 691-7791; fs.usda.gov/mbs

Finding the trailhead: From Seattle take I-5 north to exit 194. Follow Highway 2 for about 2 miles. Stay in the left lane and merge onto Lake Stevens Highway 204. Follow it for 2 miles to SR 9. Take the left onto SR 9 toward Lake Stevens. In just under 2 miles, reach SR 92 to Granite Falls. Take a right and continue for about 9 miles to the Mountain Loop Highway (MLH). Follow the MLH for 12 miles to Mount Pilchuck Road, just over the bridge crossing the South Fork Stillaguamish River. Turn right and follow the road 7 miles to the trailhead. Trailhead GPS: N48 04.215'/W121 48.887'

The Hike

The trail begins at the end of the 7-mile-long Mount Pilchuck Road, following the service road once used to access the ski area. From the parking lot, a nice little view of the Stillaguamish Valley and Green Mountain hints at the kind of vistas that await at the summit. The route briefly wanders through young forest, which quickly thins to yield ever-larger views of the valley below. A little over a mile into the trail, the former ski slopes come into view and the trail flattens into a basin below a rocky prominence known as Little Pilchuck.

▶ Whimsical references to hoarfrost are often found in descriptions of hikes and snowshoes. "Hoar" comes from Old English that was meant to describe someone growing old. This makes hoarfrost a specific type of frost, one that gives the appearance of rocks, trees, and shrubs sprouting white hair.

During the summer the route curves around the cliffs and follows the ridgeline up to a saddle between the summit and Little Pilchuck. During the winter most folks opt to head directly up the snow-covered talus field to the saddle. From here it's less than 1 mile to the lookout along the main trail. A marked scramble route to the top

View north to Three Fingers ▶

Historical Background

First climbed by a US Geological Survey crew in 1897, Mount Pilchuck has been a destination ever since. *Pilchuck* means "red water" in Chinook jargon, a name that has been given to a number of streams and rivers in Washington State, including the Pilchuck River, which runs under the south slopes of the mountain. In 1918 the Forest Service built a fire tower on the summit. Built and rebuilt over the years, today a lookout house offers shelter to hikers.

However, Mount Pilchuck wasn't always the exclusive domain of hikers and snowshoers. From 1951 to 1980 the Mount Pilchuck Ski Area drew skiers from all over the state. Although ownership changed a few times over the years, the ski area eventually sported a lodge, ski-rental building, two ski lifts, and four rope tows for hauling skiers up the mountainside. Snow levels were unpredictable, however, with some years yielding only enough snow for a single day of skiing and others so much that the lifts couldn't operate for weeks on end. Some blame the conditions, others contend that it was government ineptitude that didn't allow renewal of the lease. Whatever the cause, by 1980 the ski area was shuttered. The lodge fell into disrepair and was eventually demolished. All that remains on the mountain are a few cement ski-lift foundations and rusting metal.

that cuts out some of the distance offers a summer alternative for the more experienced and adventurous.

Once you arrive at the summit, find a comfortable spot for lunch and drink in the 360-degree views. Mount Rainer looms to the south, rising above the miniaturized cities of Seattle and Everett huddled next to Puget Sound. As you pan west over the Olympics and swing north, you can pick out Three Fingers, Mount Baker, Glacier Peak, and Green Mountain. To the east lie Big Four Mountain and Mount Dickerman, along with Mounts Index and Baring. Peer below to find Heather Lake.

In the summer hikers flock to Pilchuck. With such stunning views at the end of a fairly short trail, it's easy to see why. We highly recommend trying this in early winter, when the snow is clean and powdery and the wind has sculpted the trees to look like something out of a children's book. However, use caution in the winter months. The route is marked, but it occasionally skirts avalanche chutes, and the mountain has plenty of abrupt cliffs that can sneak up on the unwitting snowshoer. Snow also

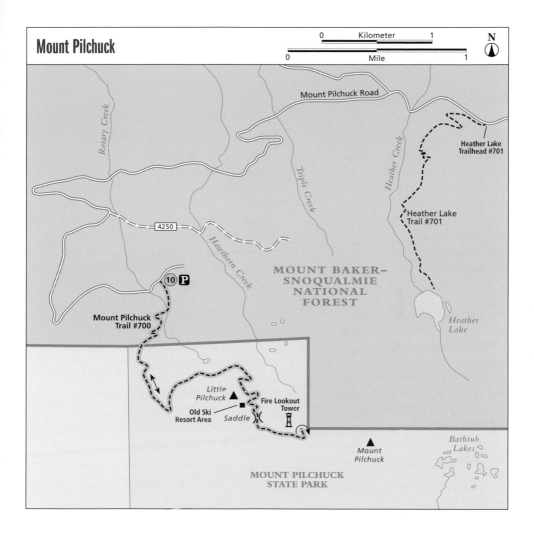

Mount Pilchuck

makes parking at the trailhead nearly impossible—simply go as far along Mount Pilchuck Road as your vehicle can, and hike the remaining miles to the trailhead.

Miles and Directions

0.0 Start hiking Mount Pilchuck Trail #700.

1.1 Emerge from the forest into a clearing for views out to Everett and the Puget Sound.

2.0 Hike through the old ski-resort slopes.

2.1 Attain the saddle on the ridge.

2.6 Reach the summit and the lookout house. Often open, the house offers shelter to hikers.

5.2 Arrive back at the trailhead.

11 Marten Creek

Explore this 6.6-mile hike along Marten Creek following a former railroad bed to an abandoned copper mine.

Start: Marten Creek Trailhead
Distance: 6.6 miles out and back
Hiking time: About 5–6 hours
Elevation gain: 1,400 feet
High point: 2,800 feet
Difficulty: Difficult due to rugged, overgrown sections of trail
Best season: May–Oct
Fees and permits: None

Maps: USGS Silverton; *Green Trails #110* (Silverton)
Trail contacts: Verlot Public Service Center, 33515 Mountain Loop Hwy. Hwy., Granite Falls, WA 98252; (360) 691-7791; fs.usda.gov/mbs
Special considerations: At 2 miles the decaying roadbed becomes more difficult to follow and is washed out in places. The full trek out to the mine may require some bushwhacking and route-finding skills.

Finding the trailhead: From Seattle take I-5 north to exit 194. Follow Highway 2 for about 2 miles. Stay in the left lane and merge onto Lake Stevens Highway 204. Follow it for 2 miles to SR 9. Take the left onto SR 9 toward Lake Stevens. In just under 2 miles, reach SR 92 to Granite Falls. Take a right and continue for about 9 miles to the Mountain Loop Highway (MLH). Follow the MLH for about 20 miles to the bridge over Marten Creek, just past the Marten Creek Campground. The signed trailhead is on the east side of the creek. There is no parking lot; find parking along the shoulder. Trailhead GPS: N48 04.331'/W121 36.370'

The Hike

The trail begins directly off the Mountain Loop Highway along Marten Creek. The first mile or so follows the now-abandoned roadbed up through a maturing forest of Douglas fir, cedar, and hemlock. The roadbed is occasionally rocky, but it is wide and generally free of blowdowns. Almost immediately the route crosses into the Boulder River Wilderness and begins switchbacking up a mountainside, carrying you past the experimental forest before swinging away from the highway and pushing deeper into the creek basin.

The road wastes little time climbing steeply 1,000 feet up through dense forest, then levels off and becomes a true trail. From here the trail crosses through a number of talus fields that offer views of the surrounding peaks, including Anaconda Peak, Three Fingers, Bald Mountain, and Long Mountain.

Unfortunately, because of current trail conditions, most hikers will not be able to catch a glimpse of Three Fingers, even on a good day. At about the 2-mile mark, the trail becomes increasingly difficult

▶ Fallen trees play an important part in forest ecosystems by providing habitat for insects and cavity nesters, which are an important part of the food chain.

Marten Creek Trailhead

to navigate: Blowdowns and washouts become more frequent, and the trail occasionally disappears. We highly recommend you bring along a GPS and be comfortable
with some bushwhacking and route finding if you are planning on continuing past
this point. If not, the 2-mile mark also has the first open view of Anaconda Peak and
the Marten Creek Valley, and it is probably a good place to settle in for a snack before
calling it a day. However, if you want a few more views and a look at an abandoned
mine, push on another 0.8 mile to Marten Creek, which can be difficult to cross
when the water is running high. Once across, follow the faint indication of the roadbed for a little less than 0.5 mile to the mine. Again, reaching the mine is not easy, and
you should not attempt it without a map or GPS.

If you're looking for a training hike or a quiet snowshoe without a lot of company,
the Marten Creek Trail is an excellent choice. Although there is not much in the way
of a destination, the first 2 miles of this trail offer forested trails, a roaring creek, some
views, and more than a little history. Beyond this point, most folks are unlikely to
enjoy the hike, at least until the trail gets some serious trail maintenance. Because of
this, we recommend you save this one for snowshoe season, as it makes a great alternative to the more popular routes along the Mountain Loop Highway.

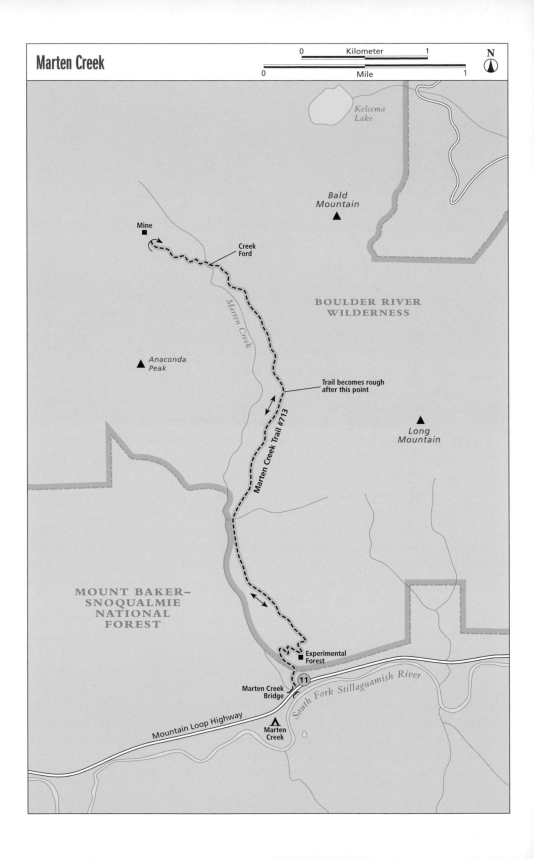

Marten Creek

0 Kilometer 1

0 Mile 1

N

Kelcema Lake

Bald Mountain

Mine

Creek Ford

BOULDER RIVER WILDERNESS

Marten Creek

Anaconda Peak

Trail becomes rough after this point

Long Mountain

Marten Creek Trail #713

MOUNT BAKER–SNOQUALMIE NATIONAL FOREST

Experimental Forest

11

Marten Creek Bridge

South Fork Stillaguamish River

Mountain Loop Highway

Marten Creek

Miles and Directions

0.0 Cross the Marten Creek Bridge and park on the right shoulder of the highway. The Marten Creek Trail #713 starts just across the road.

0.5 Douglas Fir Experimental Forest.

2.1 Arrive at the trail washout. Beyond this point the trail becomes rougher and overgrown. Route-finding skills required.

2.9 Reach the Marten Creek crossing. It's possible to find rocks to step across when the creek is running low, but it may need to be forded during the rainy months.

3.3 At the end of a deep gulch lies the old Marten Creek Mine. The mine is collapsed roughly 50 feet back into the rock.

6.6 Arrive back at the trailhead.

Historical Background

Much like nearby Monte Cristo, mining along Marten Creek boomed around the beginning of the twentieth century. At its height, dozens of claims were being worked to pull gold and copper out of the creek basin. In 1897 an Everett and Monte Cristo Railway locomotive sparked a major forest fire that consumed most of the trees on Long Mountain. Perhaps because the fire cleared so much land, the forest service chose Marten Creek as a location for one of the first experimental forests. Beginning in 1912, Douglas fir seedlings from different locations and elevations throughout Washington and Oregon were raised in nurseries. In 1915 and 1916 the young trees were transferred to the mountainside above Marten Creek, along with signs indicating where they were from and what elevation they came from, many of which are still present. The experiment was aimed at identifying and predicting different diseases that affect Douglas firs. The investigation continues to this day, making Marten Creek the oldest experimental forest in the Northwest.

Mining continued into the 1940s, when a rough road was blazed out to some of the more productive mines. Today's trail follows the remnants of this road. However, by the 1980s the mining had dropped off. In 1984 Congress designated the Boulder River Wilderness, protecting the only remaining virgin forest in the Mount Baker–Snoqualmie National Forest. Today the wilderness covers nearly 50,000 acres and is dominated by Three Fingers Mountain, which rises from the center of the protected area. Despite its size, there are only about 25 miles of trail through the Boulder River Wilderness, leaving the vast majority of the area wild and untouched.

12 Vesper Peak

This 6.6-mile hike follows mining trails up to the summit of Vesper Peak.

Start: Sunrise Mine Trailhead
Distance: 6.6-mile summit
Hiking time: About 7-9 hours
Elevation gain: 3,900 feet
High point: 6,214 feet
Difficulty: Difficult due to rugged trail and elevation
Best season: July-Sept

Traffic: Low foot traffic
Fees and permits: Northwest Forest Pass
Maps: USGS Silverton; *Green Trails Map #110* (Silverton), *#111* (Sloan Peak)
Trail contacts: Verlot Public Service Center, 33515 Mountain Loop Hwy., Granite Falls, WA 98252; (360) 691-7791; fs.usda.gov/mbs

Finding the trailhead: From Seattle take I-5 north to exit 194. Follow Highway 2 for about 2 miles. Stay in the left lane and merge onto Lake Stevens Highway 204. Follow it for 2 miles to SR 9. Take the left onto SR 9 toward Lake Stevens. In just under 2 miles, reach SR 92 to Granite Falls. Take a right and continue for about 9 miles to the Mountain Loop Highway (MLH). Take the MLH for almost 29 miles to the Sunrise Mine Road #4065 on your right. Follow the gravel road just under 2.5 miles to the end of the road and the trailhead. Trailhead GPS: N48 01.514' / W121 28.666'

The Hike

The Sunrise Mine Trail #707 begins by threading through a ragged stand of trees, with almost no underbrush. Greenery soon appears as a series of creeks and rivers cut across the rocky trail. The largest and most formidable of these is the South Fork Stillaguamish River, located about 0.5 mile down the trail. There are no permanent bridges here, so use caution crossing over rocks and logs, especially during the spring. Once you make it past the water, the trees begin to recede and the work begins. The trail slices through a valley of dense underbrush, switchbacking upward toward the cliffs above. The narrow trail is more root and rock than earth, with parts of the trail missing where sections have fallen away.

Eventually the trail plateaus and you will find yourself at the bottom of Wirtz Basin. Talus-filled and likely dotted with snowfields, the high-walled basin seems like a dead end. Ahead, Morning Star Mountain looms at the end of the basin, and to the left are the heights of Sperry Peak. You will not be able to pick out Headlee Pass until you're almost upon it, as the narrow break in the cliffs is hidden. Press onward, following the cairns over broad talus fields and winding past small pines and hemlocks. Use caution once you reach the base of the pass, where a series of tight switchbacks leads to the top and much of the trail

▶ Vesper is Latin for "evening" and is often associated with the evening prayers, or vespers, of some religious orders.

Wirtz Basin

is loose scree, raising the risk of sending rocks careening down the mountainside onto hikers below.

After you reach Headlee Pass, you may want to take a moment to poke your head over the rocks to get a taste of views to come. Once you catch your breath, follow the trail for another 0.25 mile across boulders and loose rock to Vesper Creek. Here you can follow the creek a short distance up to snowy Lake Elan (sometimes referred to as Headlee Lake or Vesper Lake) or cross and find a few welcoming campsites.

The real prize lies ahead, at the top of Vesper Peak. The trail is not easy and at times is little more than a scramble, but the rewards are worth the effort to reach the rocky summit. From the top you can pick out dozens of peaks. To the north the reddened slopes of Big Four Mountain loom above Copper Lake. As you turn east find Mount Dickerman, Mount Pugh, Sloan Peak, and Glacier Peak. Sperry Peak is right next door, while Morning Star Peak and Del Campo Peak are farther east. As you swing south pick out Mount Stuart and Mount Rainier. Continue to the west and

Vesper Peak

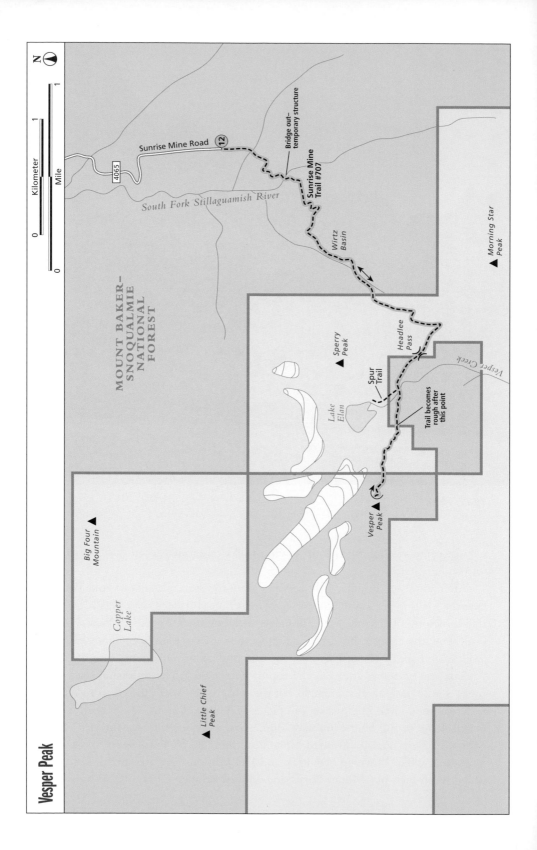

N

Kilometer
Mile

MOUNT BAKER–
SNOQUALMIE
NATIONAL
FOREST

Big Four
Mountain ▲

Copper
Lake

Little Chief
Peak ▲

Vesper Peak ▲

Lake
Elan

Sperry
Peak ▲

Spur
Trail

Headlee
Pass

Trail becomes
rough after
this point

Vesper Creek

Morning Star
Peak ▲

Wirtz Basin

Sunrise Mine
Trail #707

Bridge out–
temporary structure

South Fork Stillaguamish River

Sunrise Mine Road 12

4065

find Little Chief Peak, Whitehorse Mountain, and the Three Fingers as you complete your 360-degree turn. These are only some of the mountains—there are too many peaks to name them all. Settle in for a well-deserved break and see how many mountains you recognize.

This hike is not for everyone. It is difficult, scaling more than 4,000 feet in a little over 3 miles on rough trail. Some route-finding skills are occasionally required, depending on how snow-covered the trail is, and above Vesper Creek you can expect to encounter snow all year. With those caveats, we recommend this hike for strong hikers looking for a challenge. And because it is difficult, there is a bit less traffic on the trail, so you can expect to enjoy the views in relative solitude.

Miles and Directions

0.0 Start on Sunrise Mine Trail #707.

0.5 Cross the South Fork Stillaguamish River. The bridge is out, but rocks and logs offer a path over the river. Use caution when the river is running high.

1.2 The trail levels out at Wirtz Basin.

2.4 Arrive at Headlee Pass (4,600 feet).

2.7 Arrive at a trail junction. Just before crossing Vesper Creek, follow a path up the creek for 0.25 mile to Lake Elan.

3.3 Reach the summit of Vesper Peak.

6.6 Arrive back at the trailhead.

Historical Background

In 1889 gold was discovered around Monte Cristo. With that discovery, Monte Cristo boomed, and prospectors fanned out into nearby valleys and scaled rugged peaks looking for the next mother lode. Among those intrepid prospectors was F. M. Headlee, who is credited with discovering Barlow Pass in 1891. The Headlees were a prominent family in the area during this time. One Headlee filed the plat for the Monte Cristo townsite in 1893, and another spent decades as a Snohomish County public official. In 1897 F. M. Headlee finally found what he was looking for: His name appears on the Sunrise Prospect Mine claim along with T. E. Headlee and G. E. Humes. The mine was located near the head of Vesper Creek, though it is unclear whether this location was ever used for production. Instead it seems that the Bren Mac Mine in the Sultan River Basin was used to access most of the minerals under Vesper Peak.

13 Gothic Basin

This popular 10.5-mile hike follows trails cut to support mining operations in Gothic Basin.

Start: Monte Cristo Road
Distance: 10.5 miles out and back
Hiking time: About 7–9 hours
Elevation gain: 3,700 feet
High point: 6,000 feet
Difficulty: Difficult due to elevation
Best season: July–Sept

Traffic: Equestrian and bike use; moderate foot traffic
Fees and permits: Northwest Forest Pass
Maps: USGS Monte Cristo; *Green Trails Map #143* (Monte Cristo)
Trail contacts: Verlot Public Service Center, 33515 Mountain Loop Hwy., Granite Falls, WA 98252; (360) 691-7791; fs.usda.gov/mbs

Finding the trailhead: From Seattle take I-5 north to exit 194. Follow Highway 2 for about 2 miles. Stay in the left lane and merge onto Lake Stevens Highway 204. Follow it for 2 miles to SR 9. Take the left onto SR 9 toward Lake Stevens. In just under 2 miles, reach SR 92 to Granite Falls. Take a right and continue for about 9 miles to the Mountain Loop Highway (MLH). Take the MLH for 31 miles to Barlow Pass. Park and find the gated Monte Cristo Road on the right side of the road, opposite the trailhead parking lot. Trailhead GPS: N48 01.557' / W121 26.617'

The Hike

The hike begins along the Monte Cristo Road, the former Everett and Monte Cristo Railroad grade. Flat and wide, the grade quickly covers the 1 mile to the Weden Creek Trail #724. Once on the path toward Gothic Basin, the trail soon narrows and becomes more challenging. The miners and prospectors that cut this trail were interested in getting to their mines as quickly as possible, and the trail wastes little time before tackling the elevation.

After a long series of switchbacks through a young forest, the sheltering trees are traded for open views of the river valley and cliffs of exposed rock. As you traverse the mountainside, the trail crosses a number of creeks and waterfalls. The largest is known as King Kong's Showerbath, which makes for a great spot to take a break to cool off in the summer.

Continue to push up into the basin, where the trees almost completely recede and vast expanses of rock dominate the landscape. As you explore the basin, the trail splits. The short trail to the left descends down to an unnamed lakelet and views down onto Weden Lake. Head right to continue deeper into Gothic Basin and toward Foggy Lake. There is still some elevation to tackle, pressing up rocky gullies to arrive at the lakeshore. Almost always frozen, Foggy Lake sits beneath

▶ Barlow Pass is named for M. Q. Barlow, a surveyor who cut the first trail from Silverton to Monte Cristo.

Foggy Lake, Gothic Peak, and Del Campo Peak

the three-pronged Gothic Peak and Del Campo Peak. Clamber around the rocks and find a quiet spot to relax and enjoy the lake.

If you're up for a little more work, we recommend continuing up the shoulders of Del Campo Peak. Follow the faint trail around the east shore of the lake and soon find yourself next to a small tarn known as Tin Cup Lake. Push up the rough trail to the boulder field at the base of the summit. From here the views are spectacular. A sea of mountaintops spreads out before you. Pick out nearby Sheep Gap Mountain, Silver Tip Peak, Gothic Peak, and Crested Butte. The rest of the way up to the summit of Del Campo is somewhat technical, so make sure you've got the right experience and gear before attempting a scramble to the top.

This is a challenging hike that is not for everyone, but Gothic Basin is well worth the effort. The area is simply stunning. In the few weeks that Foggy Lake is melted out each year, its icy waters exude a gorgeous deep-blue color. There are also a number of truly amazing campsites that offer privacy and choice views. We highly recommend this hike to anyone that is comfortable with the elevation gain along a moderately rough trail. Make sure to do a little research on the conditions in the basin before you go, as the experience is better if the area is melted out.

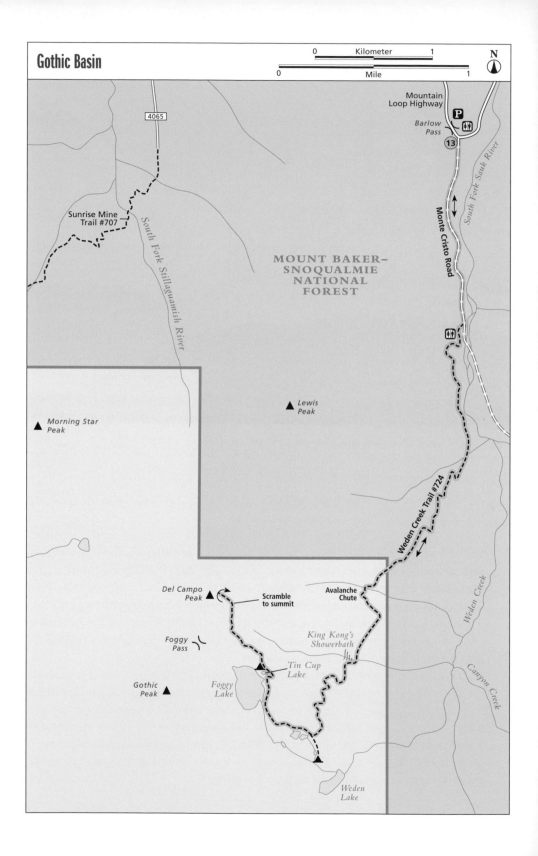

Gothic Basin

0 — Kilometer — 1
0 — Mile — 1

N

4065

Sunrise Mine
Trail #707

South Fork Stillaguamish River

Mountain
Loop Highway

Barlow
Pass

P

13

South Fork Sauk River

Monte Cristo Road

MOUNT BAKER–
SNOQUALMIE
NATIONAL
FOREST

Lewis
Peak

Morning Star
Peak

Weden Creek Trail #724

Weden Creek

Del Campo
Peak

Scramble
to summit

Avalanche
Chute

Foggy
Pass

King Kong's
Showerbath

Canyon Creek

Tin Cup
Lake

Gothic
Peak

Foggy
Lake

Weden
Lake

Historical Background

Although prominently signed WEDEN, the creek that the trail follows was named for prospector and settler Otis N. Weeden. Thus, the creek and lake that are often labeled "Weden" should actually be Weeden. It is unclear how the creek lost an e, though it may have been an intentional effort to remove the reference to Weeden because of his later crimes. On March 30, 1911, Weeden shot three of his neighbors before taking his own life in what was called the Sauk Prairie Massacre. The shootings were the result of a dispute over a small creek that all of the neighbors used for irrigation.

After gold was discovered in Monte Cristo in 1889, initial efforts to extract minerals from the area were fairly small scale. Bigger mining syndicates began arriving a few years later, starting in the areas around Del Campo Peak. In 1896 the Del Campo Mining Company began pulling gold, silver, and copper out of the area, and that same year Gothic Peak was named in honor of William Gothic, one of the first prospectors to stake a claim in Gothic Basin. Mining operations continued to expand after the turn of the century, and eventually an elaborate air tramway was constructed to transport ore from Gothic Basin down to the Everett and Monte Cristo Railroad along 7,000 feet of cable. As mining operations dwindled, the cable tramway was taken down, though traces of the cables and towers can still be found today.

Miles and Directions

0.0 Park at Barlow Pass and begin the hike by heading south on the old Monte Cristo Road. A privy is located at the trailhead.

1.1 Arrive at a privy and continue on the path to the right. Turn right again and head up the Weden Creek Trail #724.

3.1 The trail crosses an avalanche chute. During the spring melt, a creek runs down the chute.

3.6 Cross the water streaming down from the cliffs above. The falls are unoffically known as King Kong's Showerbath.

4.4 Unnamed lakelet.

4.7 Reach Foggy Lake.

4.9 Arrive at a very nice campsite next to Tin Cup Lake.

5.3 The trail ends on the slopes of Del Campo Peak, where the route becomes a 0.2-mile scramble to the summit.

10.5 Arrive back at the trailhead.

14 Monte Cristo Townsite

This 9.5-mile hike follows a railroad grade out to the gold-rush town of Monte Cristo.

Start: Monte Cristo Road
Distance: 9.5 miles out and back
Hiking time: About 5–6 hours
Elevation gain: 600 feet
High point: 2,900 feet
Difficulty: Easy, with 1 log crossing
Best season: June–Sept
Traffic: Equestrian and bike use; heavy foot traffic
Fees and permits: Northwest Forest Pass
Maps: USGS Monte Cristo; *Green Trails Map #143* (Monte Cristo)
Trail contacts: Verlot Public Service Center, 33515 Mountain Loop Hwy., Granite Falls, WA 98252; (360) 691-7791; fs.usda.gov/mbs

Special considerations: This hike's only challenge is crossing the log over the South Fork Sauk River, but that may soon be changing. A new access road will be on the other side of the river, connecting with the current road after the washout. The road is being built to support a massive cleanup effort focusing on containing the arsenic and other heavy metals churned up by Monte Cristo's mining past. The cleanup began in fall 2013 and will last into the summer 2015, and during that time the plan is to close the townsite. How the new road will be used after the cleanup is undecided.

Finding the trailhead: From Seattle take I-5 north to exit 194. Follow Highway 2 for about 2 miles. Stay in the left lane and merge onto Lake Stevens Highway 204. Follow it for 2 miles to SR 9. Take the left onto SR 9 toward Lake Stevens. In just under 2 miles, reach SR 92 to Granite Falls. Take a right and continue for about 9 miles to the Mountain Loop Highway (MLH). Take the MLH for 31 miles to Barlow Pass. Park and find the gated Monte Cristo Road on the right side of the road, opposite the trailhead parking lot. Trailhead GPS: N48 01.557' / W121 26.617'

The Hike

The hike begins at Barlow Pass, following the same railroad grade that has been in use since 1893. Flat and wide, the graveled road is an easy stroll along the South Fork Sauk River. Occasional openings in the trees reveal glimpses of the rocky prominences guarding the top of the valley: Cadet Peak, Toad Mountain, and Silvertip Mountain.

> ▶ Turntables were used to turn steam locomotives around, which, unlike diesel engines, were not configured to run well in reverse.

After about 1 mile you'll reach the washed-out bridge and the junction with the Weden Creek Trail #724 leading up to Gothic Basin. A 2006 flood further eroded the trail here, forcing

South Fork Sauk River

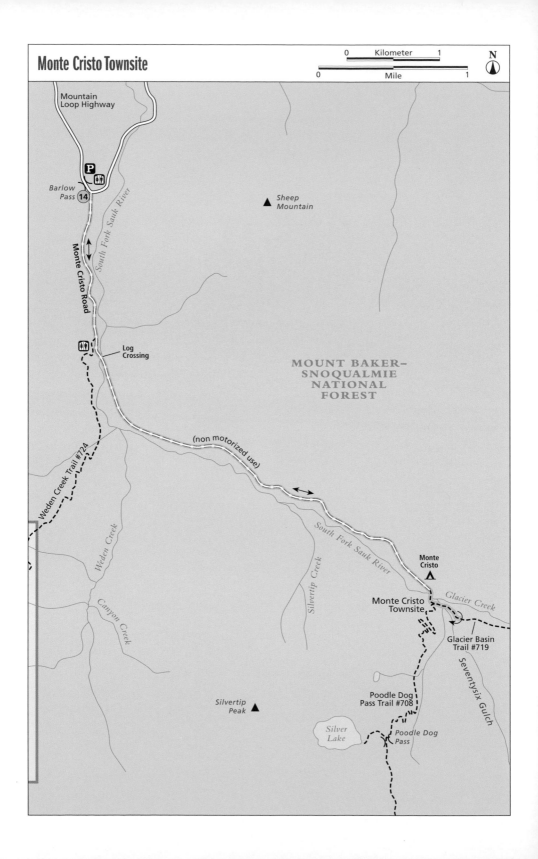

Monte Cristo Townsite

0   Kilometer   1

0   Mile   1

N

Mountain
Loop Highway

Barlow
Pass   (14)

Monte Cristo Road

South Fork Sauk River

▲ *Sheep
Mountain*

Log
Crossing

**MOUNT BAKER–
SNOQUALMIE
NATIONAL
FOREST**

Weden Creek Trail #724

(non motorized use)

South Fork Sauk River

Silvertip Creek

Weden Creek

*Monte
Cristo*
▲

Monte Cristo
Townsite

Glacier Creek

Canyon Creek

Glacier Basin
Trail #719

Seventysix Gulch

*Silvertip
Peak* ▲

Poodle Dog
Pass Trail #708

*Silver
Lake*

*Poodle Dog
Pass*

you to take a narrow path through the trees to a large log spanning the river. During the summer months the river is low enough that it is easy to wade across. Many choose to brave the log crossing—use caution if you attempt this route, as the log could be slippery.

Once across the river and back on the road, it's another 3 miles to the townsite. Along the way you might be able to pick out Twin Peaks or Monte Cristo Peak up ahead, and Lewis Peak and Del Campo Peak make appearances to the west. At about 4 miles reach the Monte Cristo Campground and the bridge over Glacier Creek just beyond, leading into the townsite. Once you arrive, take some time to explore the few remaining structures still standing and pick through the rusting artifacts from the mining days. Be sure to wander down Dumas Street—named for Alexandre Dumas, the author of *The Count of Monte Cristo*—to get an idea of how the town was laid out. Bring a healthy amount of imagination, as most of the town is long gone, leaving only signs to mark the former locations of buildings.

This is a decent hike that should be approachable for almost anyone, especially those interested in a little history. To get the most out of your visit, we recommend you stop at the Verlot Ranger Station on your way out to Barlow Pass to pick up a pamphlet that includes a map of Monte Cristo and explanations of the various marked sites in the town. After you are done touring the town, you may be looking to do a little more hiking. If that's the case, you can continue up to Glacier Falls and Glacier Basin. Or you can retrace the pre-railroad approach to Monte Cristo with a hike up to Poodle Dog Pass #708, named in honor of Frank Peabody's dog, which he evidently took with him when he climbed the pass on his way to Monte Cristo from Mineral City.

Miles and Directions

0.0 Park at Barlow Pass and begin the hike by heading south on the old Monte Cristo Road. A privy is located at the trailhead.

1.2 The bridge over the South Sauk River is washed out. Walk past the privy and find a large log spanning the river. Use caution crossing when the river is running high.

4.2 Arrive at the Monte Cristo Campground.

4.5 Arrive at Monte Cristo. The grassy clearing has an old railroad turnabout, a powerhouse, and cabins that were part of the old lodge.

4.6 Arrive at Peabody's Garage, the oldest standing structure in Monte Cristo.

4.7 Arrive at a junction. Going left leads down to what is left of a concentrator. Continuing straight leads out to Glacier Basin. Head right for a short loop through the former streets of Monte Cristo.

9.5 Arrive back at the trailhead.

Historical Background

In 1889 a prospector named Joe L. Pearsall was living in Mineral City looking to strike it rich. As the snows receded he climbed nearby Hubbart Peak to survey the area and saw something metallic shining in the afternoon sun. Pearsall gathered a few samples and had his partner, Frank Peabody, take them to Seattle for analysis. Testing indicated silver and gold. On July 4, 1889, Pearsall and Peabody staked the first claim in the area, calling it the Independence of 1776 in honor of the holiday. Today it's referred to as '76 Gulch.

News traveled quickly. Claims multiplied, and dozens of mines were opened. Peabody is credited with commenting that the minerals in the area would make them "as rich as the Count of Monte Cristo," and so the burgeoning town took up the name, hoping to attract more investors to help finance the operation. The Everett and Monte Cristo Railroad was built in 1893 to transport ore to smelters in Everett, in the process making the town more accessible to the outside world. The scale of mining operations increased exponentially, and soon a complex system of cable-bucket aerial tramways was built, allowing miners to send 230 tons of ore swinging down steep mountainsides every day for processing in Monte Cristo's concentrators.

By 1907 more than 300,000 tons of copper, gold, silver, and zinc were pulled out of the mines, worth millions of dollars. But the cost of operating the mines and keeping the railroad running was digging into profits, and many of the miners had moved on to find their fortunes in Alaska. A market collapse in 1907 put an end to mining in Monte Cristo, and attempts to revive the industry failed. In 1936 the railroad, which had long suffered washouts from seasonal flooding, was removed and Monte Cristo became something of a ghost town.

Still, attempts were made to attract tourists, using the old Royal Hotel and other remaining structures. After World War II, interest picked up and Monte Cristo saw hundreds of visitors on summer weekends, all driving down a county road built on the old railroad bed. In 1980 a flood washed out the bridge over the South Fork Sauk River, and it was never repaired. The lodge burned down in 1983, and the USDA Forest Service gained control of most of Monte Cristo in 1994. Today the Monte Cristo Preservation Society helps to maintain and highlight the history of the former mining town. The area also serves as a gateway to a number of trails in the Henry M. Jackson Wilderness.

Gear up for a 13.0-mile hike through the remains of Monte Cristo and up into a basin that once bustled with mining operations.

Start: Monte Cristo Road
Distance: 13.0 miles out and back
Hiking time: About 7–8 hours
Elevation gain: 2,200 feet
High point: 4,400 feet
Difficulty: Difficult due to steep sections of rugged trail
Best season: June–Sept

Traffic: Low foot traffic
Fees and permits: Northwest Forest Pass
Maps: USGS Blanca Lake; *Green Trails Map #143* (Monte Cristo)
Trail contacts: Verlot Public Service Center, 33515 Mountain Loop Hwy., Granite Falls, WA 98252; (360) 691-7791; fs.usda.gov/mbs

Finding the trailhead: From Seattle take I-5 north to exit 194. Follow Highway 2 for about 2 miles. Stay in the left lane and merge onto Lake Stevens Highway 204. Follow it for 2 miles to SR 9. Take the left onto SR 9 toward Lake Stevens. In just under 2 miles, reach SR 92 to Granite Falls. Take a right and continue for about 9 miles to the Mountain Loop Highway (MLH). Take the MLH for 31 miles to Barlow Pass. Park and find the gated Monte Cristo Road on the right side of the road, opposite the trailhead parking lot.

Historical Background

Situated at the base of Monte Cristo Peak, Glacier Basin was at the center of Monte Cristo's mining activity in the 1890s. The basin is named for glaciers that carved out the cirque in the distant past, and while there is almost always some snow lingering in Glacier Basin, there are no longer any glaciers. The basin is riddled with mine shafts and tunnels, with at least one long passage running underneath the basin to connect mines in Cadet Peak on the east side of the basin with Mystery Ridge on the west. When mining operations were in full swing, a massive aerial tramway hauled ore across Glacier Basin in buckets along 1,200 feet of cable to a station located on Mystery Ridge. From there the tramway sent the buckets down to Monte Cristo to concentrators that separated the ore from less-useful material. Today you can still find evidence of this tramway station on the ridge.

Glacier Basin with Monte Cristo Peak in the background

The Hike

The approach to Glacier Basin follows the old Everett and Monte Cristo Railroad grade into Monte Cristo. The trail itself follows another railroad grade that was built in the 1890s to support the mines. You'll hike past Glacier Creek tumbling down from Glacier Basin in a number of cascades of varying sizes, some hidden in between folds of rock. From the falls the trail is steep and rough; use caution as you pick your way up challenging sections.

Eventually the route begins to level out and the trail meanders along Glacier Creek into the basin. You'll soon find yourself at the end of the line, staring up at the rocky peaks that line Glacier Basin's walls. If you're hungry for more climbing, there are routes up to the ridgeline, which will give you long views of the surrounding mountains as well as Blanca Lake tucked in the neighboring valley.

This is not an easy hike, and it is likely a little too long for most day hikers. But it does make for a decent weekend backpacking trip, and you're unlikely to meet too many other folks on this less-traveled trail.

15 Goat Lake

This 10.5-mile hike travels through the Henry M. Jackson Wilderness to an alpine lake and former mine site.

Start: Elliott Creek Trailhead
Distance: 10.5-mile lollipop
Hiking time: About 6–7 hours
Elevation gain: 1,600 feet
High point: 3,200 feet
Difficulty: Moderate due to length
Best season: June–Sept

Traffic: Heavy foot traffic
Fees and permits: Northwest Forest Pass
Maps: USGS Sloan Peak; *Green Trails Map #111* (Sloan Peak)
Trail contacts: Verlot Public Service Center, 33515 Mountain Loop Hwy., Granite Falls, WA 98252; (360) 691-7791; fs.usda.gov/mbs

Finding the trailhead: From Seattle take I-5 north to exit 194. Follow Highway 2 for about 2 miles. Stay in the left lane and merge onto Lake Stevens Highway 204. Follow it for 2 miles to SR 9. Take the left onto SR 9 toward Lake Stevens. In just under 2 miles, you'll reach SR 92 to Granite Falls. Take a right and continue for about 9 miles to the Mountain Loop Highway (MLH). Follow the MLH for a little over 30 miles to the end of the pavement. Continue another 3.5 miles to FR 4080. Take a right and follow FR 4080 about 1 mile to the Elliott Creek Trailhead. Trailhead GPS: N48 03.207' / W121 24.781'

Cadet Peak over Goat Lake

Historical Background

Goat Lake sits in a cirque surrounded by Sloan, Foggy, and Cadet Peaks within the 103,591-acre Henry M. Jackson Wilderness. Originally named "Sweetleehachu" by the Sauk Indians, miners gave the lake its current name in reference to the mountain goats that roamed the basin's steep slopes in the early 1890s. As prospectors rushed into Monte Cristo and Mineral City hoping to find gold, they branched out into areas like Goat Lake hoping to strike it rich. The first claims in the basin date back to 1891, quickly followed by a road built by the Penn Mining Company in 1895.

Many tunnels were dug into Cadet Peak and Foggy Peak, though these mines produced mostly lead, silver, and zinc and very little gold. A small mining town sprang up near the lake outlet, anchored by the Penn Mining Company offices and workers' cabins, as well as a lodge operated from 1927 to 1936 by the MacIntosh family. The 266-foot waterfall just below Goat Lake is named MacIntosh Falls in honor of the family. By the 1940s the buildings were abandoned and largely forgotten, until an avalanche swept most of the buildings into the lake. Today a few structures still remain, though the bridge across Elliott Creek has long since washed away, making it a little difficult to explore the former town.

The Hike

Elliott Creek Trail #647 begins easily, following the remains of the mining road that once provided access to the lake. Within the first 0.5 mile, you'll find signs pointing to Upper and Lower Elliott. Lower Elliott follows the creek and is about 1 mile shorter than the upper trail. However, the upper trail is a smoother trail and a little easier to navigate than the lower trail. We recommend braving the rockier, muddier, and more picturesque lower trail on the way out to the lake. Save the upper trail for your return trip, when the extra mile might be worth a little less strain on your knees.

Either way, you'll cross a number of streams and bubbling cascades along the way, as the forest slowly transitions from alder, fern, and bleeding heart to old-growth cedar and moss-covered fir. At 3.5 miles you'll enter the Henry M. Jackson Wilderness and trade any semblance of road for a winding trail. Continue another mile or so to the roaring MacIntosh Falls, following the faint trail

▶ Cadet Peak was named in 1890 to honor the United States Cadets, one of the many patriotic groups for young men that eventually led to the formation of the Boy Scouts of America and US Army Cadet Corps.

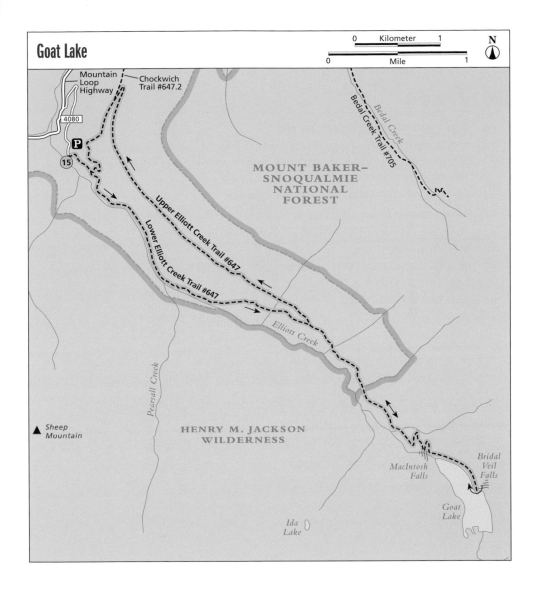

Kilometer

Mile

N

Mountain
Loop
Highway

Chockwich
Trail #647.2

4080

P

15

MOUNT BAKER–
SNOQUALMIE
NATIONAL
FOREST

Bedal Creek

Bedal Creek Trail #705

Upper Elliott Creek Trail #647

Lower Elliott Creek Trail #647

Elliott Creek

Pearsall Creek

Sheep
Mountain

HENRY M. JACKSON
WILDERNESS

MacIntosh
Falls

Bridal
Veil
Falls

Goat
Lake

Ida
Lake

out to get a closer look. Linger here for a few minutes, or push up the few remaining switchbacks to Goat Lake. Once you reach the lakeshore, follow the increasingly faint trail until you find a quiet place to settle down and have a snack. Cadet Peak sits at the far end of the lake next to Foggy Peak. If you're willing to brave the overgrown trail out to the end, you'll find Bridal Veil Falls tumbling down the cliffs of Sloan Peak.

Popular with both day hikers and backpackers, Goat Lake sees some significant traffic on summer weekends. It's easy to see why. While the trail is on the longer side, the grade is mostly gentle and the trail is clear and well maintained, making this hike approachable for most hikers. The destination is stunning: On a sunny day the reflection of snow-covered mountaintops in the lake is an impressive sight. And as if that weren't enough, getting a close-up look at massive MacIntosh Falls is more than worth a 4-mile hike. We recommend this hike for almost everyone, though be prepared to share the views with others if you go on a weekend.

Miles and Directions

0.0 Begin the hike on the Elliott Creek Trail #647.

0.2 At the junction of the Upper and Lower Elliott Trails, take the lower trail on the way in and the upper trail on the way out. Fewer people take the upper trail, so you'll enjoy a bit of solitude on the hike out.

2.5 The Upper and Lower Elliott Creek Trails reconnect here.

3.8 Follow a footpath toward Elliott Creek to the base of a raging MacIntosh Falls. Find an upward boot path to see more tiers of the giant waterfall.

4.3 Reach Goat Lake.

4.7 Brave the overgrown trail out to a small point where the trail ends. Bridal Veil Falls cascades down on your left.

10.5 Arrive back at the trailhead.

Highway 2

US Highway 2 runs from Everett to Michigan. The route follows roadbeds that were laid back in 1909, though it wasn't until 1946 that the highway was overhauled and brought into the US route system. Like the Mountain Loop Highway, Highway 2 runs through an area that has had a long relationship with mining and timber interests. Hiking in this area often brings runs through lingering traces of industry—from recovering clear-cuts to abandoned mines. The creeks and streams draining into the Snohomish and Skykomish River valleys have carved excellent opportunities to explore the mountaintops that line the highway. The skiing and snow sports at Stevens Pass make it easy to forget the feats of railroad engineering that were accomplished there, including the first railroad crossing of the Cascades in Washington and, for a time, the longest railroad tunnel in the world.

Looking out Embro Tunnel (hike 21)

16 Lord Hill Regional Park

Explore this network of trails cut through former timberlands once owned by farmer and dairyman Mitchell Lord.

Start: Lord Hill Regional Park Entrance
Distance: 3.6-mile loop
Hiking time: About 2 hours
Elevation gain: 350 feet
High point: 650 feet
Difficulty: Easy due to wide trails and little elevation
Best season: Hikeable year-round; best Apr–Oct

Traffic: Equestrian and bike use; moderate foot traffic
Fees and permits: None
Maps: USGS Maltby and Snohomish; www .co.snohomish.wa.us/documents/Departments/ Parks/maps/lordhill12_10.pdf
Trail contacts: Snohomish County Parks Department, 6705 Puget Park Dr., Snohomish, WA 98296; (425) 388-6600; www1.co .snohomish.wa.us/departments/parks/

Finding the trailhead: From Seattle take SR 522 north toward Monroe. Take the Monroe/West Main Street exit and circle around the roundabout to head west on 164th Street. Follow this road for about 3.5 miles as it changes from 164th Street to the Old Snohomish-Monroe Highway to 127th Avenue SE. Turn left and continue for 1.5 miles to 150th Street SE. Take a right and find parking at the end of the road. Trailhead GPS: N47 51.681'/W122 03.482'

The Hike

Lord Hill's trails vary from wide roads that are occasionally used by park officials to small, brush-lined paths to secluded lakeshores. Wander through a mixed forest of alder and maple interlaced with fir and hemlock as you explore trails leading to eight ponds and lakes as well as to the riverside. The park provides decent views of both the Cascades and the Olympics on a good day, and it shelters a variety of wildlife—varieties from beavers to bobcats have been seen within the park's boundaries. Routes within the park also loop together and make it easy to customize your wanderings, though not every junction is signed, making it a good idea to bring along a map to minimize any confusion.

The park is a decent hiking destination during the winter. It's close and easily accessible, but still large enough to feel like you're getting out into nature. During warmer weather this is a great place for youngsters to get out into the woods for the day, but be prepared to share the mixed-use trails with mountain bikers and equestrians. All in all, it's worth an afternoon to trek out to explore Snohomish County's largest park.

Hiking the Pipeline Trail

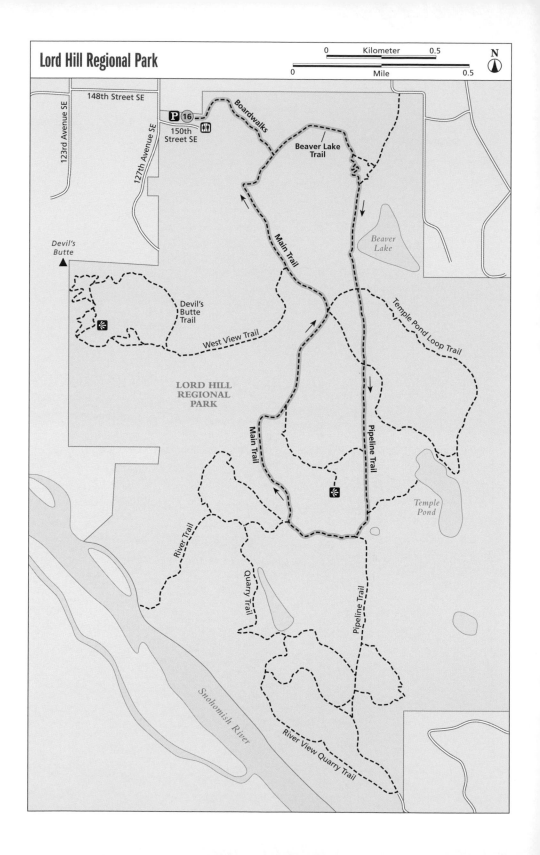

Historical Background

Lord Hill Regional Park covers most of an 800-foot volcanic ridge overlooking the Snohomish River. The prominence was named for Mitchell Lord, a farmer and dairyman who came to the Washington Territory and bought up acreage on the hill in 1879. By 1884 Lord had expanded his holdings and was raising livestock and farming 100 acres on the hill. Logging interests cut down the last of the old growth on Lord Hill by the middle of the 1930s, and large portions of the hill passed into the control of Washington's Department of Natural Resources. In the 1980s sections of the hill were again logged before the state conveyed the land to Snohomish County. In October of 1995, after building and expanding a few miles of trails, the county officially opened Lord Hill Regional Park. Since that time Lord Hill's trail network has continued to expand and today supports a variety of users including runners, hikers, bikers, and equestrians.

Miles and Directions

0.0 Turn off 127th Avenue SE into the Lord Hill parking area (privy available). Begin the hike on the connector trail to Beaver Lake Trail.

0.3 At the trail junction turn left onto Beaver Lake Trail.

0.7 At the trail junction turn right onto Pipeline Trail.

1.8 At the trail junction turn right onto the Main Trail.

2.0 Continue on the Main Trail to the right. The trail turns north back toward the parking area.

3.3 Turn left back onto the connector trail leading back to the parking area.

3.6 End back at the parking area.

17 Lake Serene and Bridal Veil Falls

Tackle this classic 8.2-mile hike past cascading waterfalls on the way up to a large mountain lake overshadowed by Mount Index.

Start: Lake Serene Trailhead
Distance: 8.2 miles out and back
Hiking time: About 4–5 hours
Elevation gain: 2,400 feet
High point: 2,600 feet
Difficulty: Moderate due to elevation
Best season: May–Oct
Traffic: Heavy foot traffic

Fees and permits: Northwest Forest Pass
Maps: USGS Index; *Green Trails Map #142* (Index)
Trail contacts: Skykomish Ranger District— Skykomish Office, 74920 NE Stevens Pass Hwy., PO Box 305, Skykomish, WA 98288; (360) 677-2414; fs.usda.gov/mbs

Finding the trailhead: From Seattle take Highway 2 out toward Index. Keep an eye out for Mount Index Road on the right near milepost 35. Take Mount Index Road for about 0.5 mile, following the signs directing you to the Lake Serene Trailhead. Trailhead GPS: N47 48.543' / W121 34.431'

The Hike

Popular for more than fifty years, the Lake Serene Trail #1068 got a makeover in the late 1990s, a reroute that smoothed the once-treacherous trail. These days the Lake Serene Trail is still a workout, with twenty-three switchbacks winding up the steep shoulders of Mount Index. But the scenery is well worth the effort. In about 8 miles, expect several crashing waterfalls, topped off with one of the best views of Mount Index in Washington, unique to the rocky shores of Lake Serene.

The trail begins innocently enough—it follows an old roadbed with a mild grade for the first portion of the hike, reserving most of the elevation for the end of the hike. Your first destination comes about 1.6 miles into the hike, just before the trail hits the switchbacks and elevation gain. Here, a well-signed path winds steeply up to Bridal Veil Falls and an expansive overview of the valley below. The glimpses of Bridal Veil Falls seen from Highway 2 as it passes under Mount Index do little justice to the experience of standing at the base of the cascade.

▶ Just past the turnoff for the town of Index is the Espresso Chalet, which sports a wooden carving of Bigfoot and marks a filming location for the movie *Harry and the Hendersons.*

From the falls, one can backtrack down to the main trail, or, for those thirsty for adventure, follow the faint boot path up the mountainside. This was the original approach hikers took up to Lake Serene before the trail was rerouted. Note that the

Mount Index above snow-covered Lake Serene

Honeymoon Mine is in this area and can be found with a little exploration. While this route shaves off almost 2 miles from the trip, it more than makes up for it in steepness. It is easy to lose track of the path, which at times is completely obscured or blocked by blowdowns. Occasional ribbons mark the way, but when in doubt, hug the creek and follow the path of least resistance. Steep, tricky, and occasionally frustrating, this route is not for the faint of heart. However, we think the effort is rewarded by an enchanting waterfall tucked halfway between Bridal Veil Falls and Lake Serene. Impressive in it its own right, the unexpected falls make a great spot to catch your breath before scaling the rest of the way to the top.

At first the satisfaction of making it up to the lake basin is euphoric in and of itself, but it is almost immediately replaced by the sight of Lake Serene spreading out beneath the imposing cliffs of Mount Index. Unlike many other questionably named places we've been to, this is no misnomer—Lake Serene lives up to its name. Once you catch your breath, follow the path as far as it will go around the lake to a popular lunch spot affectionately referred to as "Lunch Rock," or find your own little nook to take in the lake. More than likely you're going to have some company, but there is more than enough of Index to go around. Unpack your lunch and take it all in.

Historical Background

Hikers have been trekking up to Lake Serene for at least one hundred years, as maps dating back to 1912 already show a trail snaking up to the lakeshore. While the roadbed portion of the Lake Serene Trail is usually referred to as a logging road, it was probably built to support the mines that spent more than fifty years pulling copper and other minerals out of Mount Index. Before the USDA Forest Service and volunteer groups rerouted the Lake Serene Trail between 1995 and 1998, the trailhead was located at the end of this road. The old route was treacherous, causing a number of fatalities, which likely led to the official closure of the old route in 1982.

Some of the earliest visitors were likely prospectors scouring the slopes of Mount Index for signs of gold, silver, and copper. Back in 1898, the first claims were staked along Bridal Veil Creek. By 1901 mines were sending copper down the Lake Serene Trail to be hauled down to Index and, within a couple years, into the waiting railroad cars of the Great Northern Railway. One of the largest mines started as the Sixteen-to-One claim, eventually known as the Index-Independent Mine. Because the Lake Serene Mining Company operated it from 1949 to 1951, today it's often referred to as the Lake Serene Mine.

If you'd like to extend the hike, there is a side trip available along the trek up to the lake. Early in the hike a short spur leads to the old Index-Independent Mine, which is relatively safe and interesting to explore. To find it, follow the trail 1.5 miles to an unmarked trail junction. The Bridal Veil Falls Trail is 0.1 mile beyond this junction, so if you reach it, you've gone too far. Instead of continuing onto the trail, turn right for 0.2 mile to a clearing that was once the trailhead parking area. Continue straight ahead on an unmarked trail and note the large cliff and a small creek running down the hill in front of you. The mine is located at the base of the cliffs on the right-hand side of the creek.

Miles and Directions

0.0 Begin the hike on the Lake Serene Trail #1068. A privy is located at the trailhead.

0.1 At the road junction veer right and continue on the Lake Serene Trail.

1.5 Pass an unmarked junction leading to Index-Independent Mine.

1.6 At the trail junction turn right and go to up to the base of Bridal Veil Falls.

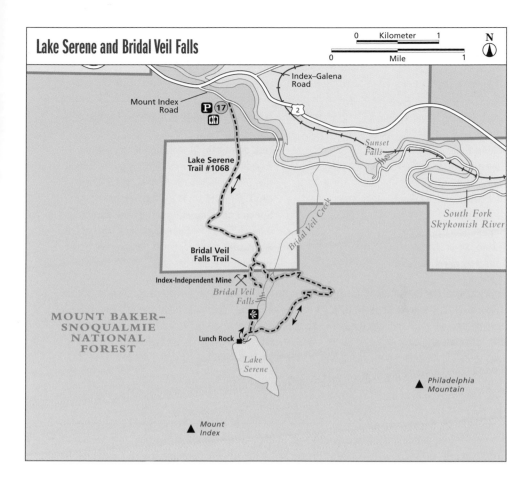

0   Kilometer   1

0   Mile   1

N

Index–Galena Road

Mount Index Road

P 17

Lake Serene Trail #1068

Sunset Falls

South Fork Skykomish River

Bridal Veil Creek

Bridal Veil Falls Trail

Index-Independent Mine

Bridal Veil Falls

Lunch Rock

MOUNT BAKER– SNOQUALMIE NATIONAL FOREST

Lake Serene

Philadelphia Mountain

Mount Index

1.9   Come to Bridal Veil Falls. Follow a short loop up wooden stairs before retracing your steps back to the Lake Serene Trail. Turn right to continue.

4.2   Reach Lake Serene. Turn right and follow a short path down Bridal Veil Creek to a viewpoint.

4.3   Arrive at the viewpoint overlooking the Skykomish River valley. Head back up to the trail and continue to the end.

4.5   Reach Lunch Rock and the perfect ending for views of Lake Serene.

8.2   Arrive back at the trailhead.

18 Index Town Wall

Explore a former quarry site turned rock climbing area on this short hike.

Start: Parking along Avenue A
Distance: 2.5 miles out and back
Hiking time: About 3–4 hours
Elevation gain: 1,300 feet
High point: 1,800 feet
Difficulty: Difficult due to steep and rugged trail
Best season: Apr–Oct
Traffic: Rock climbers; low foot traffic
Fees and permits: None

Maps: USGS Index; *Green Trails Map #142* (Index).
Trail contacts: Skykomish Ranger District– Skykomish Office, 74920 NE Stevens Pass Hwy., PO Box 305, Skykomish, WA 98288; (360) 677-2414; fs.usda.gov/mbs
Special considerations: This hike travels through areas frequented by rock climbers. Be aware that climbers could be above or below you, and exercise caution.

Finding the trailhead: From Seattle take Highway 2 to the Index turnoff near milepost 34. Follow the Index-Galena Road for about 1 mile to the bridge. Take a left across the river, proceeding through town to Index Ave. Turn left, crossing the railroad tracks and following Index Ave. as it turns left and becomes 2nd Street. Take the next right onto Avenue A and follow it out of town for 0.5 mile to find the parking area on the right. Park and hit the trail. Trailhead GPS: N47 49.058'/W121 34.275'

The Hike

The trickiest part of the hike is getting to the trailhead. A large parking area is 0.5 mile outside of town to the west. There are a number of names for the road leading to the lot, and depending on your map it might be noted as "Ave A," "Old Gold Bar–Index Road," or "Reiter Road." Luckily, it is the only road leading downriver from Index, so it shouldn't be too hard to find. Look for the lot on the right. If you cross railroad tracks, you've gone too far.

Once you've parked, take the obvious trail up to the railroad tracks, cross them, and avoid being lured toward the prominent sign to the left. Instead head right and follow the tracks for a couple hundred yards until you meet a road turning toward the wall. Follow this to a clearing, the wall, and the white doors of a tunnel drilled back in 1984. Once here, head right into the trees to find the trailhead.

The trail is fairly straightforward once you're on it. Switchback up through the young forest, always choosing the path that continues uphill. The route is a steady uphill slog the entire way, relentlessly climbing to the top of the cliffs, with no real reprieve until you reach your destination. The boot path spills out onto an old forest road at the Forks of the Sky State Park boundary.

▶ Sport climbing is a type of rock climbing that makes use of anchors that have been permanently mounted to the rock.

View from the top of the wall at the North Fork Skykomish River

Head to the right to get to the views you've been climbing for. The largest viewpoint is likely to be occupied, so push past along the faint network of climbers' trails until you find a good stop for lunch. The tiny town of Index is below. Mount Index and Baring Mountain dominate the southern skyline, and you can make out Gunn Peak and Merchant Peak to the east.

This is a fun little hike, good for a day when you don't have a lot of time, with some great rewards on a short, if somewhat challenging, route. There is more to see and explore in the 1,300-acre Forks of the Sky State Park for those who want to do a little extra. Obviously, use caution while up on the cliffs. It's a 500-foot sheer drop to the bottom. This area is an extremely popular climbing spot, so be aware that there are likely climbers below.

Historical Background

Before Index was incorporated in 1907, the area between Sultan and Index was home to the Skykomish Indians. The town was named for Mount Index, which was said to look like an index finger pointing to the sky. Of course what we call Mount Index today looks nothing like that. Originally the nearby fingerlike Baring Mountain was called Mount Index and today's Mount Index was known as West Index Mountain before the names were switched to the present arrangement.

Despite some confusion over what to name the surrounding mountains, the town flourished with the Monte Cristo strike of 1889, as many prospectors passed through Index on their way to Mineral City and Monte Cristo. At the turn of the century, the Index Town Wall was heavily quarried, creating what is now referred to as the "Lower Wall." Much of the rock was shipped off for building materials, including some that ended up as the steps of the state capitol in Olympia. The quarry owners still have ownership of parts of the Lower Wall, but a coalition of climbers acquired the option to purchase the area in 2009 and continues to work toward purchasing the parcel.

The Index Town Wall began to be known as a climbing area in the late 1950s, and by the early 1960s many routes had been hammered into the cliffs. Over the years, the cliffs became one of the most popular and easily accessible climbing features in the state. In 1984, over the protests of the climbers, a mine-cutting machine was tested at the base of the Upper Wall, boring a 200-foot tunnel into the granite. In the late 1990s the University of Washington leased the tunnel from the state and used it to complete underground physics experiments. Today one can still see the barricaded tunnel entrance, sealed behind metal doors.

Miles and Directions

0.0 Park in the gravel lot. Head up the path toward the railroad tracks.

0.1 Cross the railroad tracks, turn right, and follow a gravel road along the tracks.

0.2 Arrive at a quarry-drilling test site and small camping area. The trail leads off to the right.

0.5 At the junction with a spur trail to a climbing area, turn right.

0.6 At the trail junction turn left to continue to the top. Heading right leads to the base of the main wall.

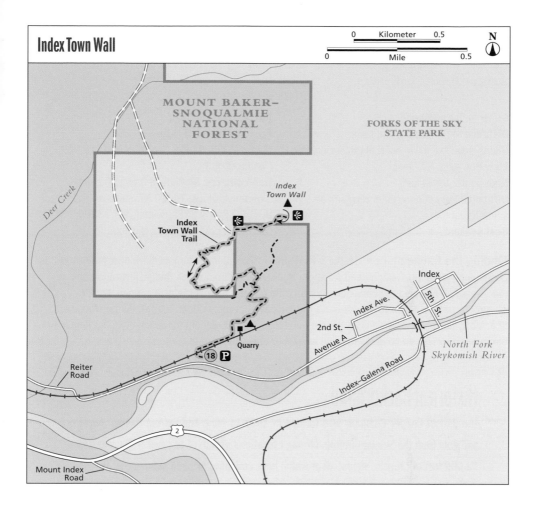

Index Town Wall

MOUNT BAKER–
SNOQUALMIE
NATIONAL
FOREST

FORKS OF THE SKY
STATE PARK

Deer Creek

*Index
Town Wall*

Index
Town Wall
Trail

Index

5th St.

Index Ave.

2nd St.

Avenue A

Quarry

Index-Galena Road

*North Fork
Skykomish River*

Reiter
Road

18   P

2

Mount Index
Road

1.1   The trail ends at a road fenced with a park-boundary sign. Turn right, crossing over the fence and continuing up the road.

1.2   The road ends in a small clearing and at the top of Index Town Wall, overlooking Index and the Skykomish Valley.

1.3   Arrive at another small overlook.

2.5   Arrive back at the trailhead.

D Honorable Mention: Sunset Mine

Explore the crumbling foundations and remaining mine shafts left behind by the Sunset Copper Company.

Start: Trout Creek Road
Distance: 4.0 miles out and back
Hiking time: About 3–4 hours of exploration time
Elevation gain: 800 feet
High point: 1,650 feet
Difficulty: Easy due to gentle elevation and smooth trail
Best season: Apr–Oct

Traffic: Low foot traffic
Fees and permits: None
Maps: USGS: Baring; *Green Trails Map #143* (Monte Cristo)
Trail contacts: Skykomish Ranger District–Skykomish Office, 74920 NE Stevens Pass Hwy., PO Box 305, Skykomish, WA 98288; (360) 677-2414; fs.usda.gov/mbs

Finding the trailhead: From Seattle take Highway 2 to the Index turnoff. Drive past Index and continue on the Index-Galena Road for about 5 miles to the Trout Creek Bridge, just before the road washout. Just past the bridge take a right onto a forest road. If the gate is open, decide whether to park your vehicle here or brave the 2 miles of pothole-ridden road to the mill foundation. Most four-wheel-drive vehicles should be able to make it without too much difficulty. Remember that the mines can be dangerous, so keep your explorations safe.

Historical Background

The Sunset Copper Company was formed in 1897 to mine and extract copper, silver, and gold from the Sunset outcrop. Mining operations expanded to cover 960 acres and 12,000 feet of tunnels, almost all of which have collapsed or been submerged. Ownership of the area changed hands a number of times before operations ceased and the property was ceded to the USDA Forest Service in 1985. By that time more than thirteen million tons of copper had been hauled out of the ground. Today all that remains of the production site is the crumbling cement foundation of the copper mill.

The Hike

Tromping around Sunset Mine is more a stroll through history than it is a hike, but what it lacks in distance, it more than makes up for in the fun of investigating the mines. Obviously, all tunnels and openings should be approached with caution, but the two large stopes have collapsed enough that they are now fairly shallow and do not go back much more than 200 feet. Lingering wooden beams and platforms seem to be the most unstable, so we avoided getting too close to them. All it all, the area is fun to explore. If you're looking for a longer hike, there are more claims along Trout Creek farther past the Sunset Mine; just keep following the road to find them.

Minerals inside Sunset Mine

19 Blanca Lake

Enjoy a 7.5-mile hike into the Henry M. Jackson Wilderness to a unique alpine lake.

Start: Blanca Lake Trailhead
Distance: 7.5 miles out and back
Hiking time: About 5–7 hours
Elevation gain: 3,400 feet (2,700 feet in, 700 feet out)
High point: 4,700 feet
Difficulty: Difficult due to elevation
Best season: June–Sept

Traffic: Heavy foot traffic
Fees and permits: Northwest Forest Pass
Maps: USGS Blanca Lake; *Green Trails Map #143* (Monte Cristo)
Trail contacts: Skykomish Ranger District– Skykomish Office, 74920 NE Stevens Pass Hwy., PO Box 305, Skykomish, WA 98288; (360) 677-2414; fs.usda.gov/mbs

Finding the trailhead: From Seattle take Highway 2 out past Skykomish to milepost 50. Take a left onto FR 65, also known as the Beckler River Road. Continue for almost 7 miles to a junction and the pavement end. From here continue north for just under 6 miles to a five-way intersection known as Jack Pass. Take the second left and continue 2.5 miles to FR 63. Turn right and drive 2 miles to the trailhead. Trailhead GPS: N47 54.902' / W121 18.750'

The Hike

Nestled in the Henry M. Jackson Wilderness at the bottom of a cirque formed by Kyes, Monte Cristo, and Columbia Peaks, Lake Blanca is something of a hidden treasure. At least it was at some point. Today the Blanca Lake Trail #1052 is very popular, drawing dozens of hikers down miles of gravel forest roads every weekend.

The trail begins pleasantly enough, gliding quickly through forests of hemlock and sword fern. Within a few tenths of a mile, you enter the Wild Sky Wilderness and the trail quickly steepens, signaling the beginning of the 3-mile ascent. Surprisingly, the trail is well maintained here, largely free of the jutting rocks and roots more typical of trails in the area. As you climb, the water-loving ferns slowly recede and are replaced with heartier huckleberry, eventually yielding to lush meadows at the top.

While the lower trail is completely tree covered, the meadows offer your legs some respite and some of the first views of the hike. On a good day you'll see Glacier Peak looming in the near distance through the occasional break in the tree line. Once you push through the meadows to the top of the saddle and some of the best vistas, the trail begins a fairly steep descent down to the lakeshore. The route drops about 600 feet, quickly passing Virgin Lake and a

▶ Before 1944 Kyes Peak was called Goblin Peak or Goblin Mountain. But on Christmas Eve 1944, Commander James E. Kyes was killed when his ship was torpedoed. The mountain was renamed in his honor, as he made the first recorded ascent of Kyes in 1920. A memorial to Commander Kyes can also be found in Monte Cristo.

host of decent campsites following a much rougher and narrower trail. The expected jumble of rocks and roots are in full attendance, making the path a little more slippery and precarious. Luckily, the Washington Trails Association has done some trail work here to make the hike more navigable.

The trail spills you out at the top of the cirque, the vibrant green-blue waters of Blanca Lake standing out in sharp contrast to the sheer granite walls surrounding the lake. The snowfield in the distance is Columbia Glacier, which fuels the lake with runoff and glacial silt, helping to give the lake its distinctive color. While most folks end the hike here, we suggest you continue down the trail to the lakeshore and Blanca's outlet, Troublesome Creek. Supposedly the trail continues around the lake to the glacier, though it requires fording Troublesome Creek.

Starting from the creek and running clockwise, the ridgeline climbs up Columbia Peak, then to Monte Cristo Peak just to the right of the glacier, before running into the imposing crags of Kyes Peak. Claim some space and take it all in. Or if you're thirsty for adventure and you feel very confident in your rock-climbing skills, clamber down the rocks along Troublesome Creek to Blanca Lake Falls, a reportedly enormous series of waterfalls, some dropping hundreds of feet to the rocks below. We didn't see them when we were there.

Historical Background

In 1963 Senator Henry M. "Scoop" Jackson became chair of the Senate's Committee on Interior and Insular Affairs, a position he held until 1981. From that position Senator Jackson oversaw legislation that created "wilderness" as we know it today. The Wilderness Act of 1964 set aside 9 million acres of wilderness and established the process for designating and protecting areas in the future. In 1968 Senator Jackson spearheaded the creation of North Cascades National Park, and in the following year he helped pass the National Environmental Policy Act, the law that mandates the use of Environmental Impact Statements for construction and development projects. Senator Jackson passed away in 1983, and the 1984 Wilderness Act established the Henry M. Jackson Wilderness to honor his legacy of preserving Washington's wild areas.

Today the Henry M. Jackson Wilderness protects 103,591 acres of forests and peaks. Roughly 50 miles of trail provide access to a few of the sixty or so lakes that dot the region. Portions of the wilderness include areas of the Mount Baker-Snoqualmie and Wenatchee National Forests. The area is bordered by the Glacier Peak Wilderness to the north and the Wild Sky Wilderness to the south.

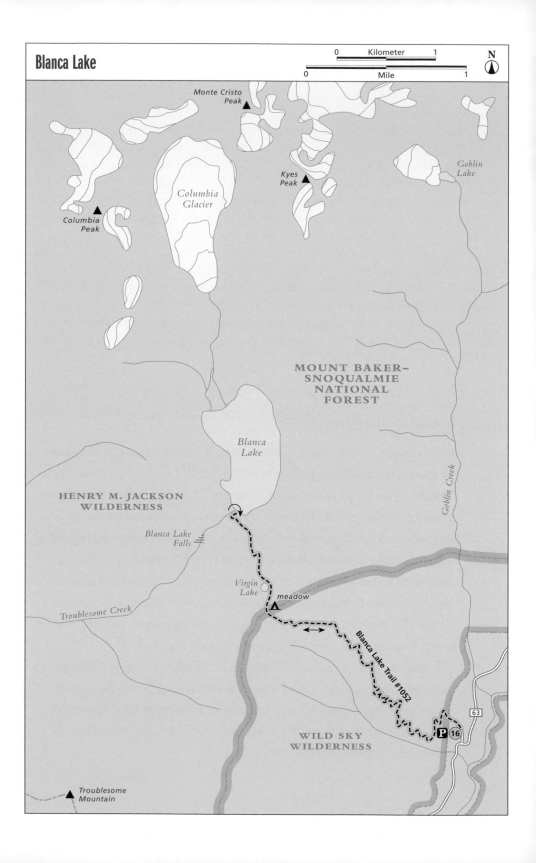

Blanca Lake

0 — Kilometer — 1
0 — Mile — 1

N

Monte Cristo
Peak ▲

Kyes
Peak ▲

Goblin
Lake

Columbia
Glacier

Columbia
Peak ▲

MOUNT BAKER–
SNOQUALMIE
NATIONAL
FOREST

Blanca
Lake

HENRY M. JACKSON
WILDERNESS

Goblin Creek

Blanca Lake
Falls

Virgin
Lake

meadow

Troublesome Creek

Blanca Lake Trail #1052

P 16

63

WILD SKY
WILDERNESS

Troublesome
Mountain ▲

Blanca Lake and Monte Cristo Peak

We recommend this hike for most hikers, though some will find the elevation gain a little too taxing. Of course, as we mentioned, Lake Blanca attracts quite a few hikers, and you can expect quite a bit of company when you make the trek. However, this isn't a hike to do early in the season to avoid the crowds, because the lake needs to thaw to reveal its trademark colors. This is definitely a destination for those hikers looking for something a little different—Lake Blanca looks nothing like your typical alpine lake.

Miles and Directions

0.0 Start from the parking lot for the Blanca Lake Trail #1052.

3.0 Come to a small plateau with a meadow and campsites. View Kyes Peak immediately to the north.

3.1 Arrive at Virgin Lake.

3.8 Reach Blanca Lake.

7.5 Arrive back at the trailhead.

Explore the Wild Sky Wilderness on this 8.0-mile summit.

Start: Johnson Ridge Trailhead #1067
Distance: 8.0 miles out and back
Hiking time: About 4–5 hours
Elevation gain: 2,600 feet (2,300 feet in, 300 feet out)
High point: 5,540 feet
Difficulty: Difficult due to elevation and rough trail
Best season: June–Oct

Traffic: Low foot traffic
Fees and permits: None
Maps: USGS Captain Point; *Green Trails Map #144* (Benchmark Mountain)
Trail contacts: Skykomish Ranger District—Skykomish Office, 74920 NE Stevens Pass Hwy.; PO Box 305; Skykomish, WA 98288; (360) 677-2414; fs.usda.gov/mbs

Finding the trailhead: From Seattle take Highway 2 out past Skykomish to milepost 50. Take a left onto FR 65, also known as the Beckler River Road. Continue for almost 7 miles to a junction, taking a sharp right up FR 6520 and following it for almost 3 miles to an unsigned junction. Veer left here, continuing on FR 6520 for another 4 miles to the next junction. Here take a right up FR 6526 and follow it for about 0.25 mile to the last junction, taking a left up to a small trailhead at road's end.

Historical Background

Just inside the Wild Sky Wilderness, Scorpion Mountain anchors one end of Johnson Ridge, surrounded by such prominences as Captain Point, Lichtenberg Mountain, Mount McCausland, Eagle Rock, and Scrabble Mountain. Such evocative names might be expected to have interesting stories behind them. Much to our surprise, we were unable to dig up much in the way of history beyond vague hints of a once-expansive trail system branching off from Johnson Ridge. It would seem that remnants of trails can still be found leading out to Mount Fernow, Alpine Baldy, and Beckler Peak. Perhaps the section that sees the most traffic is the Kelly Creek Trail, running between Captain Point and Scorpion Mountain, which is still used by a few intrepid hikers a year.

Yellow glacier lilies in the snowmelt on Scorpion Mountain

The Hike

Just inside the Wild Sky Wilderness, Scorpion Mountain anchors one end of Johnson Ridge, surrounded by such prominences as Captain Point, Lichtenberg Mountain, Mount McCausland, Eagle Rock, and Scrabble Mountain. The trail begins steeply, following a decommissioned logging road for 0.3 mile before a short but steep ascent to the ridgeline. Once on the ridgeline, the trail eventually enters extended sections of subalpine old-growth fir and hemlock just as you gain the summit of Sunrise Mountain. From the summit the trail immediately plummets a few hundred feet down the side of Sunrise to follow a saddle to the foot of Scorpion. Forgoing any pretense of a switchback, the trail heads straight up the mountainside, gaining 500 feet in 0.3 mile to reach the edge of the meadows. Continue up to the summit for Scorpion Mountain's big views.

This can be a challenging hike. The elevation gain is not insignificant, especially with all the ups and downs. Yet the amazing views Scorpion Mountain offers are more than worth the extra workout. The lengthy drive down forest roads keeps this hike a little under the radar, so don't expect to be sharing the views with a lot of company.

F Honorable Mention: Tonga Ridge

Popular for its wildflowers and huckleberries, this 5.5-mile out and back also has great views and is approachable for most hikers.

Start: Tonga Ridge Trailhead
Distance: 5.5 miles out and back
Hiking time: About 4-6 hours
Elevation gain: 1,200 feet
High point: 5,480 feet
Difficulty: Moderate due to steep sections of rugged trail
Best season: May-Oct; huckleberries ripen Aug-Sept

Traffic: Heavy foot traffic
Fees and permits: Northwest Forest Pass
Maps: USGS Scenic; *Green Trails Map #175* (Skykomish), *#176* (Stevens Pass)
Trail contacts: Skykomish Ranger District—Skykomish Office, 74920 NE Stevens Pass Hwy., PO Box 305, Skykomish, WA 98288; (360) 677-2414; fs.usda.gov/mbs

Finding the trailhead: From Seattle take Highway 2 out past Skykomish just beyond milepost 50. Take a right onto FR 68, also known as the Foss River Road. Continue for about 3.5 miles to a junction, taking a left onto FR 6830 and following it for almost 7 miles to the signed 310 spur. Head right onto the spur and drive a little over 1 mile to the end of the road and the trailhead.

Mount Daniel from the summit of Mount Sawyer

The Hike

The well-maintained Tonga Ridge Trail #1058 is largely free of rocks and roots and offers glimpses of the Foss River and Burn Creek valleys early in the hike. The trail ambles through meadows and stands of evergreen, gliding over the ups and downs of the ridge without much difficulty. After about 2 miles you'll reach a relatively large meadow that older maps mark as Lake Sawyer. Today the small lake is gone, but it still serves as a useful landmark for finding the unmarked trail to the summit of Mount Sawyer. As you enter the trees just past the onetime lake, look for a small, steep track heading upward. After a short scramble you'll find yourself on a narrow path, switchbacking up the shoulders of the mountain.

Before long, reach the wooded summit, with broad vistas stretching to the north and south. Find a good rock and settle to soak up the views. For those looking for a longer day, you can continue past Mount Sawyer up to Sawyer Pass and follow boot paths down to Fisher Lake and Ptarmigan Lake beyond. This is a great all-season trail that we recommend to all hikers. The trail is also fairly easy and should be approachable for hikers of all ages and experience levels, which tends to draw in the crowds. You can expect to share the trail with a lot of other folks on this popular hike, and the limited parking at the trailhead can be a challenge on a crowded day.

Historical Background

Back around the early twentieth century, mining and timber interests were pulling trees and ore out of the valleys near Skykomish at breakneck speed. Forest fires were among the biggest threats to these industries, because fire would destroy resources and camps and cut off access to the outside world. The forest service responded by building fire lookouts throughout the region in an attempt to find and contain fires before they spread out of control. In the Skykomish Ranger District, there were numerous lookouts, including a fire lookout camp on Tonga Ridge throughout the 1920s, likely in response to a fire that seared the trees off Mount Sawyer in 1914. A ranger named George Sawyer spent his life in the forests of the Skykomish District helping keep watch for those fires, and after his death in 1930, Mount Sawyer was named in honor of his service.

20 Beckler Peak

Take on this 7.5-mile hike up to the site of a former fire lookout.

Start: Jennifer Dunn Trailhead
Distance: 7.5-mile summit
Hiking time: About 3-4 hours
Elevation gain: 2,300 feet
High point: 5,062 feet
Difficulty: Moderate due to elevation gain
Best season: May–Sept
Traffic: Moderate foot traffic
Fees and permits: Northwest Forest Pass

Maps: USGS Skykomish; *Green Trails Map #175* (Skykomish)
Trail contacts: Skykomish Ranger District– Skykomish Office, 74920 NE Stevens Pass Hwy., PO Box 305, Skykomish, WA 98288; (360) 677-2414; fs.usda.gov/mbs
Special considerations: FR 6066 is a 1-lane gravel road with occasional pullouts; use some extra caution navigating the traffic at this trailhead.

Finding the trailhead: From Seattle take Highway 2 out past Skykomish. At 2 miles past the ranger station, take a left onto FR 6066, which is signed but easy to overshoot if you're not paying attention. Continue for just under 2 miles to a junction. Bear right and continue about 5 miles to the trailhead at road's end. Trailhead GPS: N47 43.446'/W121 16.014'

The Hike

From the trailhead the route follows a series of logging roads through a young forest of alder and maple. Wide switchbacks and decent roadbeds make the first 2 miles of the hike fairly easy, though the grade is steeper than one might expect from a logging road. Hike past splashing creeks and catch the occasional glimpse of the landscape through the trees. Reach the saddle after crossing through a section of clear-cut and enter a very different, much older forest. Look for the mossy logs that were part of the log cabin that once stood in the saddle.

▶ Although used almost interchangeably, a "pass" is the route between two mountains, while a "saddle" is one name for the topographic feature that the pass utilizes.

The transition is nearly instant. Suddenly you're on a quiet trail through mature firs and hemlock, leaving behind the dusty logging road and the road noise of the highway. The trail becomes a little more difficult here as switchbacks tighten and gain elevation more quickly. Continue following the ridgeline as the trees begin to thin and a series of rock steps help smooth out the final push up to Beckler's exposed East Peak.

These stone steps were built by trail volunteers near the summit. ▶

Historical Background

Beckler Peak was named for Elbridge H. Beckler, a well-known railroad engineer who oversaw the extension of the Great Northern Railway through Washington from 1889 to 1893. Industry followed the railroad, and before long a crude fire lookout was built near the top of Beckler's West Peak, little more than a rough platform nailed to the top of some trees. It wasn't until 1924 that the makeshift platform was replaced with a log cabin and lookout tower by the Civilian Conservation Corps. It remained in use until it burned down in 1958 and was abandoned.

For years a number of trails led to the lookout site and Beckler Peak's prominences. Most of these trails were worn into the mountain by hikers, hunters, and lovers of the outdoors. One such was Norm McCausland, a Skykomish District ranger who had a cabin at Harlan Saddle—the low point between Beckler Peak and Alpine Baldy. McCausland died in 1982, but his cabin continued to be a popular destination on Beckler Peak, even as logging companies moved in and replaced many of the old trails with roads. Today the cabin is little more than a jumbled pile of moss-covered logs, but if you're looking for it, it's hard to miss this former landmark.

There is some controversy over which of Beckler's three major Peaks—East, Middle, or West—is the most prominent. Although they are all about the same height, each peak has a set of advocates claiming the title. We don't have a favorite and assume you can get the same spectacular view from each of them, though official trails lead only to the East Peak. On a good day you can pick out Mount Rainier, but there's plenty to see much closer. Glacier Peak looms large to the north, along with Sloan Peak, Frog Mountain, and Evergreen Mountain. Pick out Scorpion Mountain as you turn east toward nearby Mount Fernow and Alpine Baldy. Turn south to the Skykomish Valley and the town of Skykomish below. To the west you can pick out Mount Index, Baring Mountain, Merchant Peak, and Eagle Rock.

This trail delivers a great view without too much effort—a combination that has already made it very popular. The East Peak does not have a lot of room. Still, the route is in great condition and the nearly 360-degree views are excellent. We recommend you find your way out to Beckler Peak before long.

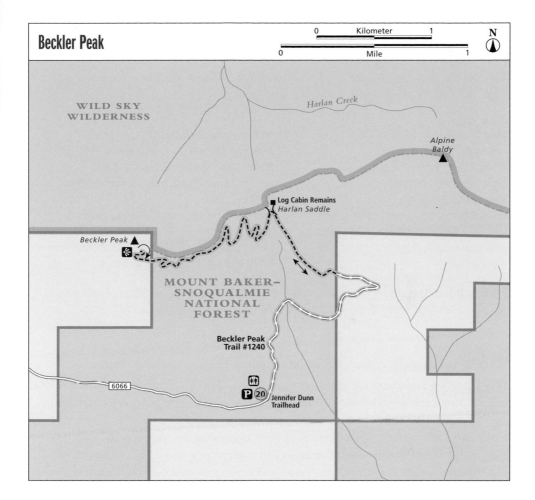

Miles and Directions

0.0   Begin at the Jennifer Dunn Trailhead for Beckler Peak Trail #1240. A privy is available here.

1.4   The trail transitions from old forest road to boot path and enters the canopy of a second-generation forest.

2.0   Arrive at Harlan Saddle and the faint remains of a log cabin.

3.7   Look for the viewpoint overlooking the valley at the end of a switchback.

3.8   Arrive at the summit of Beckler Peak. To the north the Wild Sky Wilderness spreads out, with Glacier Peak dominating the skyline. To the west find Mount Index and Baring Mountain.

7.5   Arrive back at the trailhead.

21 Iron Goat Trail

This hike follows sections of the Great Northern Railway line to tunnels and the work sites used during construction of the railroad.

Start: Iron Goat Interpretive Site
Distance: 6.3-mile loop
Hiking time: About 5–6 hours
Elevation gain: 700 feet
High point: 2,800 feet
Difficulty: Moderate due to some rugged side trails
Best season: May–Sept; popular for snowshoeing

Traffic: Moderate foot traffic
Fees and permits: Northwest Forest Pass
Maps: USGS Scenic; *Green Trails Map #176* (Stevens Pass); irongoat.org/images/IGT2007.pdf
Trail contacts: Skykomish Ranger District–Skykomish Office, 74920 NE Stevens Pass Hwy., PO Box 305, Skykomish, WA 98288; (360) 677-2414; fs.usda.gov/mbs

Finding the trailhead: From Seattle take Highway 2 out just past milepost 58 and look for the Iron Goat Interpretative Site on the left. Trailhead GPS: N47 42.682′/W121 09.709′

The Hike

Officially completed in 2007, the Iron Goat Trail follows portions of an abandoned railroad route, allowing hikers to peek into tunnels, visit former work camps, and explore some of the history of the area. There are multiple trailheads, one at each end of the park and one roughly in the middle. We recommend a central approach, beginning at the Scenic Trailhead and the Iron Goat Interpretive Site. Almost immediately you have the choice of following the grade out toward the work-camp site known as Corea or taking the Windy Point Crossover to the upper grade. The Crossover trail is only about 1 mile, but be warned that the trail is very new, very steep, and difficult to navigate with snowshoes. If you're snowshoeing, we recommend you skip the shortcut and dive into the trail.

Although the roar of Highway 2 never fully recedes, the forest is welcoming and pleasant. Volunteers have put an incredible amount of effort into adding signs and information to explain the remaining vestiges of the railroad. You'll quickly encounter impressive concrete retaining walls built to anchor snowsheds to the mountainside and replicas of mileposts marking your distance from St. Paul, Minnesota. Crumbling

▶ Although the Great Northern Railroad's engineers likened their locomotives to "iron goats" scaling the steep slopes of the Rockies and Cascades, this is not the reason the railroad adopted the mountain goat as its logo in 1921. It was chosen as a symbolic link between the railroad and Glacier National Park, which played a prominent role in the railroad's advertising campaigns.

Hiking toward Twin Tunnel

tunnels yawn invitingly along the route, necessitating more than a few side trips to peer cautiously into the darkness.

With 9 miles of trail and three different trailheads, the Iron Goat Trail has more than enough to explore. The trail between Martin Creek Trailhead and Scenic Trailhead is ADA accessible and stroller friendly in the summer months, and it is an easy snowshoe in the winter. If you want a little extra, take a cutoff trail up to the Embro work camp or out to Windy Point. The trail doesn't have the remoteness and hushed silence that some of us associate with snowshoeing, but it is perfect for a last-minute destination or a first-time snowshoe.

Miles and Directions

0.0 Park at the Iron Goat Trail Interpretive Site. More parking is available across the highway. Iron Goat Trail #1074 begins near the caboose. A privy is located at the trailhead.

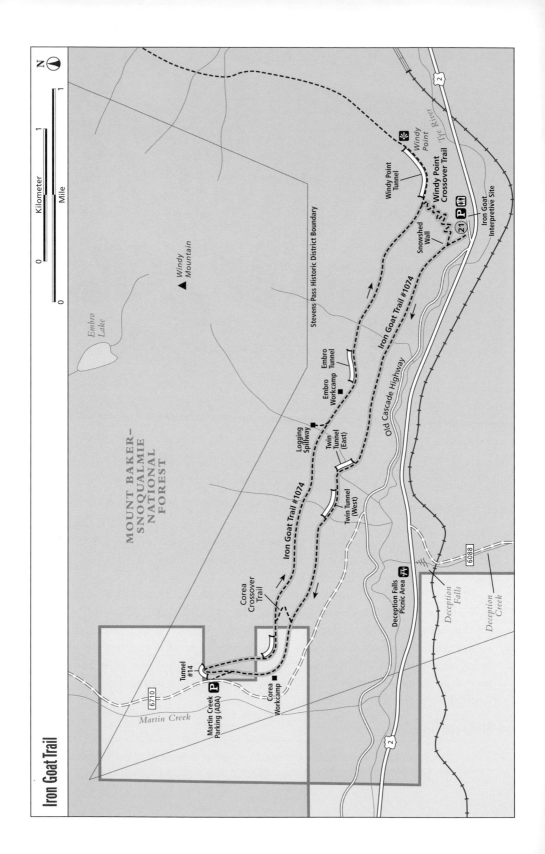

Iron Goat Trail

0.1 Arrive at a junction with the Windy Point Crossover Trail. Head down and to the left to avoid the steep sections of the Windy Point Trail.

0.3 Come to the foundation of a snowshed designed to minimize avalanche damage.

1.2 Arrive at the east entrance of Twin Tunnel. Follow the path to explore the tunnel and read the interpretive sign.

1.7 West entrance of Twin Tunnel.

2.8 Reach the Tunnel #14 west portal.

4.2 Arrive at a trail junction. (*Option:* Just beyond the snowshed foundation is a spur trail leading to the site of an old logging spillway. The trail is short and worth the side trip.)

4.4 Arrive at the western portal of Embro Tunnel. Although you may see light coming from the other end of the tunnel, there is no safe route through the tunnel.

5.4 Reach the aptly named Windy Point Tunnel and junction with the Windy Point Crossover Trail. Head down to complete the loop or continue another 0.25 mile out to Windy Point for big views of the valley.

6.3 Arrive back at the trailhead.

Historical Background

In 1893 the former Great Northern Railway finally connected Seattle to Chicago and the Midwest. Constructing a route over Stevens Pass was no easy feat, requiring a series of switchbacks and tunnels to navigate the steep grade. After the route was complete, the railroad still needed to contend with heavy annual snows that often delayed trains for days. Over time even more tunnels and snowsheds were built to lessen the impact of the snow, yet winters continued to plague the railway. On March 1, 1910, a massive avalanche tumbled down Windy Mountain toward Wellington Station and two snowbound trains full of passengers waiting for plows to clear snow from the tracks. The snow swept the trains down into the Tye Creek basin, killing nearly a hundred people—one of the worst railroad accidents in the history of the United States.

The railroad reacted to the disaster by building more snowsheds for a few years before eventually admitting defeat and blasting miles of tunnel under Stevens Pass, bypassing and abandoning the higher route entirely by 1929. For sixty years the rail bed languished, until the early 1990s, when efforts led by Ruth Ittner and the Mountaineers worked to reclaim the route and establish the Iron Goat Trail. At one hundred years after the first train crossed over Stevens Pass, the Iron Goat Trail opened on October 2, 1993.

22 Surprise and Glacier Lakes

This 9.5-mile hike travels out to a pair of alpine lakes that were once a popular destination for visitors to and residents of the former community of Scenic.

Start: Surprise Creek Trailhead
Distance: 9.5 miles out and back
Hiking time: About 6–7 hours
Elevation gain: 2,700 feet
High point: 4,900 feet
Difficulty: Moderate due to elevation and steepness
Best season: June–Sept

Traffic: Heavy foot traffic
Fees and permits: None
Maps: USGS Scenic; *Green Trails Map #176* (Stevens Pass)
Trail contacts: Skykomish Ranger District—Skykomish Office, 74920 NE Stevens Pass Hwy., PO Box 305, Skykomish, WA 98288; (360) 677-2414; fs.usda.gov/mbs

Finding the trailhead: From Seattle take Highway 2 out past Skykomish toward Stevens Pass. Just past milepost 58 look for an unmarked road on your right just beyond the Iron Goat Interpretive Site. Turn onto the access road and follow it across the Tye River to the Burlington Northern Santa Fe railroad tracks. Cross the tracks and head to the right, paralleling the tracks for a short distance to a spur road heading into the trees. Follow this road a few tenths of a mile to the trailhead. Trailhead GPS: N47 42.488' / W121 09.385'

The Hike

The Surprise Creek Trail #1060 begins along a service road running beneath a set of massive power lines. The road quickly transitions into shaded trail, and within 0.5 mile or so the route passes into the Alpine Lakes Wilderness. Almost immediately you are greeted by expansive stairs, wooden boardwalks, and bridgework. Large portions of the lower trail are composed of this boardwalk, the product of hundreds of hours of trail work. Climb your way past giant cedars and massive hemlocks as you cross creeks and pass the occasional waterfall. In about 1 mile reach Surprise Creek, currently spanned by a single log. Use caution crossing during the winter, when it could be easy to slip into the fast-flowing creek.

Beyond the creek the trail continues its fairly mild climb up the valley for another 1 mile. At this point the trail becomes more serious, climbing nearly 1,000 feet in a series of tight switchbacks. The switchbacks eventually begin to level out as the canopy gives way to wider expanses and your first glimpses of Thunder Mountain. As you near the lake, the trail dips down to cross over Surprise Creek again before climbing up to the rocky shores of Surprise Lake, nestled beneath the shoulders of Spark Plug Mountain.

Find a spot to settle down for a snack, or continue onward to Glacier Lake, connecting with the Pacific

▶ Boardwalks are commonly used in trail building in areas of high erosion, steep grade, and seasonal flooding to minimize the need for long-term maintenance.

Snow-covered trees are reflected in Surprise Creek.

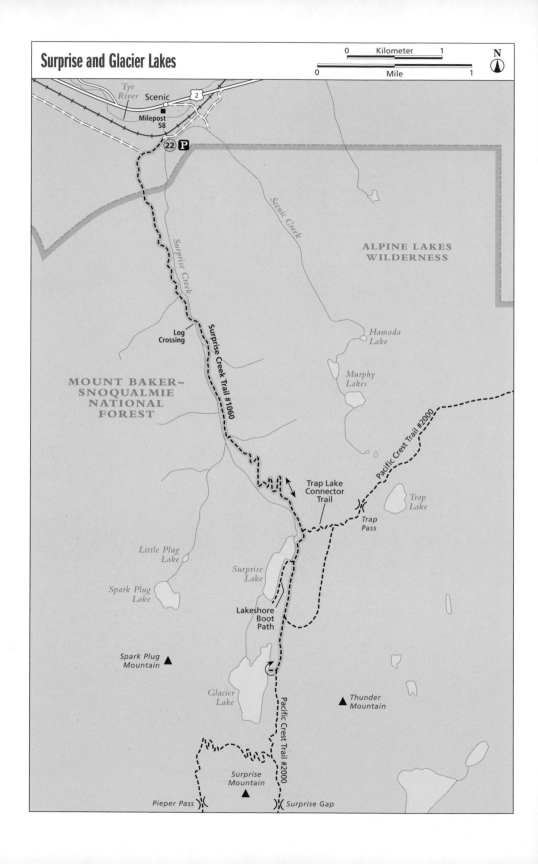

Surprise and Glacier Lakes

Historical Background

Surprise Lake is one of two glacier-fed lakes tucked into a narrow valley between Spark Plug Mountain and Thunder Mountain. The lake is in a depression and was named for the "surprise" that comes with finally reaching the lake after cresting the small ridge that surrounds it. Along with nearby Glacier Lake, the duo is collectively known as Scenic Lakes, named not just for their scenic beauty but also the nearby community of Scenic.

Back in the late 1880s when the Great Northern Railway was working on connecting Seattle to the Midwest, railroad workers enjoyed the natural hot springs found near the tracks. One of the first railroad stops on the west side of Stevens Pass was called Madison, but that name was quickly changed to Scenic when a hotel was built in 1904 to take advantage of the hot springs. The Scenic Hot Springs Hotel lasted until 1908, when it caught fire and burned to the ground. The owners were undaunted and rebuilt the hotel the next year, when it became nationally famous for its baths. A small settlement sprung up around the hot springs, becoming Washington's highest-elevation community west of the Cascades. The hotel was demolished in 1928 as part of the construction of Great Northern Railway's Cascade Tunnel.

Crest Trail along the way. The trail winds up through trees that refuse to reveal more than tantalizing glimpses of the really big views of the nearby peaks before dropping down to Glacier Lake. Tucked in a bowl at the feet of Surprise Mountain and Spark Plug Mountain, boulder-lined Glacier Lake offers pristine views and more than one campsite for those looking to stay a little while. Still yearning for some more trail time? Head back to Surprise Lake and take the signed spur trail up to Trap Pass for some incredible views.

We recommend this hike for anyone looking for an engaging hike any time of the year. It is a little long for more casual hikers, and the elevation gain is not insignificant, but most of the work is a short series of switchbacks at around the 3-mile mark. However, if enough time is budgeted, this hike should be attainable for almost every hiker. The lakes are more than worth the effort, and the hike even makes for a decent little backpacking weekend. While Surprise Lake is popular in the summer, few people make the trek in the winter, making this a good time to do some exploring and get the lakes all to yourself.

Miles and Directions

0.0 Begin at Surprise Creek Trailhead #1060.

0.2 At the trail junction turn left off the road and onto the trail.

1.1 Cross over Surprise Creek on a downed log.

3.8 Arrive at a trail junction with a connector trail that leads to the Pacific Crest Trail.

3.9 Reach Surprise Lake.

4.3 Arrive at a junction with the Pacific Crest Trail. Continue going straight ahead to Glacier Lake.

4.7 At the trail junction turn right, following a short spur trail to Glacier Lake.

4.8 Reach Glacier Lake.

9.5 Arrive back at the trailhead.

23 Skyline Lake

Enjoy a short, 3.0-mile hike and popular snowshoe route up to an alpine lake.

Start: Stevens Pass Ski Area
Distance: 3.0 miles out and back
Hiking time: About 4-5 hours
Elevation gain: 1,400 feet
High point: 5,400 feet
Difficulty: Moderate due to elevation
Best season: June–Sept; also popular for snowshoeing

Traffic: Moderate foot traffic
Fees and permits: None
Maps: USGS Labyrinth Mountain; *Green Trails Map #176* (Stevens Pass)
Trail contacts: Skykomish Ranger District–Skykomish Office, 74920 NE Stevens Pass Hwy., PO Box 305, Skykomish, WA 98288; (360) 677-2414; fs.usda.gov/mbs

Finding the trailhead: From Seattle take Highway 2 out 64.4 miles to the Stevens Pass Ski Area. Find parking in the lots on the north side of the highway. Trailhead GPS: N47 44.846'/W121 05.301'

The Hike

The trail begins in the ski area parking lot and follows a gravel service road up the mountainside. During the winter this road is often groomed or otherwise cleared. Follow the road past ski huts and under electrical wires for about 0.25 mile to a green Washington Department of Transportation building. From here you have a choice: You can continue to follow the road as it slowly switches back up the mountain, or you can head straight uphill and cut a lot of distance. This approach also has some great views and gets you into the trees before connecting with the road just below the ridgeline. From here the trail veers west toward nearby Skyline Lake and the rocky pinnacle rising above it.

▶ Hiking in the tracks of cross-country skiers is poor trail etiquette; skiers count on using their tracks on the way back out.

If you're hungry for views, continue around the lake and push up another 300 feet through boulder-strewn forest to get them. To the north, Glacier Peak rises above nearby Tye Peak, Lichtenberg Mountain, and Union Peak. As you turn toward the east, pick out Mount Howard, Rock Mountain, Mount Mastiff, and nearby Big Chief Mountain. Continue to turn clockwise to find Mount Daniel, Mount Hinman, Big Chiwaukum, and finally Cowboy Mountain directly across the valley. To the west, Windy Mountain stands close by. Want more? You can continue to follow the ridgeline for another 1 mile to reach the Sky Mountain high point.

Snowshoeing near the summit ▶

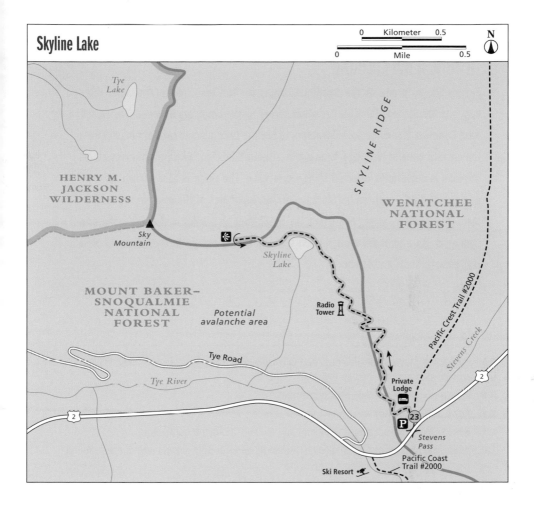

Skyline Lake

Tye Lake

HENRY M. JACKSON WILDERNESS

Sky Mountain

SKYLINE RIDGE

WENATCHEE NATIONAL FOREST

Skyline Lake

MOUNT BAKER–SNOQUALMIE NATIONAL FOREST

Potential avalanche area

Radio Tower

Pacific Crest Trail #2000

Stevens Creek

Tye Road

Tye River

Private Lodge

Tye River

P 23

Stevens Pass

Pacific Coast Trail #2000

Ski Resort

This short hike packs a lot into just a few miles. We definitely recommend taking the more direct route when snowshoeing, because it gets you to the views faster and is a lot more rewarding than trudging up a service road. This is an understandably popular destination in the winter, so expect company. Although there is some elevation gain involved, the different approaches mean that you can easily tailor this hike so that even a first-timer will be able to make it to the lake, while the expert can explore the more challenging sections.

A word of caution if you visit this area during the winter months: Stick to the western end of the ridge and avoid the southern slopes—there have been multiple avalanche fatalities there over the years. And when you reach the lake, stick to the shores and resist the temptation to march across the frozen surface. It's impossible to tell if the ice has started to melt or is otherwise weak.

Historical Background

Skyline Ridge is one of the unofficial names for the long, rocky, U-shaped ridge opposite the Stevens Pass Ski Area that serves as the boundary between Chelan and King Counties. The name probably refers to Skyline Lake, a small lakelet tucked under the eastern base of the ridge. Then again, although labeled "Skyline" on many maps, the lake is sometimes referred to as Dozer Lake. The ridge is also known to some as Heather Ridge, perhaps in reference to the abundance of the plant in the area. To further add to the naming confusion, the 5,482-foot high point of the ridge is known simply as Sky Mountain, though most snowshoers do not go farther than the first jagged 5,400-foot prominence.

Miles and Directions

0.0 Park at the Stevens Pass Ski Area on the north side of Highway 2. The trail begins along a service road near the middle of the lot.

0.1 Pass a private lodge along the access road.

0.8 Arrive at the radio tower.

1.1 Reach Skyline Lake. Follow the trail around the lake along the north shore.

1.5 Attain the 5,400-foot prominence on Skyline Ridge for a 360-degree view of the surrounding mountaintops and Skyline Lake below.

3.0 Arrive back at the trailhead.

Interstate 90

Where other highway corridors followed in the wake of industry, much of I-90's story is wrapped up in attempting to connect the western and eastern portions of Washington. As Washington grew, the need to find a reliable way over the Cascades grew along with it. For decades anyone trying to reach the Puget Sound was forced to either find passage by ship or travel to Portland before heading north. After years of searching, Snoqualmie Pass was identified as a viable route and today handles the majority of the traffic moving across the mountains. Partially due to the sheer volume of traffic traveling through the corridor, nearly every peak between North Bend and Snoqualmie Pass has a trail winding to a summit and likely a junction with another trail leading out into the Alpine Lakes Wilderness. And because cruising down four lanes of interstate at 70 mph eats up miles in a hurry, many of the hikes in this area can be reached quickly and easily.

Lake Easton and Little Kachess Lake (hike 32)

24 Soaring Eagle Regional Park

Explore this network of trails carved into land that was held in trust by the state for more than one hundred years.

Start: Soaring Eagle parking area
Distance: 4.2-mile loop
Hiking time: About 2–3 hours
Elevation gain: 200 feet
High point: 520 feet
Difficulty: Easy, almost flat trail
Best season: Hikeable year-round; best Mar–Nov
Traffic: Equestrian and bike use; low foot traffic

Fees and permits: None
Maps: USGS Fall City; your.kingcounty.gov/ftp/gis/web/vmc/recreation/bct_soaringeagle _brochure.pdf
Trail contacts: King County Parks and Recreation Division, 201 S. Jackson St., #700, Seattle, WA 98104; (206) 296-8687; kingcounty.gov/recreation/parks.aspx

Finding the trailhead: From Seattle take SR 520 until it ends, and head right on Redmond Way. Follow Redmond Way out to 244th Street and head right. Continue on 244th until you reach East Main Street. Take a left and follow East Main Street until you reach the Soaring Eagle parking lot. The trailhead is at the far end of the lot. Trailhead GPS: N47 36.712' / W121 59.437'

The Hike

Like many regional trail systems, Soaring Eagle is a cobweb of connected trails that cover most of the park. To prevent confusion, each of the twenty-eight trail intersections is signed and most have a map letting you know where you are. To see as much of the park as possible, make a large loop starting from the main entrance. Although housing developments are initially visible, they quickly fade into the trees as you wander deeper into the park.

The grade is gentle and the trails are mostly in good repair, allowing you to enjoy the surroundings. Birds are plentiful and fill the trees with constant movement. The landscape is surprisingly fluid—widely spaced stands of alder and maple change quickly to more densely packed swaths of fir and hemlock; these yield to sections of marshy wetlands.

The park is very popular for biking and trail running, so be prepared to share the trail. The main Pipeline Trail is wide and flat, making it possible to bring the whole family out, stroller and all. If you're looking for new places to bring the dog, this is a good option as well. On the other hand, there is relatively little actual hiking in the park, so those looking for a good hill climb should choose a different hike.

▶ The pileated woodpecker is common in this area. It's one of the largest woodpeckers in the world.

A moss-covered stump is a legacy of the area's logging past. ▶

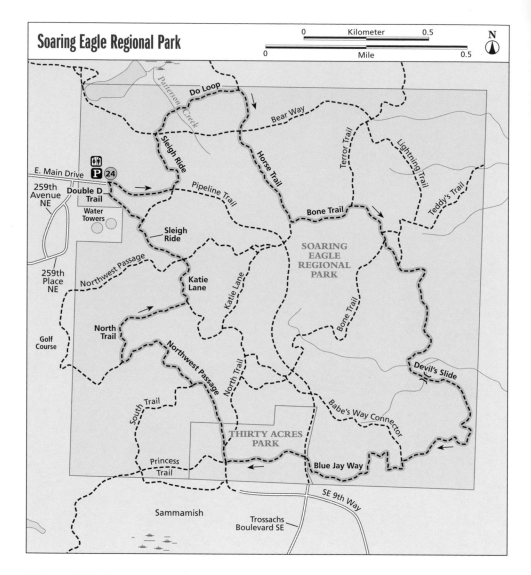

Miles and Directions

0.0 Begin the hike on the Pipeline Trail. A privy is located at the trailhead.

0.2 Turn left onto Sleigh Ride Trail.

0.3 At the junction with Creek Bed Trail, continue straight on Do Loop Trail.

0.7 At the junction with Bear Way Trail, continue straight on Horse Trail.

1.0 Turn left onto Bone Trail.

1.3 Veer left onto Devil's Slide Trail.

Historical Background

Soaring Eagle's boundaries form an almost perfect square, a legacy dating back to the early 1800s when Washington State was first surveyed. Those surveys divided the state into townships, each with thirty-six sections of 1 square mile each. One section in every township was held in trust by the state for the building of schools, preventing development in that section. This is exactly what happened to Soaring Eagle, which was managed by the Department of Natural Resources until 1993. In that year King County acquired the 600 acres from the DNR and slowly set about developing the area into a regional park. Grand plans of play fields were mothballed due to lack of funding, and instead the mixed forest and wetlands were allowed to survive, supporting a variety of wildlife—including deer, bears, and many types of birds.

2.3 At the junction with Babe's Way Connector Trail, continue straight on Blue Jay Way.

2.9 Turn right onto North Trail.

3.0 Continue straight on Northwest Passage Trail.

3.4 Turn right onto North Trail.

3.7 Turn left onto Katie Lane.

3.8 Turn right onto Sleigh Ride Trail.

4.0 Turn left onto Double D Trail.

4.2 End back at the parking area.

25 Dirty Harry's Peak

Tackle this 8.0-mile summit trek named to honor the exploits of an infamous independent logger.

Start: Gates of the State Fire Training Academy
Distance: 8.0-mile summit
Hiking time: About 4–5 hours
Elevation gain: 3,400 feet
High point: 4,680 feet
Difficulty: Difficult due to elevation and rugged trail
Best season: May–Oct

Traffic: Low foot traffic
Fees and permits: Discover Pass
Maps: USGS Bandera; *Green Trails Map #206* (Bandera)
Trail contacts: Snoqualmie Ranger District– North Bend Office, 902 SE North Bend Way, Bldg. 1, North Bend, WA 98045; (425) 888-1421; fs.usda.gov/mbs

Finding the trailhead: From Seattle take exit 38 off I-90 and head right. Follow the remnants of old US 10 for 2 miles past Olallie State Park and back under I-90. Find the gate for the State Fire Training Academy, warning you that it closes at 4 p.m. Park in the paved lot just outside the gates; the Washington State Patrol, which manages the academy, prefers that hikers do not attempt to park on the shoulder near the trailhead. From the lot follow the road over a bridge for about 0.75 mile to a bend in the road. The trail is on the right, marked by two large concrete roadblocks. Trailhead GPS: N47 25.866' / W121 37.943'

The Hike

The unmarked trail begins directly off the road leading to the State Fire Training Academy. The rough and rocky trail is what remains of Harry Gault's logging road after rain and weather have stripped away much of the soil, exposing the small boulders just beneath the surface. During most of the year, water is a prevalent theme, either cutting across the road or running directly down it, transforming the trail into a streambed. As you progress up the tree-lined trail, logging discards become common; buckets and cable are often found languishing at the trailside.

The first 1.5 miles are very moderate; most hikers will have no problem getting to the junction at 2,500 feet, where an old oil drum serves as a marker. From there follow a side trail to the right for roughly 0.25 mile to a rocky outcropping that overlooks I-90 known as Dirty Harry's Balcony. McClellan Butte

▶ The Washington State Fire Academy specializes in high-risk fire training, such as that needed for aircraft fires.

looms large dead ahead, while Mount Defiance and Bandera Mountain crouch to the east. Many hikers find the views here to be more than satisfying and decide to call it a day here. For those hungry for more elevation, return to the junction and continue upward to the peak.

Looking down at Interstate 90 from Dirty Harry's Balcony

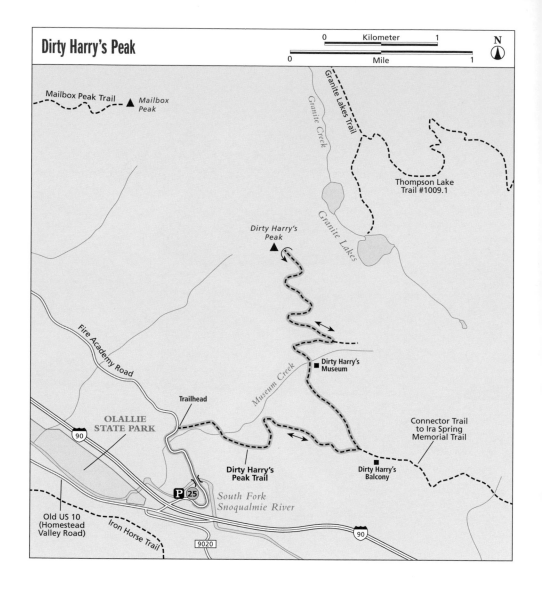

0 Kilometer 1

0 Mile 1

N

Granite Lakes Trail

Granite Creek

Mailbox Peak Trail ▲ Mailbox
Peak

Thompson Lake
Trail #1009.1

Dirty Harry's
Peak
▲

Granite Lakes

Fire Academy Road

Museum Creek

■ Dirty Harry's
Museum

Trailhead

OLALLIE
STATE PARK

90

Connector Trail
to Ira Spring
Memorial Trail

Dirty Harry's
Peak Trail

■ Dirty Harry's
Balcony

P 25

South Fork
Snoqualmie River

Old US 10
(Homestead
Valley Road)

Iron Horse Trail

90

9020

From the Balcony the trail is wetter, rockier, and steeper. It is also unabashedly uphill. It rarely gives more than a few dozen yards of level ground before ratcheting upward again. At 3,000 feet the trail meets Museum Creek, so named for "Harry's Museum," a fabled collection of rusted logging equipment secreted away nearby. Find the collection by bushwhacking up Museum Creek to another logging road and following that to the museum. Whether you decide to go hunting for the museum or not, keep an eye out for the occasional window cut out of the alders, yielding more views of McClellan Butte and Mount Washington.

As you near the summit, the canopy opens as older trees give way to a swath of young Douglas firs and the lingering evidence of the clear-cutting done by Harry decades earlier. Scramble up some boulders to find yourself on something of a precipice with a sheer drop of a couple hundred feet to the Granite Lakes below. That's Baker to the far north, past Bessemer and Russian Butte. To the east you should be able to make out Glacier Peak. While the view is impressive, one can only imagine the panorama that Harry's chainsaw may have briefly created. Most of the views in other directions have been reclaimed by the recovering forest, though the shadow of Mount Rainier looms unobscured to the south.

The roughness of the former logging road—large rocks, often made slippery by water—and uncompromising inclines after the Balcony make this a difficult hike. It's definitely attainable by most prepared hikers—just make sure to bring the hiking poles to steady you over water hazards and rock. If the full trip up to the summit is more than you want to tackle, the hike up to the Balcony is a fine hike unto itself. This hike is also less traveled than the more popular hikes nearby, which means you're likely to get these big views all to yourself.

Historical Background

Dirty Harry's Peak sits at the eastern end of a ridge that begins with Mailbox Peak. Back in 1977, Harvey Manning—the late author of many, many popular guidebooks—had his first encounter with the logging roads that Harry Gault carved into the mountainsides up and down the I-90 corridor. Mr. Gault, or "Dirty Harry" as he was known to his friends, made his living by buying up the right to cut timber in areas where the trees were either too difficult to access or the quality of the wood was too poor to be commercially viable for big logging companies. By ramming treacherous roads straight up mountainsides and employing now illegal clear-cut logging practices, Dirty Harry cut enough corners that he was able to turn a profit. However, his practices visibly scarred the forests, and Dirty Harry became famous for his clashes with the USDA Forest Service and the Weyerhaeuser Company. After Manning experienced firsthand the logging roads and logging equipment that Gault left behind, he began popularizing the area by naming it in honor of Dirty Harry. Today you can still find plenty of artifacts left behind by Harry, including rusting trucks and cables hidden in the underbrush.

Miles and Directions

0.0 Park in the large paved area just outside the Fire Academy gates. The hike begins by heading past the gates along the paved Fire Academy Road.

0.3 Cross over the South Fork Snoqualmie River. There is a rope swing under the bridge—this is a popular swimming hole during the summer.

0.7 Arrive at the trailhead. Cement blocks mark the beginning of Dirty Harry's Trail.

2.0 Come to a trail junction. Head right for Dirty Harry's Balcony, a viewpoint 0.25 mile down the trail. The main trail continues to the left.

2.6 Just before crossing Museum Creek, turn right and uphill into the underbrush. Bushwhack up about 30 feet to find an old logging road. Follow the logging road uphill to the right for about 0.25 mile to get to Dirty Harry's Museum. Retrace your steps back to the main trail.

3.0 Arrive at a trail junction. Head left to continue switchbacking up to the summit. The path to the right leads to a dead end.

4.0 Reach the summit of Dirty Harry's Peak.

8.0 Arrive back at the trailhead.

26 McClellan Butte

Climb one of the most distinctive peaks along the I-90 corridor on this 10.0-mile summit hike.

Start: McClellan Butte Trailhead
Distance: 10.0-mile summit
Hiking time: About 6-7 hours
Elevation gain: 3,600 feet
High point: 5,162 feet
Difficulty: Moderate, with steep sections of trail
Best season: May-Oct
Traffic: Moderate foot traffic

Fees and permits: Northwest Forest Pass
Maps: USGS Bandera; *Green Trails Map #206* (Bandera)
Trail contacts: Snoqualmie Ranger District— North Bend Office, 902 SE North Bend Way, Bldg. 1, North Bend, WA 98045; (425) 888-1421; fs.usda.gov/mbs

Finding the trailhead: From Seattle take I-90 out to exit 42. At the stop sign turn right and follow FR 55 for less than 0.5 mile to the McClellan Butte spur, heading uphill on your right. Follow the spur to the trailhead parking lot. Trailhead GPS: N47 24.733' / W121 35.354'

The Hike

The McClellan Butte Trail #1015 hits the grade almost immediately, quickly crossing the Iron Horse Trail and FR 9020 within the first mile. Relentlessly, the trail forges upward under branches of hemlock and cedar trees, through talus fields, and over streams of runoff. At the right time of year, as the snow recedes, wildflowers mob any open space between the rocks in avalanche chutes on the east face of the mountain. As you continue to gain elevation, you'll slowly leave the trail improvements behind and be forced to negotiate the still rocky and root-gnarled route to the top.

Two-thirds of the way through the hike, the trail abruptly turns behind the mountain, revealing Chester Morse Lake and views of Mount Rainier in the distance before again turning to continue up the west face. Here snow lingers much later in the year. The unexpected snow can cause complications for the unprepared, so bring along some hiking poles to give you extra stability as you traverse the steeply slanted snowfields. This is also the location of an unmarked junction with a boot path that leads out to Mount Kent.

The trail officially ends about 100 feet below the exposed summit, on a small, sparsely treed plateau. Perhaps it was here that the long-gone 1930s-era fire-lookout cabin once stood. The views here are almost as good as can be had if you continue on: Mount Kent and Bandera Mountain to the east, Putrid Pete's Peak and Mount Defiance directly across the valley, and Mount Washington, Mailbox Peak, and Mount Si can be seen to the west. To the south, Mount Rainier dominates the skyline above

▶ The first recorded ascent of nearby Mount Kent was on April 10, 1938, by a group of Mountaineers.

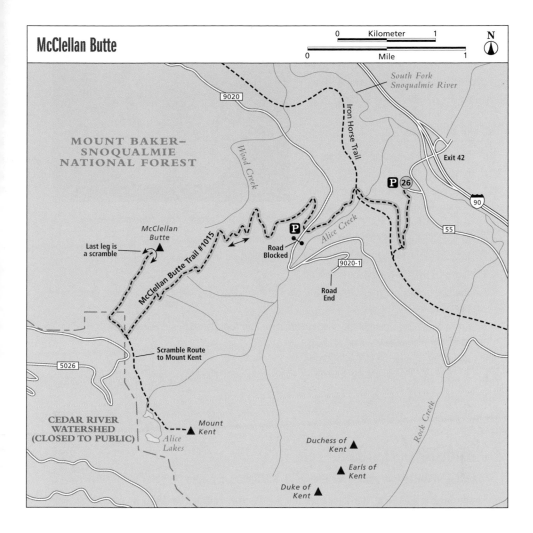

Kilometer

Mile

N

South Fork
Snoqualmie River

9020

MOUNT BAKER–
SNOQUALMIE
NATIONAL FOREST

Wood Creek

Iron Horse Trail

Exit 42

P 26

90

McClellan
Butte

Last leg is
a scramble

McClellan Butte Trail #1015

P

Road
Blocked

Alice Creek

55

9020-1

Road
End

Scramble Route
to Mount Kent

5026

CEDAR RIVER
WATERSHED
(CLOSED TO PUBLIC)

Alice
Lakes

Mount
Kent

Duchess of
Kent

Earls of
Kent

Rock Creek

Duke of
Kent

the watershed. Experienced hikers can scramble up the last hundred feet, mindful of the long drop at the end of the rocks. Here and there you'll walk over rusting pipes and cables, all that remains of the radio beacons that once guided planes through the pass. McClellan Butte has claimed more than a few lives over the years, so use your best judgment before clambering up.

McClellan Butte is the perfect alternative to Mount Si if you're looking for a good training hike without the crowds. In high summer and early fall, once all the snow has finally melted away, the hike should not pose too much difficulty for the whole family to reach the top. Although the hike is a steady uphill climb, frequent openings in the tree line offer ideal places to catch your breath before pushing onward. And while

◀ *Talus field below the summit of McClellan Butte*

the views are similar to many of the other peaks in the area, the combination of the allure of the exposed crags and the minimal mileage needed to get there makes this a great hike.

Miles and Directions

0.0   Begin at the McClellan Butte Trailhead #1015.

0.4   Continue right at the junction with the short trail that leads up to a different point on the Iron Horse Trail.

1.0   At the junction with the Iron Horse Trail, cross the Iron Horse Trail and continue straight on McClellan Butte Trail.

1.5   Cross FR 9020 and continue straight.

4.1   The trail swings northwest around the back of the ridge. A faint route out to Mount Kent begins here.

4.9   Arrive at the beginning of the short scramble to the top. Use extreme caution, especially when the rock is wet.

5.0   Reach the summit of McClellan Butte.

10.0   Arrive back at the trailhead.

Butterflies are common along the McClellan Butte Trail.

Historical Background

McClellan Butte was named for George B. McClellan, a future Civil War general who undertook a survey of the Cascades for the Pacific Railroad in 1853 in search of an appropriate mountain pass for the proposed transcontinental railway. This early survey proved inadequate, with McClellan overlooking a number of viable options, including Snoqualmie Pass, near where his namesake butte now resides. Perhaps unsurprisingly, in keeping with his dubious prowess as a surveyor and general, geologically speaking McClellan Butte is not a butte at all. Instead, it is a "horn peak," a classic glacial formation much like the Matterhorn of the Swiss Alps. The volcanic rock that makes up McClellan Butte was slowly eroded over millions of years by ice age glaciations, forming the sharp-peaked precipice we see today.

27 Mount Defiance and Mason Lake

This 10.5-mile trek past alpine lakes climbs to an expansive vista at the summit of Mount Defiance.

Start: Ira Spring Memorial Trailhead
Distance: 10.5 miles to the summit; 6.8 miles to Mason Lake
Hiking time: About 6–7 hours to the summit
Elevation gain: 2,200 feet to Mason Lake; 3,400 feet to the summit
High point: 5,584 feet
Difficulty: Difficult due to rugged trail beyond Mason Lake and elevation gain
Best season: May–Oct

Traffic: Moderate foot traffic to Mason Lake; low foot traffic to Mount Defiance
Fees and permits: Northwest Forest Pass
Maps: USGS Bandera; *Green Trails Map #206* (Bandera)
Trail contacts: Snoqualmie Ranger District— North Bend Office, 902 SE North Bend Way, Bldg. 1, North Bend, WA 98045; (425) 888-1421; fs.usda.gov/mbs

Finding the trailhead: From Seattle take I-90 to exit 45, going left under the freeway to FR 9030. Follow FR 9030 for about 1 mile until the road splits. Veer left onto FR 9031 and follow it for 2 more miles until the road terminates in a parking lot. Trailhead GPS: N47 25.475' / W121 34.991'

The Hike

The trail begins on the bones of a repurposed fire road, with a grade suitable for conveying heavy machinery up a mountainside. A few streams need to be forded before the trail becomes serious, leaving the young forest behind for a much steeper path up the mountain. The dusty trail moves beyond the pines for ever-larger glimpses at the valley below. Once the trail sheds the last of the trees, enormous views are your compensation for being fully exposed to the elements.

At just under 3 miles, the Mason Lake Trail and the Bandera Mountain Trail diverge. Continue upward and to the west through subalpine meadows and talus fields, reaching the Ira Spring Memorial plaque just before the short descent down to Mason Lake. The lakeshore offers an abundance of campsites and the possibility of a refreshing dip before pressing on to the heights of Defiance. Near the 4-mile mark, you hit the Mount Defiance Trail #1009 and things become rough; rotted roots and rocks exposed by the runoff from melting snow make the trail more difficult to navigate. As you gain elevation you will eventually emerge onto the meadows of Mount Defiance, famously brimming with lush fields of wildflowers in the late spring and early summer. Watch for a small rock cairn marking the spur trail to the summit.

The spur is more of a goat trail, chipped straight from the mountain face on a direct route to the

▶ *Kulla Kulla* is Chinook jargon that roughly means "bird."

Looking down from the summit to Lake Kulla Kulla, Mason Lake, and Little Mason Lake

summit. There you are richly rewarded with panoramic views of the Alpine Lakes Wilderness as well as a bird's-eye view of the Snoqualmie Valley below. On the best of days, five volcanic peaks can been seen: Adams, Baker, Glacier, Rainier, and St. Helens. Lakes are liberally sprinkled throughout the bowl between Bandera and Defiance—the largest is Lake Kulla Kulla, with Blazer Lake and Rainbow Lake just to the east. Little Mason Lake is nestled below familiar Mason Lake. To the northeast you can make out a portion of Pratt Lake resting at the base of Pratt Mountain. Cast an eye across I-90 to look down on craggy McClellan Butte. To the west a treeless ridge known as West Defiance (aka Putrid Pete's Peak) extends out from the summit, looming over Spider Lake below.

Miles and Directions

0.0 Start at Ira Spring Memorial Trailhead #1038 (privy available).

0.2 Arrive at a junction with a trail that leads out to Dirty Harry's Balcony (Dirty Harry's Peak Trail). Head right to continue on the main trail.

0.8 Arrive at a small waterfall on Mason Creek.

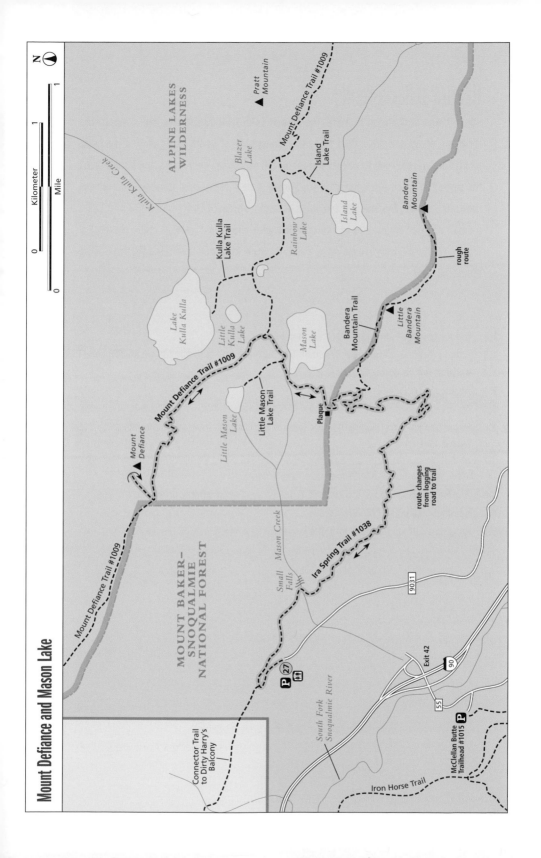

Mount Defiance and Mason Lake

Mount Defiance Trail #1009

Connector Trail to Dirty Harry's Balcony

MOUNT BAKER–SNOQUALMIE NATIONAL FOREST

Mount Defiance

Lake Kulla Kulla

Little Kulla Kulla Lake

Kulla Kulla Creek

ALPINE LAKES WILDERNESS

Kulla Kulla Lake Trail

Blazer Lake

Pratt Mountain

Rainbow Lake

Mount Defiance Trail #1009

Island Lake Trail

Island Lake

Mount Defiance Trail #1009

Little Mason Lake

Little Mason Lake Trail

Mason Lake

Bandera Mountain Trail

Bandera Mountain

Little Bandera Mountain

rough route

Plaque

route changes from logging road to trail

Small Falls

Mason Creek

Ira Spring Trail #1038

South Fork Snoqualmie River

P 27

9031

Exit 42

90

55

McClellan Butte Trailhead #1015

P

Iron Horse Trail

N

0   Kilometer   1

0   Mile   1

Historical Background

Since it was first blazed in 1958, the Mason Lake Trail #1038 has had a reputation for being steep and dirty. Over the years thousands of boots badly eroded the trail, and hikers were forced to negotiate long uphill stretches over rocks and boulders. At the urging of wilderness advocate Ira Spring, a new route was proposed to address the trail damage, the steep grade, and the rocky obstacle course. In 2003 and 2004 a small army of volunteers in coordination with the forest service made the trail a reality. With Ira Spring's passing in 2003, the new trail was dedicated the Ira Spring Memorial Trail.

1.5 The logging road ends and a steeper trail begins.

2.8 At the junction with Bandera Mountain Trail, turn left and continue on the Mason Lake Trail.

3.0 Arrive at the Ira Spring Memorial.

3.4 Reach Mason Lake.

3.5 Arrive at the campsites near the shore of Mason Lake.

3.6 At the trail junction head right to continue to the summit. The path to the left leads to Little Mason Lake.

3.7 At the trail junction turn left onto the Mount Defiance Trail #1009. The path to the right leads to Lake Kulla Kulla, Island Lake, and beyond.

5.0 Arrive at the spur trail to the summit. Turn right and head steeply uphill.

5.2 Reach the summit of Mount Defiance.

10.5 Arrive back at the trailhead from the summit.

G Honorable Mention: Bandera Mountain

Tackle this classic summit for expansive and unbroken views of surrounding peaks and lakes.

Start: Ira Spring Memorial Trailhead
Distance: 7.8-mile summit
Hiking time: About 6–7 hours
Elevation gain: 3,100 feet
High point: 5,241 feet
Difficulty: Moderate due to elevation gain
Best season: May–Oct
Fees and permits: Northwest Forest Pass

Traffic: Moderate foot traffic
Maps: USGS Bandera; *Green Trails Map #206* (Bandera)
Trail contacts: Snoqualmie Ranger District–North Bend Office, 902 SE North Bend Way, Bldg. 1, North Bend, WA 98045; (425) 888-1421; fs.usda.gov/mbs

Finding the trailhead: From Seattle take I-90 to exit 45, going under the freeway to FR 9030. Follow FR 9030 for about 1 mile until the road splits. Veer left onto FR 9031 and follow it for 2 more miles until the road terminates in a parking lot.

View to the west

Historical Background

Bandera has long been a name entwined with the history of Snoqualmie Pass. Though officially recognized by the US Geographic Board as Bandera Mountain only in 1920, a nearby train station along the Chicago, Milwaukee, St. Paul and Pacific Railroad named "Bandera" had been in operation since 1909 and would continue service up until 1980. In 1948 the Bandera Airstrip was dedicated, marking the first emergency airfield in the pass, which is still actively used today. The original trail up the mountain was first blazed to provide access for crews fighting a large fire around Mason Lake in the summer of 1958, and was later popularized by Harvey Manning.

The Hike

Bandera Mountain. Words that often are followed by "steep" and "dry." But another word associated with Bandera keeps hikers coming back: "breathtaking."

Beginning at the Ira Spring Memorial Trail #1038, the path starts casually, following a repurposed logging road. At just over 1 mile, you leave the gentle logging road and the hike begins in earnest, the grade sharpening and the trail beginning to switchback. Whatever time of year, this section of the trail offers a front-row seat to the ever-expanding mountainous panorama, courtesy of the fires that have kept much of the mountainside free of trees. Once you reach the ridgeline, peek over the edge at Mason Lake tucked in a bowl beneath Mount Defiance, then follow the rocky path to the false summit to take in the view.

Mount Rainier presides over a sprawling landscape of lesser peaks. McClellan Butte and Mount Gardner are just across the snaking ribbon of concrete that is I-90. You can make out the rocky outcroppings of Dirty Harry's Balcony just above I-90 to the west. From here you can climb off the first summit and continue on to the true summit to get better views of Granite Mountain and Snoqualmie Pass.

28 Kendall Peak and Kendall Katwalk

This classic hike along the Pacific Crest Trail leads out to the dynamite-carved Katwalk.

Start: Pacific Crest Trailhead at Snoqualmie Pass
Distance: 12.2 miles out and back
Hiking time: About 6–8 hours
Elevation gain: 3,000 feet
High point: 5,784 feet
Difficulty: Moderate due to mileage
Best season: May–Sept

Traffic: Moderate foot traffic
Fees and permits: Northwest Forest Pass
Maps: USGS Snoqualmie Pass; *Green Trails Map #207* (Snoqualmie Pass)
Trail contacts: Snoqualmie Ranger District—North Bend Office, 902 SE North Bend Way, Bldg. 1, North Bend, WA 98045; (425) 888-1421; fs.usda.gov/mbs

Finding the trailhead: From Seattle take exit 52 off I-90 and veer left toward Alpental. Take a right onto a small spur road marked PACIFIC CREST TRAIL and follow it to the parking lot. Trailhead GPS: N47 25.672' / W121 24.810'

The Hike

Descriptions of this popular section of the Pacific Crest Trail usually conjure images of a vertigo-inducing shimmy across an exposed cliff face hundreds of feet in the air. The reality is much more tame and pales in comparison to the stunning panorama from the top of Kendall Peak.

Something about the obvious intrusion of man onto a fairy tale–like landscape has attracted hikers and backpackers for decades. The trail to the Katwalk begins in mixed fir and hemlock that quickly yield to thick patches of huckleberry and salmonberry flanking the path. The grade is fairly mild through long, lazy switchbacks, although the trail soon becomes rocky and root riddled. The path becomes slightly steeper before crossing long stretches of talus and subalpine meadow, with accompanying open views of the pass and surrounding landscape. This hike is particularly enjoyable during the spring and early summer, when the meadows are brimming with color from wildflowers.

▶ Dynamite was invented by Alfred Nobel and is usually made with nitroglycerin, diatomaceous earth, and sodium carbonate.

As you continue beneath the shadow of Kendall Peak, keep an eye out for a tight set of switchbacks just past the 5-mile mark. Here take the unmarked boot path straight up the mountainside to the summit. Though a bit of a scramble beset with loose rock, the path is fairly well defined and easy to follow. You'll quickly gain the narrow ridgeline and cautiously follow it to the top, keeping one eye on the rubble at the bottom of the cliffs hundreds of feet below.

Historical Background

The Pacific Crest Trail (PCT) spent the better part of sixty years under construction. A coalition of hiking and youth groups conceived an approximate route in the 1930s as a Pacific coast counterpart to the Appalachian Trail. From the 1930s until 1968, the route was blazed and explored, receiving federal recognition as a scenic trail under the 1968 National Trail Systems Act. Various trail organizations, land management agencies, and an army of volunteers then worked to link regional trails from Mexico to Canada to form the PCT. By the early 1970s one of those regional trails—the Cascade Crest Trail—was rerouted to meet the PCT trail standards. Finding the current route less than ideal, and finding no reasonable alternative, the choice was made to blaze the trail with dynamite, blasting a path from the sheer granite wall. And so the Kendall Katwalk was born.

The view is tremendous. The weatherworn spires and crags of the Alpine Lakes Wilderness fill the horizon like a sea of crumbling sandcastles. Red Mountain commandeers the landscape to the north, with Mount Thompson just beyond. In the distance to the south, Mount Rainier provides the backdrop for Mount Catherine and the Snoqualmie ski slopes. Look down on Guye Peak and the pass to the west and the shores of Keechelus Lake to the east. While enjoying the views, take a moment to find the cast-iron tube containing a Mountaineers summit registry.

Once you've had your fill, scramble back down to the main trail and continue on to the Katwalk, which is farther down the trail than anyone expects. Don't be surprised to meet a lot of folks confused and wondering if they'd somehow missed the infamous Katwalk. Our advice: Just keep following the trail—you will know when you reach the Katwalk. The views are great, though we highly recommend taking the time to scramble up Kendall Peak, where the panorama dwarfs what you can see from the Katwalk.

◀ *Kendall Katwalk*

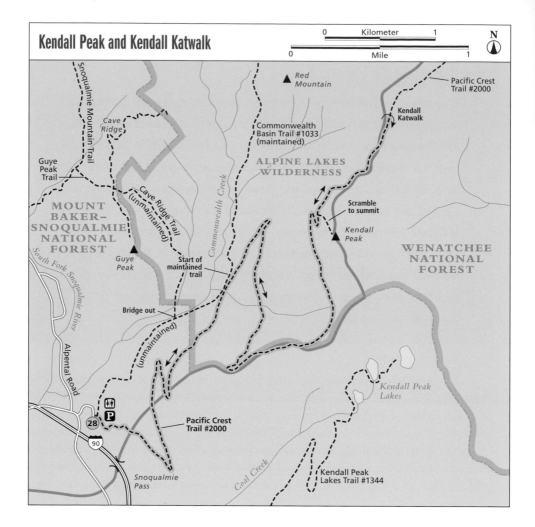

Kendall Peak and Kendall Katwalk

Miles and Directions

0.0   Follow Pacific Crest Trail #2000. A privy is located at the trailhead.

0.1   At the junction with Commonwealth Basin Trail #1033 (unmaintained), continue straight.

2.4   Arrive at a junction with a connector trail that leads down to the Commonwealth Basin Trail. Continue up and to the right on the Pacific Crest Trail.

5.3   *Option:* Scramble route up to Kendall Peak. Look for the obvious boot path cutting up to the rocks above.

6.1   Reach Kendall Katwalk.

12.2   Arrive back at the trailhead.

29 Snoqualmie Mountain

This short but challenging 3.0-mile summit climbs the tallest peak in Snoqualmie Pass.

Start: Snow Lake Trailhead
Distance: 3.0-mile summit
Hiking time: About 6-8 hours
Elevation gain: 3,100 feet
High point: 6,278 feet
Difficulty: Difficult due to steep, rough trail
Best season: June-Sept
Traffic: Low foot traffic

Fees and permits: Northwest Forest Pass
Maps: USGS Snoqualmie Pass; *Green Trails Map #207* (Snoqualmie Pass)
Trail contacts: Snoqualmie Ranger District–North Bend Office, 902 SE North Bend Way, Bldg. 1, North Bend, WA 98045; (425) 888-1421; fs.usda.gov/mbs

Finding the trailhead: From Seattle take I-90 to exit 52. From the exit take a left onto Alpental Road for about 2 miles to a large gravel parking lot. The dirt road is across the road to the right, near the Snow Lake Trailhead. Trailhead GPS: N47 26.717' / W121 25.404'

The Hike

This unimproved trail has all the challenges that come along with that honor. The trail begins a few feet from the Snow Lake Trailhead, up an unsigned dirt road. Keep an eye out to take a small side trail branching to the right, about 0.1 mile up the road. If you reach a shed, you've gone too far. Once on the narrow trail, be prepared for a rough ride. The route takes advantage of rocky streambeds, cuts through groves of encroaching alder, and climbs over talus fields and up ridges of loose rock. Fortunately, vegetation is nearby to steady your balance or provide a helping hand. After about 1 mile a signed junction in a talus field marks the routes to Snoqualmie Mountain and Guye Peak. Veer left over the rocks for Snoqualmie Mountain.

Historical Background

Snoqualmie Mountain quietly rises above the rest of the Snoqualmie Pass peaks, clocking in at 6,278 feet. Despite being the highest peak in the pass, its broad, rounded slopes make it appear smaller than it is. Snoqualmie Mountain and the surrounding area were already abuzz with activity by the time a USGS survey led by Albert H. Sylvester made the first recorded summit climb back in 1898. While miners' boots originally pounded out most of the trails in the area, it was Mountaineers who put Snoqualmie Mountain on their list of peaks to bag in the 1920s and kept the trail from being lost.

Looking down at Snow Lake

When you're not watching the ground for obstacles, catch occasional pocket views of the ski slopes of Alpental and Snoqualmie Pass. The vegetation rapidly changes from lowland underbrush to mountain forest and finally to sparse alpine wildflowers and trees. The transition to the open air roughly marks the halfway point. From here the trail switchbacks up the exposed ridge to the summit, and the views get more impressive with every step. In summer a few patches of trees lend some relief from the sun, but expect a hot and dusty trudge to the top.

Although challenging, Snoqualmie Mountain dishes out a phenomenal panorama. On a good day Mount Rainier commands the skyline. Starting at Rainer's snowy slopes to the south, turn clockwise to follow the long, craggy ridgeline that begins with Denny Mountain, becomes the Tooth, then extends to Hemlock Peak and Bryant Peak before culminating above Snow Lake in a massive mountain that sprouts Chair Peak, Kaleetan Peak, and Mount Roosevelt. Swing past Snow Lake and check out the seemingly gentle ridges of the Middle Fork Snoqualmie Valley, and on the best of days catch a glimpse of Glacier Peak in the distance. Nearby Lundin Peak and the distinctive Red Mountain sit almost directly opposite Rainier, at about 12 o'clock, along with Mount Thompson, Kendall Peak, and Alta Mountain. Cave Ridge and Guye Peak sit to the east, 3 o'clock, with Keechelus Lake beyond.

▶ *Snoqualmie* means "people of the moon" in Coast Salish.

We highly recommend this hike for those who are up for a little punishment. There will definitely be some folks on the trail, but they will only be a tiny percentage of the hikers clogging the parking lot bound for Snow Lake. There is plenty of

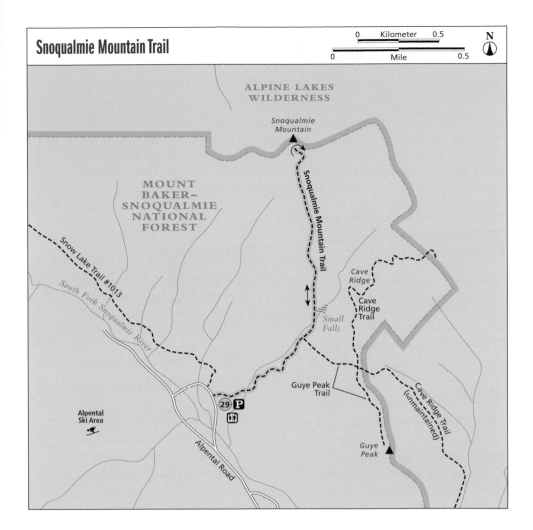

room at the top to find a place to settle down, argue about the names of peaks, and enjoy a hard-earned lunch.

Miles and Directions

0.0 The hike begins along an unsigned dirt road to the right of the Snow Lake Trailhead.

0.1 Turn right off the dirt road onto the trail.

0.2 The trail joins a creek bed, following it upward. Be prepared for water during wetter months.

0.6 At the trail junction head left to continue toward Snoqualmie Mountain. The trail to the right leads to Guye Peak.

0.7 Arrive at small creek crossing and waterfall.

1.5 Reach the summit of Snoqualmie Mountain.

3.0 Arrive back at the trailhead.

30 Silver Peak Loop and Twin Lakes

Explore an 8.6-mile loop featuring streams, lakes, and unbroken 360-degree views from the summit.

Start: Cold Creek Trailhead
Distance: 8.6-mile loop
Hiking time: About 5–6 hours
Elevation gain: 3,000 feet
High point: 5,605 feet
Difficulty: Difficult due to elevation and sections of loose trail beyond Twin Lakes
Best season: June–Sept

Traffic: Moderate foot traffic
Fees and permits: Northwest Forest Pass
Maps: USGS Lost Lake; *Green Trails Map #207* (Snoqualmie Pass)
Trail contacts: Snoqualmie Ranger District–North Bend Office, 902 SE North Bend Way, Bldg. 1, North Bend, WA 98045; (425) 888-1421; fs.usda.gov/mbs

Finding the trailhead: From Seattle take I-90 to Hyak exit 54 and head right. Take a left into the ski area parking lot and head toward the houses at the far end. Pass a small water-treatment plant on your way to FR 9070. Continue to a T intersection and turn left. Find the Cold Creek Trailhead roughly 2.5 miles from the beginning of the road on the left. Trailhead GPS: N47 21.814'/W121 25.356'

The Hike

The trail begins by following Cold Creek up to Twin Lakes, cutting a narrow swath through a young forest still thick with undergrowth. Within 1 mile the shores of Twin Lakes appear, often reflecting within their waters the eventual goal: the rocky cornice of Silver Peak. Veer to the left, following a path that rapidly deteriorates into a rock-ridden game trail in need of some maintenance. Don't be surprised to find a Washington Trails Association work crew in the midst of being issued axes and adzes, readying for another pitched battle against trail degradation.

From Twin Lakes the route begins to aggressively gain elevation, quickly switch-backing up to the Tinkham Peak ridgeline, where the trail intersects with the Pacific Crest Trail #2000. Continue to the right, beginning a long traverse around the bowl beneath Tinkham and eventually Silver Peak. Access to the peak itself is via an inter-mittently marked but well-worn spur trail. At this point you can choose to tackle the mountain or continue on the loop back to Twin Lakes. Note that a short portion of the return route is along FR 9070, so do not be confused when the trail runs aground on the road; simply head to the right for a few tenths of a mile before connecting up with the Mount Catherine Trail #1348.

For the more adventurous, the last leg of your journey to the summit is rough. Loose rock, steep slopes, and windy conditions make it easy to misstep or lose

▶ Huckleberries are common in this area, so bring along a container to collect them in late summer.

The slopes of Silver Peak

your balance. Be prepared to scramble a bit to reach the top, but rest assured that your efforts will be well rewarded. From the breezy precipice you have a commanding 360-degree view of the Snoqualmie Valley. Beyond Tinkham and Abiel Peaks to the southwest, the massive profile of Mount Rainier demands attention. Below, the blue-green of Annette Lake resides in the forested bowl between Silver Peak and Humpback Mountain. To the east, nearby Mount Catherine obscures parts of Keechelus Lake. While ski slopes and clear-cuts dominate the foreground to the north, look beyond the forests to the array of mountaintops before you: Denny, Snoqualmie, Kendall, and Red. Look down into the Snoqualmie Valley past Granite Mountain, Mount Defiance, and McClellan Butte to see the faint and distant indications of North Bend.

Miles and Directions

0.0 Start at the Cold Creek Trail #1303 Trailhead located at a sharp bend on FR 9070.

0.6 At the trail junction with Mount Catherine Trail #1348, head left on Cold Creek Trail #1303 and find Twin Lakes shortly afterward.

2.1 At the junction with Pacific Crest Trail #2000 (PCT), head right and continue on the PCT. Veering downhill leads to Mirror Lake.

2.9 Turn left onto Silver Peak Trail. The spur trail is unsigned; keep an eye out for a rock cairn marking the trail.

Silver Peak Loop and Twin Lakes

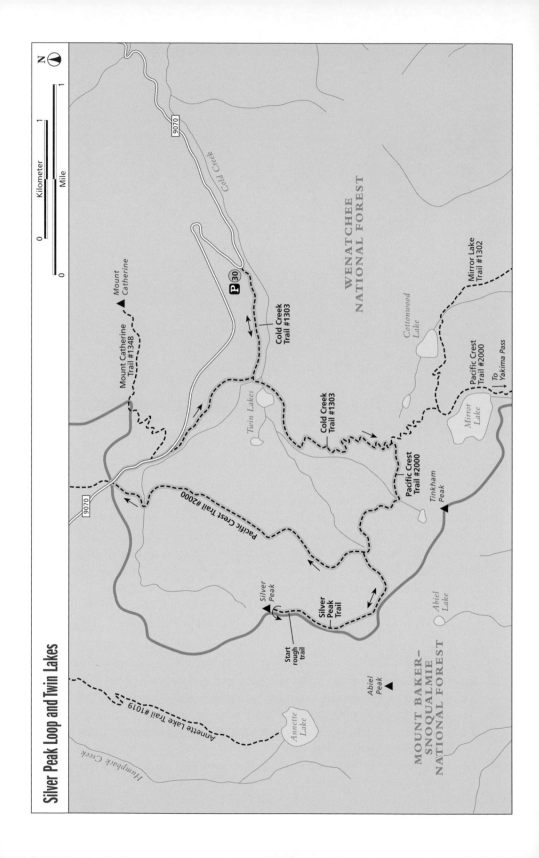

3.9   Arrive at a small saddle before the steep scramble to the top.

4.1   Reach the summit of Silver Peak.

5.2   Retrace your steps back to the main trail and take a left onto PCT #2000.

6.9   Turn right and follow FR 9070 for 0.3 mile to the Mount Catherine Trail #1348.

7.2   Head right and downhill off FR 9070 onto Mount Catherine Trail #1348.

8.0   Turn left back onto Cold Creek Trail #1303 for the final leg of the hike.

8.6   Arrive back at the trailhead.

Historical Background

Silver Peak has long been popular with hikers, spanning back to the first recorded ascent by the US Geological Survey in 1899. Since that time thousands of snowshoers, mountaineers, and backpackers have enjoyed the relative ease of access to one of the tallest peaks in the Snoqualmie region as well as the expansive views from the top.

Looking south from Silver Peak's summit, the two nearest peaks are Abiel Peak and Tinkham Peak. The Cedar River runs along the base of these peaks, creating a low-elevation basin known as Yakima Pass. Both peaks were named by the Mountaineers in honor of Lieutenant Abiel W. Tinkham, a railroad surveyor who worked under Governor Isaac Stevens as a member of the Stevens Railroad Survey and is credited with being the first person to snowshoe across Yakima Pass in 1854.

It may not look like much now, but Yakima Pass was once a busy thoroughfare. In addition to Snoqualmie Pass, Yakima Pass was heavily utilized by Native Americans as a means of crossing the Cascades. Snoqualmie was mainly used for foot traffic, while Yakima, with lighter snow accumulations, was preferred for horse traffic. As Europeans made their way west, Yakima Pass became a popular trade route for the Hudson Bay Company and early explorers in the early 1800s. Until 1856 both passes were often referred to as "Snoqualmie Pass," causing a great deal of confusion for those attempting to find a rail route through the mountains. In 1853 the area was surveyed by Captain George McClellan of McClellan Butte fame, who deemed today's Snoqualmie Pass "impassable" and recommended Yakima Pass as an option. The following year Tinkham went through Yakima Pass as well, never finding Snoqualmie Pass but collecting enough information to raise questions about McClellan's findings. Tinkham's findings prompted further surveys of the area, and in 1856 J. H. H. Van Bokkelen managed to locate and survey the Snoqualmie Pass we use today.

31 Rachel Lake and Alta Mountain

Take this 10.0-mile hike of alpine lakes, ridgelines, and big summit views.

Start: Rachel Lake Trailhead
Distance: 10.0-mile summit
Hiking time: About 7–8 hours
Elevation gain: 3,800 feet
High point: 6,151 feet
Difficulty: Difficult due to steep elevation and rugged trail
Best season: June–Oct

Traffic: Moderate to heavy foot traffic to Rachel Lake; low foot traffic to Alta Mountain
Fees and permits: Northwest Forest Pass
Maps: USGS Chikamin Peak; *Green Trails Map #207* (Snoqualmie Pass)
Trail contacts: Cle Elum Ranger District, 803 W. 2nd St., Cle Elum, WA 98922; (509) 852-1100 or (425) 888-1421; fs.usda.gov/okawen

Finding the trailhead: From Seattle take I-90 to exit 62. Turn north and drive 5 miles to the Lake Kachess campground. Take a left onto Box Canyon Road #4930. Continue for 4 miles and turn left into the Rachel Lake Trailhead parking area. Trailhead GPS: N47 24.050' / W121 17.020'

The Hike

The Rachel Lake Trail #1313 has always been a rough one. The trail bed is more rock and root than actual packed earth—a tangled mess full of trips and tangles, loose rock, and unstable footing. Over the years many an agency has tried in vain to find a better route to the lake, but thus far it has fallen to volunteer groups such as the Washington Trail Association to do their best to smooth out the path to the top. Despite their admirable efforts, the trail remains challenging to navigate.

The trail begins on a gentle grade, hugging Box Canyon Creek for the first 3 miles, crossing numerous streams and cascades as well as dozens of creekside cul-de-sacs, perfect for taking a break from the trail and clambering around on the rocks. Beneath a thin veneer of dust, stands of pine and cedar are surrounded by endless stretches of blue huckleberry, something of a contrast to the forests on the other side of Snoqualmie Pass. The last mile to the lake contains most of the elevation gain, meandering around boulders and occasionally piggybacking on streambeds. As you get closer to the lake, the trail begins to splinter, creating a network of interwoven side paths branching off to picnic nooks and secluded campsites along the shore.

Press up toward Alta Mountain, but pause on the exposed ridgeline to take in Rachel Lake, quietly nestled against Rampart Ridge, with Box Canyon stretching out into the distance. At the saddle the route ends in a T intersection, joining a length of trail that spans the entire length of the ridge from

▶ In Chinook jargon *alta* means "now" or "the present," but it translates to "high" in Spanish and Italian.

Ridgeline trail up to Alta Mountain

Rampart Lakes up to the top of Alta Mountain. Veer to the right through brush and meadows to another intersection, where the trail splits. Head left up to Alta, or if it is not a day for a summit, continue to the right out to Lila Lake.

The trail up Alta Mountain is fairly well defined at lower elevations, but as you trudge up the steep slope, the path gets muddled on exposed rock. False summits abound on the way to the top; time and again you will attain a ledge only to find more mountain to climb. Marked with a gigantic cairn, the summit is breathtaking. The landscape unfolds in all directions. Alaska and Lila Lakes can be seen to either side. The Rampart Lakes shimmer in the distance to the south, just below Mount

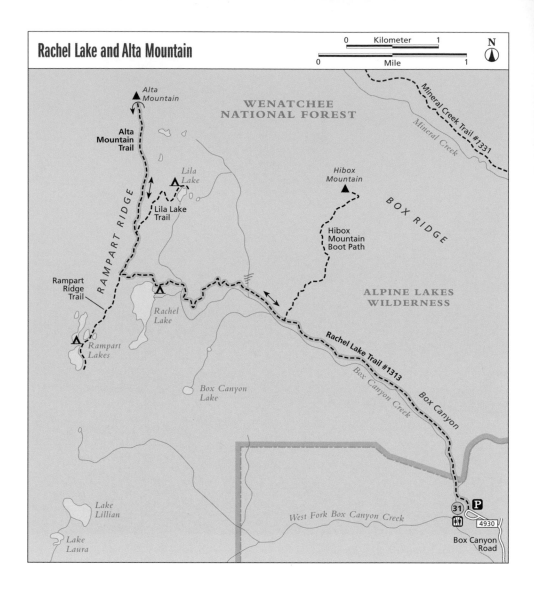

Margaret. To the east the distinctive profile of Hibox Mountain grabs your attention. To the north Chikamin Peak, Four Brothers, and Mount Thompson can be seen. As your eyes sweep west, Alaska Mountain stands above Alaska Lake and Red Mountain can be seen peeking up over Kendall Peak. Snoqualmie Mountain can be seen in the distance, with Denny Mountain just to the south.

Although the trail is challenging, making this hike feel more difficult than the elevation gains would suggest, the beauty and the view more than make up for the effort. Rachel Lake and Rampart Ridge hold more than can be seen in a day, making this hike perfect for a short backpacking excursion.

Historical Background

Back before Washington was a state, it was part of the Oregon Territory, and settlers carved out their lands on either side of the Washington Cascades. By 1853 Washington's population had grown to the point that it was reorganized as a separate government known as the Washington Territory. Almost immediately, the new government began to tackle the need to connect the eastern and western portions of the territory. Surveyors and explorers set about finding suitable passage through the Cascades, eventually finding many routes, including Snoqualmie Pass. Box Canyon was explored during this time and was named for the way Rampart Ridge and Keechelus Ridge "box" you in as you try to cross the Cascades.

It is possible that some trails may have been cut during these early explorations of Box Canyon, but the trail to Rachel Lake was more likely blazed by adventurous fishermen who followed Box Creek in the hopes of finding the next fishing hole. Over the years, the trail was improved and the fishing expanded by volunteers stocking a few of the Rampart Lakes. While the lakes brought in the fishermen, Alta Mountain drew hikers hungry to bag another peak. The Mountaineers have records of a summit of the mountain as far back as 1902 and maintained a summit register on the mountaintop from 1929 to 1989 and from 1998 to 2000.

Miles and Directions

0.0 Start at the Rachel Lake Trailhead #1313 in the northeast part of the parking area. A privy is located at the trailhead.

2.0 At the trail junction with the Hibox Trail spur, look for the unsigned but obvious and well-worn boot path leading uphill. Continue on the main trail.

2.3 Scramble up the creek to the right to a stunning waterfall.

3.4 Reach Rachel Lake. Head right, avoiding the false trails that are closer to the lakeshore. Find the small forest service sign that reads RAMPART LAKES 1 and that marks the main trail.

3.6 At the trail junction turn right to head toward Lila Lake and Alta Mountain. Heading left will take you to the Rampart Lakes.

3.9 At the trail junction head up and to the left to continue to Alta Mountain. The trail to the right leads to Lila Lake.

5.0 Reach the summit of Alta Mountain.

10.0 Arrive back at the trailhead.

32 Kachess Ridge Beacon

This 4.7-mile loop hike travels up to the site of a retired airway beacon.

Start: Kachess Ridge Trailhead
Distance: 4.7-mile loop
Hiking time: About 4–5 hours
Elevation gain: 2,200 feet
High point: 4,600 feet
Difficulty: Difficult due to very steep sections of rugged trail
Best season: May–Oct

Traffic: Low foot traffic
Fees and permits: None
Maps: USGS Kachess Lake; *Green Trails Map #208* (Kachess Lake)
Trail contacts: Cle Elum Ranger District, 803 W. 2nd St., Cle Elum, WA 98922; (509) 852-1100 or (425) 888-1421; fs.usda.gov/okawen

Finding the trailhead: From Seattle take I-90 to exit 70. Take a left over the freeway and turn left onto West Sparks Road. Continue for 0.5 mile to FR 4818 (signed KACHESS DAM ROAD) and take a right. Follow FR 4818 for 1 mile to an unmarked road on the right. Follow this road for 0.5 mile to the small parking area at the trailhead. Trailhead GPS: N47 16.046' / W121 10.457'

The Hike

The Kachess Ridge Trail #1315 immediately begins to ascend the steep slopes of the Silver Creek drainage. Firs, pines, and underbrush line this first portion of the trail but quickly thin to reveal glimpses of the rocky cliffs of nearby Easton Ridge. Occasional talus fields offer wider views. Depending on the time of year, the hike's fist wildflowers appear here and hint at the abundance to come.

As you continue upward, at about 1.5 miles start looking for a faint path leading off toward a vista at the end of a switchback. It may have rocks or branches blocking the path, but it is otherwise unmarked. Once you find it you have a choice: You can take the official route that switchbacks to the right and follows Silver Creek to the Kachess Beacon Trail junction. Alternatively, you can continue straight ahead on the faint path to a challenging and relentlessly direct route up the edge of the ridge to the beacon that offers stunning views of the valley and surrounding mountains. The official route is longer but has long stretches of level ground before climbing up to the ridgeline. We recommend heading straight ahead for quick access to the views. This is also the best approach in the spring, when the official route will still be mired in snow.

▶ It is common to see raptors riding the thermals that rise from the valley below the beacon.

Whether you choose to enjoy broad vistas or the roar of Silver Creek, both routes climb approximately 1,200 more feet of elevation before you reach the beacon. Dig in and push up to the top for your reward. Kachess Lake spreads out below, dwarfing

Lake Easton from the beacon ▶

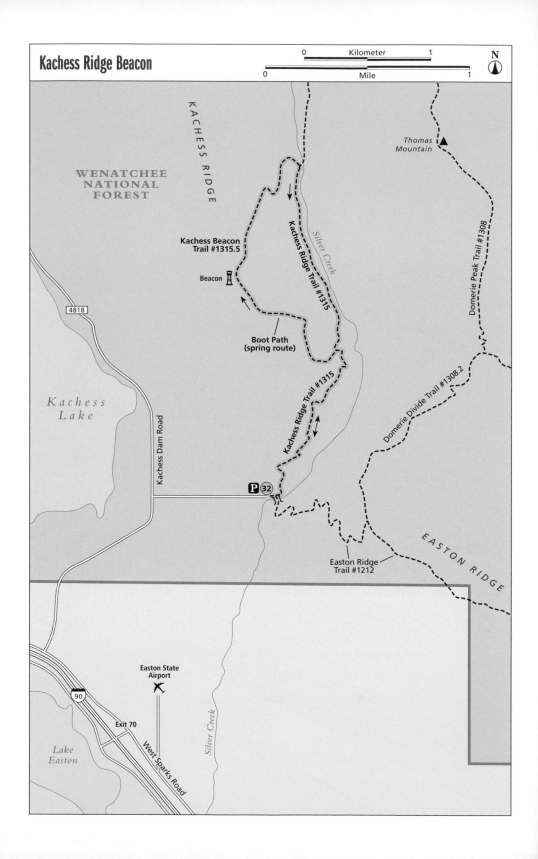

Kachess Ridge Beacon

0   Kilometer   1

0   Mile   1

N

K A C H E S S   R I D G E

Thomas Mountain

WENATCHEE
NATIONAL
FOREST

Kachess Beacon
Trail #1315.5

Kachess Ridge Trail #1315

Silver Creek

Domerie Peak Trail #1308

Beacon

Boot Path
(spring route)

4818

Kachess Ridge Trail #1315

Domerie Divide Trail #1308.2

*Kachess
Lake*

Kachess Dam Road

P 32

Easton Ridge
Trail #1212

E A S T O N   R I D G E

Easton State
Airport

90

Exit 70

West Sparks Road

Silver Creek

*Lake
Easton*

nearby Lake Easton. To the west, rising from the base of the lake, is Amabilis Mountain. On a good day you'll see Mount Rainier poking up over mountains to the southwest. Directly to the south is Easton Ridge, followed by Domerie Peak and Mount Baldy as you continue east. Pick out your other favorite mountaintops and peaks as you settle in for a break. If you still want more, you can continue along the ridgeline for another mile to reach Kachess Ridge's 5,194-foot high point.

Kachess Ridge has a great deal to offer. It is easily accessible from the freeway, but surprisingly few hikers are to be found along the trail. And because it is east of the pass, it is an ideal early-season hike. *A word of caution, however:* The spring route up the ridge is steep and challenging, so we don't recommend it for the inexperienced. Either approach makes for a hard hike, but the views are worth the extra effort.

Miles and Directions

0.0 Start from the Kachess Ridge Trailhead #1315.

0.1 At the trail junction with Easton Ridge Trail, head left for the Kachess Ridge Trail.

1.1 At the end of the switchback, leave the main trail and continue straight ahead on a boot path.

1.9 Reach the site of the Kachess beacon. To continue the loop, head north on Kachess Beacon Trail #1315.3.

2.7 At the trail junction with the Kachess Ridge Trail #1315, turn right and follow Silver Creek downstream.

4.7 Arrive back at trailhead.

Historical Background

Sometimes known as "Little Kachess," the high point on Kachess Ridge is probably best known for its abandoned airway beacon. For a short time beginning with the installation of beacons on Mount Catherine and McClellan Butte in 1934, a series of lighted beacons was strung across Snoqualmie Pass every 10 miles, allowing pilots to deliver mail and cargo after the sun went down. The "lighted airway" was part of a nationwide effort that began in the 1920s and sought to modernize air traffic by installing around 1,500 beacons.

Within a few years the popularity of radio quickly made lighted towers obsolete, prompting the removal of two of the Snoqualmie beacons in 1940. The FAA officially shut down the last beacon in 1973, though Montana still operates its own lighted route. The Kachess beacon, likely manufactured by the International Derrick & Equipment Company (IDECO), features a small shed below a 20-foot tower that held a small electrical plant or acetylene tanks to power the beacon.

This 6.5-mile summit hike travels to the site of the fire tower that once kept watch over the town of Easton below.

Start: Kachess Ridge Trailhead
Distance: 6.5 miles out and back
Hiking time: About 4-5 hours
Elevation gain: 2,200 feet
High point: 4,500 feet
Difficulty: Moderate due to elevation gain
Best season: May-Oct

Traffic: Low foot traffic
Fees and permits: None
Maps: USGS Easton; *Green Trails Map #208* (Kachess Lake)
Trail contacts: Cle Elum Ranger District, 803 W. 2nd St., Cle Elum, WA 98922; (509) 852-1100 or (425) 888-1421; fs.usda.gov/okawen

Finding the trailhead: From Seattle take I-90 to exit 70. Take a left over the freeway and turn left onto West Sparks Road. Continue for 0.5 mile to FR 4818 (signed KACHESS DAM ROAD) and take a right. Follow FR 4818 for 1 mile to an unmarked road on the right. Follow this road for 0.5 mile to the small parking area at the trailhead.

A small dam on Silver Creek

The Hike

The Easton Ridge Trail #1212 begins from the same small trailhead as the Kachess Ridge Trail. However, the Easton Ridge Trail is a little trickier to find. From the Kachess Ridge junction, head toward Silver Creek and drop down to the water to find a sturdy bridge crossing the creek near an old wooden dam. From here the trail begins a series of tight switchbacks straight up the mountainside, climbing roughly 1,200 feet in the first mile or so. Climb onward and upward until you reach the high point. Still looking for more trail time? You can continue down the ridge, attempting to follow what remains of the old trail, or you can double back to the Domerie Divide Trail and do some further exploring.

Easton Ridge works well for an early-season hike. At a lower elevation and located east of Snoqualmie Pass, it tends to melt out quickly. Although there is a bit of elevation gain, most hikers should be able to tackle Easton Ridge, making it a great alternative on a sunny weekend. We recommend you tackle this hike in late June or July, when the wildflowers will be in their full glory.

Historical Background

Easton Ridge is named for the nearby town of Easton, located just below the ridge to the southwest. Settled in 1886, Easton was platted in 1902 and served as an important railroad stop along the Northern Pacific Railway. It was named for its proximity to the east end of the Stampede Tunnel—the long-gone railroad town of Weston once served the other side of the tunnel. By the 1930s airplanes were also flying over Snoqualmie Pass, following a string of beacons like the one on Kachess Ridge. During this time an airstrip was constructed by the federal government as an emergency landing field for military transports. You can pick out from the trail the long green rectangle that is the Easton Airport—it's used today for those able to land on its unpaved, grassy surface.

In 1934 a fire tower was constructed on Easton Ridge to help guard the town against unexpected forest fires. It was probably around this time that the beginnings of the Easton Ridge Trail were blazed, once stretching from one end of the ridge to the other. But when the fire tower was destroyed in 1948, parts of the trail began to fade soon after. Today, while the trail to the top is fairly clear, only faint sections beyond the top remain, leading down the ridge to the trail's eastern end.

33 Hex Mountain

Take on this 5.0–mile hike up to a summit featuring impressive views of Cle Elum Lake.

Start: Sasse Mountain Trailhead
Distance: 5.0-mile summit
Hiking time: About 3–4 hours
Elevation gain: 1,500 feet
High point: 5,030 feet
Difficulty: Moderate due to steep elevation gains
Best season: May–Oct

Traffic: Equestrian, biking, motorcycle, and off-highway-vehicle (OHV) use; low foot traffic
Fees and permits: Northwest Forest Pass
Maps: USGS Cle Elum Lake; *Green Trails Map #208* (Kachess Lake)
Trail contacts: Cle Elum Ranger District, 803 W. 2nd St., Cle Elum, WA 98922; (509) 852-1100 or (425) 888-1421; fs.usda.gov/okawen

Finding the trailhead: From Seattle take I-90 to exit 80. Head left over the freeway following Bullfrog Road to SR 903. Follow 903 for 10 miles through Roslyn and along Cle Elum Lake to FR 4305 (about 0.25 mile before the Wish-poosh Campground). Turn right onto FR 4305 and follow it for 0.5 mile to the first intersection. Veer left and continue on FR 4305 for another mile, watching for a sign pointing left to Sasse Mountain. From here it is another mile to the end of the road and the Sasse Mountain Trailhead. Trailhead GPS: N47 18.133'/W121 03.706'

The Hike

The trail begins with a hike up a rise overlooking Cle Elum Lake, a decent preview of the panoramas to come. The dusty Sasse Mountain Trail #1340 (mistakenly marked #1302 at the trailhead) continues through grassy clearings born when the area was logged years ago, climbing small ridges and descending down the other side. Occasionally the trail cuts across one of the many logging roads that pervade the area. Thankfully, the maze of roads and trails is signposted at every intersection to minimize confusion.

▶ Western tanagers are American songbirds that prefer relatively open coniferous forests and mixed woodlands. They migrate alone or in groups of up to thirty birds, foraging on native fruits and insects.

Continue onward and upward to the nearly treeless summit to take in views in every direction. Directly across the lake a series of peaks runs eastward from Mount Baldy to Thomas Mountain, ending with North Peak at the west end of the lake. Beyond North Peak you can pick out Thorpe Mountain, Red Mountain, and eventually Mount Rainier. To the west are Sasse and Jolly Mountains. As you turn northward, Elbow Peak and Yellow Hill make up the two ends of the closest ridgeline. To the east the Cascade foothills quickly level out into the flat expanses of eastern Washington. Pick your favorite view and settle in for a snack.

Hex Mountain summit ▶

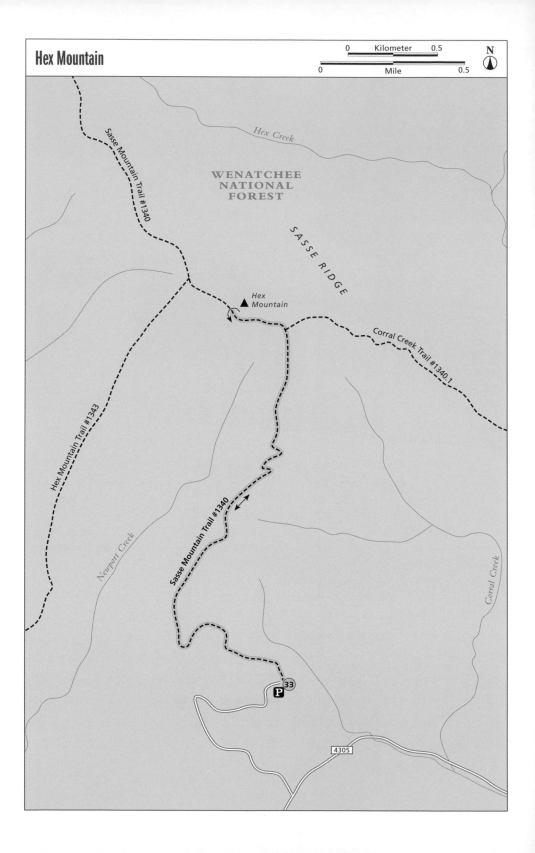

Hex Mountain

0   Kilometer   0.5

0   Mile   0.5

N

Hex Creek

WENATCHEE
NATIONAL
FOREST

SASSE RIDGE

Sasse Mountain Trail #1340

▲ Hex
Mountain

Corral Creek Trail #1340.1

Hex Mountain Trail #1343

Sasse Mountain Trail #1340

Newport Creek

Corral Creek

P 33

4305

Hex Mountain is a popular snowshoe destination, beginning from SR 903 in the winter and winding 3.5 steep miles up the mountainside. While the hike is less grueling in the summer, many hikers avoid it later in the season because parts of the trail open up to motorcycle traffic. While this can be a significant deterrent for some, hiking midweek minimizes your chances of encountering motorcyclists. And even if you have to share the trail, it's likely only for a few minutes before the smell of gas dissipates and the sounds of the forest return. Moreover, motorcycles are not allowed all the way up the trail, allowing you some respite near the summit.

Short and rewarding, this is a great hike to take your reluctant hiking friends on. The trail is in great shape and not at all rough, with only an occasional blowdown along the way. The elevation gain might be a little strenuous for some—about 600 feet per mile—but should be approachable for most. And the views will be enough to

Western tanager

placate any complaints. As an added bonus, the motorcycles do a decent job of keeping other hikers at bay—don't expect too much company on this one. Ideally, hit this one during the workweek to dodge the motorized traffic.

Miles and Directions

0.0   Begin at the Sasse Mountain Trail #1340 Trailhead (mistakenly marked #1302).
2.3   At the trail junction with Corral Creek Trail #1340.1, continue heading up the ridge.
2.5   Reach the summit of Hex Mountain.
5.0   Arrive back at the trailhead.

Historical Background

Hex Mountain is one of many prominences along the ridges surrounding Cle Elum Lake. In 1886 the Northern Pacific Railway built a station near a newly mapped township, dubbing it "Clealum." The name was an anglicization of *tie-el-lum,* the name local tribes had given to a nearby river, meaning "swift water." The town incorporated in 1902 as Clealum but six years later changed it to the now-familiar Cle Elum. Eventually this name was applied to both the river and the lake. In 1933 the Cle Elum Dam was built to better control the water levels in Cle Elum Lake, ensuring a steady irrigation supply in the summer.

Highway 410

Like I-90, Highway 410's story is wrapped up in finding a reliable passage through the Cascades. Back in 1897 the state built a wagon road through Naches Pass, one of the first permanent routes across the mountains. Eventually that wagon road was incorporated into the state highway system, making portions of Highway 410 among the oldest in Washington. But Highway 410 isn't all about route finding: The area has a rich mining history to explore, including the townsites of a few long-abandoned mining communities. Today the highway provides access to Mount Rainier National Park as well as to the skiing and other snow-sport opportunities at Crystal Mountain. Something of a jack-of-all-trades, the White River Valley and area around Highway 410 have a little bit of everything, from mountaintops and waterfalls to forested lakes and abandoned mines.

A wooden bridge crosses the Greenwater River (hike 36).

34 Franklin Townsite

Take a tour through the once-thriving coal-mining community of Franklin.

Start: Green River Gorge Bridge
Distance: 2.2 miles out and back
Hiking time: About 2-3 hours
Elevation gain: 300 feet
High point: 800 feet
Difficulty: Easy with little elevation
Best season: Hikeable year-round; best Mar–Oct

Traffic: Low foot traffic
Fees and permits: None
Maps: USGS Cumberland
Trail contacts: Franklin Tours, The Black Diamond Historical Society, PO Box 232, Black Diamond, WA 98010; (253) 852-6763; blackdiamondmuseum.org

Finding the trailhead: From Seattle take I-5 south to I-405. Take exit 4 off the 405 onto SR 169. Follow SR 169 for 18 miles to Lawson Street in Black Diamond. Take a left and follow Lawson as it changes into Green River Gorge Road. About 3.5 miles from Black Diamond, as the road bends toward the Green River Gorge Bridge, find a chain-link gate on the right. This is the access point. Find parking on the roadside or at the nearby cemetery. Trailhead GPS: N47 18.062'/W121 57.067'

The Hike

The trickiest part of a trek to Franklin is finding it. Although the Franklin townsite is owned by King County Parks, there is no motorized access and there is not much in the way of parking. Access, just after you cross the Green River Gorge Bridge, is marked by a chain-link gate covered in No Parking signs. There is room for one vehicle on the opposite side of the road a little closer to the bridge. If that is taken, most people drive down to a little cemetery 0.25 mile or so back toward Black Diamond. Once you're parked, head back to the chain-link fence. You'll see a yellow gate in the distance, which is the beginning of King County Park property. The property in between is private, but King County has an easement along the road, so just stick to the gravel road and head toward the gate.

Things are easy once on the trail. Head up to a signed junction complete with an ore cart donated by the Palmer Coking Company. Veer left for the mine and cemetery. While there are some foundations on the right, you need permission from Palmer before doing much in the way of exploring on their land.

Brush past sword fern and salal as you follow the road up to the mineshaft. Dropping 1,300 feet into the ground, the shaft was popular among spelunkers and other explorers, but after a couple of accidents, the state sealed the shaft in the 1980s. After you've taken a moment to drop a few rocks down the pit, move on toward the cemetery. The trail is a little rougher here and not quite as wide,

▶ The Class III and IV rapids of the Green River Gorge make it a popular destination for whitewater rafting.

Historical Background

Sometime in the late 1880s, those who were mining coal in Black Diamond branched out to the Green River and began work in the hills around Franklin. Connected by railroad to the rest of the world in 1885, Franklin even got its own US post office in 1886. Labor disputes intensified in May 1891 when hundreds of African-American miners were recruited from the Midwest to replace striking white miners. Unfortunately, the new arrivals were not told about the strike and upon arrival were issued a firearm—supposedly as a defense against local Native Americans. Tensions quickly mounted and two died in a resulting riot, which was only quelled in July when Governor Elisha Ferry called in the National Guard.

A few years later, in 1894, Franklin was rocked by the second-worst mining disaster in Washington's history. The disaster came just two years after forty-five miners were killed in an explosion near Roslyn in the Northern Pacific Mine No. 1. In Franklin thirty-seven miners suffocated when a coal fire broke out in the mine. Miscommunication and poor management led first to the shutdown of the fan that supplied air to the miners, then to opening doors that changed the airflow in the mineshaft. This trapped the coal smoke 1,000 feet below the surface and killed the miners. Later, evidence surfaced that the fire was intentionally set, though the arsonist was among those that perished.

At the turn of the century, as oil continued to replace coal, demand fell and families began to leave Franklin. The post office closed in 1916, and mining largely ceased by 1919. World War II created enough demand for coal that the Palmer Coking Company sporadically mined around Franklin from the late 1940s until 1971, when the coal-car bridge spanning the Green River was dynamited and removed. Today the Black Diamond Historical Society leads tours of Franklin, and cleanup efforts by local school and Scout troops keep the area accessible.

but it is still an easy stroll to the ivy-covered cemetery. Along the way you'll pass a section of rusting trestle that once supported the 8-inch wooden pipe that supplied water to the town. Without much warning, you will suddenly notice a few marble tombstones rising out of the brush. Take a moment to explore and reflect on the community that once thrived here.

This mine cart was donated for exhibit by the Palmer Coking Company.

Franklin is a fun little adventure on those days when you cannot make it out to the mountains. While it is not exactly a traditional hike, it is a walk steeped in the history of this state. Its obscurity and somewhat confusing access makes it likely that you'll have the townsite to yourself and lends a feeling of remoteness. There is also much more to explore in Franklin—it's possible to head down to the site of the coal bridge or get permission from Palmer to hike to the top of Franklin Hill. A day spent tromping around Franklin is well worth the trip.

Miles and Directions

0.0 Start at the Green River Gorge Bridge. Parking is very limited at a small pullout on the west side of the bridge.

0.1 Cross the gravel parking area to the yellow gate marked WASHINGTON STATE PARKS and head up the road.

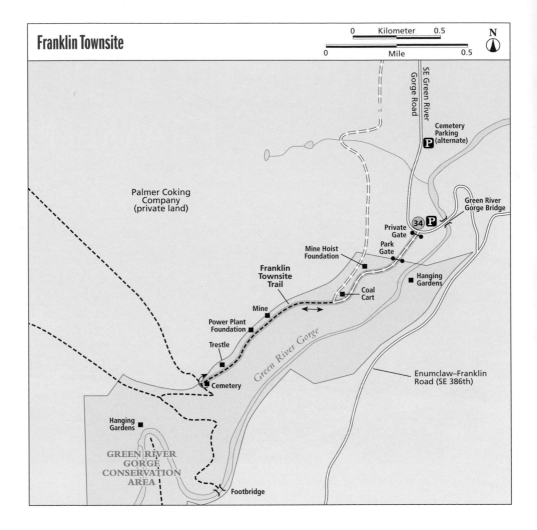

Franklin Townsite

- **0.5** At the road junction and Franklin coal cart, turn left for the mine and the cemetery. Head right to find the foundation of a mine hoist.
- **0.7** Arrive at the now-sealed Franklin Mine.
- **0.8** Reach the power plant foundation.
- **1.0** The small trestle here once supported the 8-inch wooden pipe that supplied water to the town.
- **1.1** Arrive at the town cemetery.
- **2.2** Arrive back at the trailhead.

35 Mud Mountain Rim Trail

Enjoy an easy, family-friendly, 5.0-mile tour of the White River Gorge.

Start: Mud Mountain Dam Recreation Area

Distance: 5.0 miles out and back

Hiking time: About 3–4 hours

Elevation gain: 400 feet

High point: 1,300 feet

Difficulty: Easy, well-maintained trails

Best season: Hikeable year-round; best May–Oct

Traffic: Equestrian and bike use; moderate foot traffic

Fees and permits: None

Maps: USGS Enumclaw; *Green Trails Map #237* (Enumclaw)

Trail contacts: Snoqualmie Ranger District–Enumclaw Office, 450 Roosevelt Ave. E., Enumclaw, WA 98022; (360) 825-6585; fs.usda.gov/mbs

Finding the trailhead: From Seattle take I-5 south to SR 18 exit 142A. Follow SR 18 into Auburn and take the SR 164 exit. Head left on SR 164 through Enumclaw to Highway 410. Head left onto Highway 410 for about 7 miles to the well-signed Mud Mountain Road. Take a right and continue about 2 miles to the Mud Mountain Dam Recreation Area. You can opt to park inside the gates during the summer, but keep an eye on the time—they close, and lock, at 4 p.m. Trailhead GPS: N47 08.702'/W121 56.041'

The Hike

The trail begins at the entrance to the Mud Mountain Dam Recreation Area, following the fence for a short distance to the bluffs above the White River. As the name suggests, the route hugs the rim of the White River Gorge, offering glimpses

Historical Background

Before the Mud Mountain Dam was built, farmers from Enumclaw to Puyallup would endure nearly annual flooding of the White River. For decades farmers attempted to control the waters by dynamiting new river channels, pushing the flow away from their land and onto others'. As Washington's population grew, the flooding problem became more acute, and the Army Corps of Engineers was called in to find a solution. Their recommendation of an earth-fill dam located 7 miles southeast of Enumclaw was authorized by Congress in 1936. The project, which would eventually entail 2.3 million cubic yards of sand, rock, and gravel, was delayed by World War II and was not completed until 1948. Since that time the dam has saved potentially hundreds of millions of dollars in flood damage.

Mudflats on White River

of waterfalls and distant vistas through cottonwoods, alders, and the occasional ever-green. Although the trail crosses a number of roads that lead down to the river, trail makers do a decent job of minimizing confusion. Depending on how much exploring you're up for, you may find yourself wandering through mixed forests and marshes down to the sandy riverside.

This gentle multiuse trail is open to bikers, equestrians, and hikers. Accessible all year, it's a perfect option for an off-season hike. The playground and picnic area make for a nice family outing during the summer, and the Rim Trail is toddler friendly enough to bring the whole family along. Although the trail is over 6 miles long, multiple access roads break up the distance, offering the opportunity to explore the trail in smaller sections. Relatively close to civilization and easy, this hike is a good excuse to dust off your gear and get a jump on hiking season.

▶ Trilliums are often found in this area, but refrain from picking these flowers, as it can take years for the plant to recover from the loss of its flower.

◀ *On the banks of the White River*

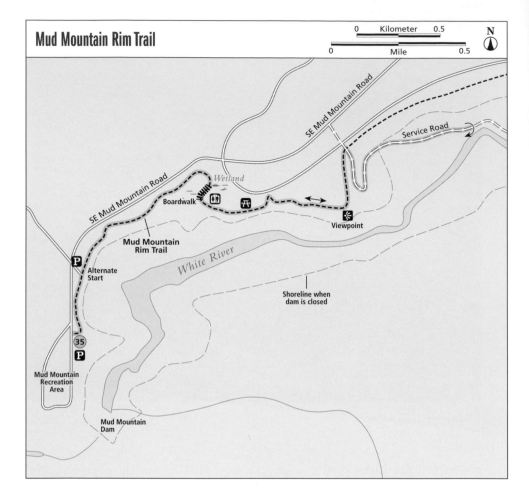

Mud Mountain Rim Trail

Miles and Directions

0.0 Start at the Mud Mountain Rim Trailhead just outside the gate for the park.

0.3 Alternate starting point for the hike when the main park is closed. Park in the small dirt lot to the left of the gate.

0.8 The trail briefly turns into a road. Continue to the right, following the signs to reconnect with the trail.

1.0 Walk across makeshift boardwalks through wetlands.

1.1 The trail reconnects with an old roadbed. Turn left on the road and follow it a few hundred feet to a privy.

1.3 A picnic table provides a stopping point for a snack before continuing along the trail.

1.7 Catch glimpses of a cascading waterfall spilling down to the White River across the canyon.

1.9 Arrive at a gravel service road. The trail continues straight ahead. Head right for a closer view of the river and the mudflats.

2.5 Reach the White River.

5.0 Arrive back at the trailhead.

36 Echo and Greenwater Lakes

Explore the Norse Peak Wilderness on this hike through dense forest to placid mountain lakes.

Start: Greenwater Lakes Trailhead
Distance: 13.0 miles out and back to Echo Lake; 4.0 miles out and back to Greenwater Lakes
Hiking time: About 5 hours for Echo Lake; about 2.5 hours for Greenwater Lakes
Elevation gain: 1,900 feet (1,600 feet in and 300 feet out) to Echo; 500 feet to Greenwater
High point: 4,100 feet to Echo; 3,000 feet to Greenwater
Difficulty: Moderate to Echo; easy to Greenwater

Best season: Apr–Oct
Traffic: Moderate equestrian traffic; heavy foot traffic
Fees and permits: Northwest Forest Pass
Maps: USGS Noble Knob; *Green Trails Map #239* (Lester)
Trail contacts: Snoqualmie Ranger District— Enumclaw Office, 450 Roosevelt Ave. E., Enumclaw, WA 98022; (360) 825-6585; fs.usda.gov/mbs

Finding the trailhead: From Seattle take I-5 south to SR 18 exit 142A. Follow SR 18 into Auburn and take the SR 164 exit. Head left on SR 164 through Enumclaw to Highway 410. Turn left onto Highway 410 and drive about 20 miles through the town of Greenwater, past the fire station to FR 70 on the left. Follow FR 70 a little over 9 miles to FR 7033. Take a right and follow the road to the trailhead. Trailhead GPS: N47 06.344' / W121 28.503'

The Hike

From the trailhead the Greenwater Lakes Trail #1176 begins on a very wide, gentle path. The first 2 miles to Greenwater Lakes is almost entirely flat, helping to quickly pull you deeper into the forest. Expect to cross half a dozen bridges along the way, as the trail follows the path of least resistance up the river valley. Before long you'll find yourself at the first of the Greenwater Lakes, which tends to feel a little more like a widening in the river than a true lake. A few campsites can be found here if you follow small side trails around the lake.

Continue a few tenths of a mile to upper Greenwater Lake and cross the Norse Peak Wilderness boundary. Here the trail temporarily leaves the banks of the river, the forest transitions away from alders and vine maples toward old-growth firs and cedars, and the crowds begin to thin. The trail becomes a little rockier and steeper, though it is still very well maintained. Past the boundary the trail hits a junction with the Lost Lake Trail #1185, heading up to the right. Continue to the left for Echo Lake.

▶ Norse Peak was originally named Swede Butte, but the name was changed because forest service officials considered it "inappropriate."

Greenwater Lake

Now the grade becomes more difficuilt as the trail climbs a ridge above the Greenwater River. Near the top of the rise, the Maggie Creek Trail #1186 splits off to the left. Keep climbing to the top and down the other side to Echo Lake. The forested shores of the lake do not offer huge views, but plenty of campsites lie along the lake. From here, if you're looking for a longer, more challenging day, you can continue onward to Corral Pass and Noble Knob.

Rushing rivers, placid lakes, and wild forests continue to bring hikers out to the Greenwater Lakes Trail. This hike is very approachable for almost anyone. It's a great option for young campers on their first overnight or backpacking experience. Beyond the lakes the trail does become more difficult, gaining a fair amount of elevation, so be prepared for more of a workout. Those looking to get away from the crowds will want to avoid this approach to Echo Lake, which can also be accessed via the Corral Pass Trailhead. Still, we definitely recommended this hike for getting the whole family on the trail or getting those reluctant friends out on a hike.

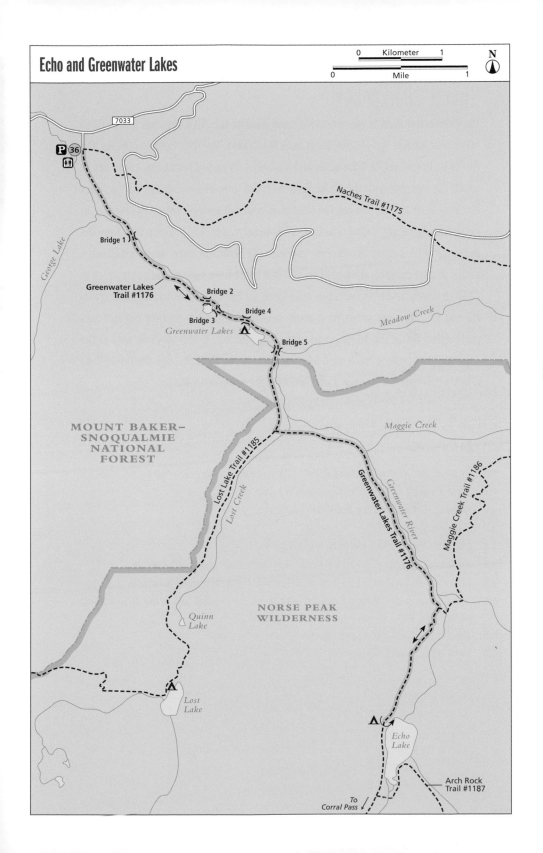

Echo and Greenwater Lakes

0 Kilometer 1
0 Mile 1

N

7033

P 36

Naches Trail #1175

George Lake

Bridge 1

Greenwater Lakes
Trail #1176

Bridge 2

Bridge 3

Bridge 4

Greenwater Lakes

Bridge 5

Meadow Creek

Maggie Creek

MOUNT BAKER–
SNOQUALMIE
NATIONAL
FOREST

Lost Lake Trail #1185

Lost Creek

Greenwater Lakes Trail #1176

Greenwater River

Maggie Creek Trail #1186

Quinn
Lake

NORSE PEAK
WILDERNESS

Lost
Lake

Echo
Lake

Arch Rock
Trail #1187

To
Corral Pass

Historical Background

The Greenwater River is your constant companion on this hike. The river and the trail begin near Naches Pass in the Norse Peak Wilderness. The river flows down into Hidden Lake, drains out to Echo Lake, and continues down to Greenwater Lakes before eventually merging with the White River near the town of Greenwater. Naches Pass has long been a route though the Cascades, with the earliest recorded crossing by Europeans following Native American trails occurring in 1841. Since that time the desire to build a more permanent road over the pass has been nearly constant. A series of road-building attempts resulted in a short-lived wagon route completed in 1853 that was almost immediately abandoned for Snoqualmie Pass. Still, the dream did not die. Proposed plans for a route over the pass were actually codified into Washington law in the 1970s, making the nonexistent SR 168 officially part of the state highway system. Today such a highway would run right through the Norse Peak Wilderness—over 50,000 acres of wilderness set aside in 1984.

Miles and Directions

0.0 Begin at the Greenwater Lakes Trail #1176 Trailhead. A privy is located at the trailhead.

0.8 Cross Bridge 1.

1.6 Arrive at Bridge 2 and the first Greenwater Lake.

1.7 Cross Bridge 3.

1.9 Come to upper Greenwater Lake and Bridge 4.

2.3 Arrive at Bridge 5. Cross into the Norse Peak Wilderness shortly after bridge.

2.9 At the junction with Lost Lake Trail #1185, follow the path leading down and to the left.

5.2 At the junction with Maggie Creek Trail #1186, continue uphill and to the right on Greenwater Lakes Trail.

6.5 Reach Echo Lake and an open camping area.

13.0 Arrive back at the trailhead.

37 Kelly Butte

Tackle a 3.4-mile summit hike climbing up to a restored fire lookout with big views of surrounding peaks.

Start: Kelly Butte Trailhead
Distance: 3.4-mile summit
Hiking time: About 2–3 hours
Elevation gain: 1,100 feet
High point: 5,400 feet
Difficulty: Moderate due to some elevation gain and rugged trail
Best season: May–Oct
Traffic: Moderate foot traffic
Fees and permits: None

Maps: USGS Lester; *Green Trails Map #239* (Lester)
Trail contacts: Snoqualmie Ranger District—Enumclaw Office, 450 Roosevelt Ave. E., Enumclaw, WA 98022; (360) 825-6585; fs.usda.gov/mbs
Special considerations: From the trailhead it's possible for some vehicles to continue the last 0.75 mile to the base of Kelly Butte, but the road is very narrow, so we recommend you park and walk it.

Finding the trailhead: From Seattle take I-5 south to SR 18 exit 142A. Follow SR 18 into Auburn and take the SR 164 exit. Head left on SR 164 through Enumclaw to Highway 410. Turn left onto Highway 410 and drive about 20 miles through the town of Greenwater, past the fire station to FR 70 on the left. Follow FR 70 a little over 8 miles to FR 7030. Take a left onto the gravel road and continue about 4 miles to a T intersection. Take a left and continue 1 mile to the next intersection, again veering to the left. Continue for about 0.5 mile to another intersection, this time heading right. Find the signed trailhead on the left in about 1 mile. Trailhead GPS: N47 09.789'/W121 28.451'

The Hike

The trail begins steeply, climbing past the rocks and crags of the butte. There are two approaches. The old route starts at the end of the logging road, where ropes have been strung to help you up the steep scramble. The new route is much tamer and begins a hundred yards from the road's end. Either way, the trails quickly connect and switchback through logged meadows dotted with sun-bleached stumps and snags. In summer the meadows are bursting with wildflowers, bear grass, and mountain blueberry, and if you're lucky, you may even come across a mountain goat or two. The views begin almost immediately and grow steadily larger as the trail flattens and you begin the short traverse to the lookout. On a clear day you can't miss Mount Rainier, Glacier Peak, Mount Baker, and Mount Stuart.

▶ Rhizomes in bear grass are able to survive fires, which is why the plant is often the first to sprout and thrive in burn zones.

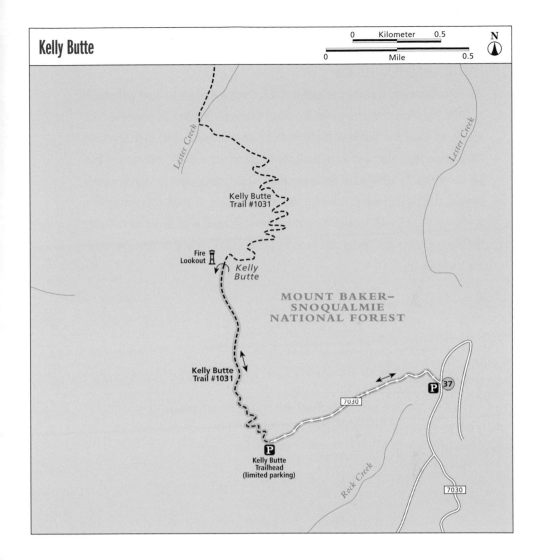

0   Kilometer   0.5

0   Mile   0.5

N

Lester Creek

Kelly Butte
Trail #1031

Fire
Lookout

Kelly
Butte

MOUNT BAKER–
SNOQUALMIE
NATIONAL FOREST

Kelly Butte
Trail #1031

7030

37

Kelly Butte
Trailhead
(limited parking)

Rock Creek

Lester Creek

7030

This is a fun little hike, quickly delivering a short workout and some views. Despite the steep start, this hike is approachable for almost every hiker. The most challenging part of the hike is actually finding it. There are quite a few unmarked logging roads to deal with, and it is fairly easy to get turned around. Once you find the road to the trailhead, we really encourage you to park at the makeshift lot near the KELLY BUTTE TRAIL sign. While you can probably make it down the somewhat overgrown road to the base of the butte, the road is extremely narrow and there are no pullouts, making it impossible for two cars to pass each other. If you happen to

Cliffs near the Kelly Butte trailhead

Historical Background

The Kelly Butte Fire Lookout was built in 1926, though it was torn down and rebuilt in 1950. The lookout watched over the small Green River Valley communities that sprung up along the Northern Pacific Railway when it built a line over Stampede Pass. Towns like Lester and Nagrom slowly shrank along with the railroad and timber industries. By 1980, when the towns were all but abandoned, the forest service stopped staffing the lookout and it fell into disrepair. Then, in 2006, with money from the Forest Fire Lookout Association and the forest service, work began on restoring the lookout. Today the lookout has been restored and is enjoyed by both day hikers and backpackers.

encounter another car going in the opposite direction, one of you will have to reverse all the way to the end of the road to make room.

Miles and Directions

0.0 The hike begins on a on a narrow forest road leading to the trailhead.

0.7 Turn right onto the steep trail heading up the butte.

1.7 Reach the summit of Kelly Butte and the restored fire lookout.

3.4 Arrive back at the trailhead.

Combine this short hike up to a former fire lookout with other nearby hikes.

Start: Colquhoun Trailhead
Distance: 1.0-mile round-trip summit (2.0 miles round-trip from FR 7036)
Hiking time: About 1 hour
Elevation gain: 600 feet (900 feet from FR 7036)
High point: 5,200 feet
Difficulty: Moderate due to steep and narrow trail
Best season: May–Oct
Traffic: Very low foot traffic
Fees and permits: None

Maps: USGS Lester; *Green Trails Map #239* (Lester)
Trail contacts: Snoqualmie Ranger District– Enumclaw Office, 450 Roosevelt Ave. E., Enumclaw, WA 98022; (360) 825-6585; fs.usda.gov/mbs
Special considerations: The spur road to the trailhead is a narrow, rough road that requires a high-clearance vehicle. Either park at the junction and hike the 0.5 mile to the trailhead, or drive to the end of the road and park in the small turnaround at the end of the road.

Finding the trailhead: From Seattle take I-5 south to SR 18 exit 142A. Follow SR 18 into Auburn and take the SR 164 exit. Head left on SR 164 through Enumclaw to Highway 410. Turn left onto Highway 410 and drive about 20 miles through the town of Greenwater, past the fire station, to FR 70 on the left. Take a left and follow FR 70 for about 8.5 miles to FR 7030. Take a left and continue about 4 miles to FR 7036. Take a right and continue 0.5 mile to unmarked Road #7036-110 on your right.

The Hike

This rocky and narrow trail begins at the end of a forest road, switchbacking steeply 600 feet up to the ridgeline. Although the trees have grown to obscure some of the

Historical Background

Colquhoun Peak was named by the owner of a summer home near Greenwater. The owner's son drowned in a lake near the peak, and it was named in his honor. It's not clear whether it was named for the boy's first name or last. Colquhoun is an unusual first name, though Scotland's Colquhoun clan traces its lineage back hundreds of years. Either way, in the 1930s the forest service built a fire lookout here, similar to the cabin on nearby Kelly Butte. It served for a few decades before it was destroyed in 1958. Today all that remains of the lookout are a few cables, some bits of metal, and shattered glass.

Summit views to the north

view at the summit, there are still long views over a sea of mountaintops, including nearby Kelly Butte, Sawmill Ridge, Pyramid Peak, and Mount Rainer.

It's a short hike, but Colquhoun Peak works as a good addition to a day of hiking, delivering excellent views in very little time. Combining a trip to Colquhoun Peak with a trek up Kelly Butte or Blowout Mountain can make for a decent day of hiking and exploring this area. As an added bonus, this trail also does not see a lot of foot traffic, mostly because it is a little tricky to find. So expect to savor Colquhoun Peak's views without anyone else around.

38 Snoquera Falls

Explore a Depression-era Civilian Conservation Corps base camp turned Boy Scout summer camp on this 3.8-mile loop up to an impressive waterfall.

Start: Camp Sheppard parking area
Distance: 3.8-mile loop
Hiking time: About 3–4 hours
Elevation gain: 900 feet
High point: 3,400 feet
Difficulty: Easy, with some elevation gain
Best season: Apr–Oct; waterfall most impressive Apr–May

Traffic: Moderate to heavy foot traffic
Fees and permits: Northwest Forest Pass
Maps: USGS Sun Top; *Green Trails Map #238* (Greenwater).
Trail contacts: Snoqualmie Ranger District–Enumclaw Office, 450 Roosevelt Ave. E., Enumclaw, WA 98022; (360) 825-6585; fs.usda.gov/mbs

Finding the trailhead: From Seattle take I-5 south to SR 18 exit 142A. Follow SR 18 into Auburn and take the SR 164 exit. Head left on SR 164 through Enumclaw to Highway 410. Head left onto Highway 410 for 32 miles to Camp Sheppard, just past the Dalles campground. Trailhead GPS: N47 02.154' / W121 33.595'

The Hike

The Snoquera Falls Trail #1167 begins at the Camp Sheppard parking lot, immediately plunging into the forest and weaving through the outskirts of the camp. Ignore the amphitheater and nature trail and instead push on to the signed trail junction less than 0.25 mile down the path. We recommend taking a right for a counterclockwise approach to this loop—mostly because you get to the waterfall a little faster this way. Despite being a little rocky and narrow, the trail is well maintained and free of blowdowns.

Travel beneath mossy, second-generation forest and through the occasional talus field as you switchback up the trail. Once you reach the falls, you have a choice: You can continue over the creek to a rough path hugging the cliff side up to the base of the waterfall, or you can watch the water tumble hundreds of feet down the rock face from a distance. Up close it's difficult to get a feeling for the waterfall as a whole, but what you can get near is worth the extra effort. There's enough room at the top to have a snack, enjoy the crashing water, and look out over a sea of evergreens stretching out into the distance. Keep in mind that Snoquera Falls are snow driven, meaning that during high summer they will be reduced to a trickle and will not be as impressive as they are during the spring and fall.

This is a great hike that we would recommend to almost anyone. It's not often that such

▶ Nearby, the horse-tailed Skookum Falls tumble down the opposite side of the valley and are viewable from a parking area on the side of Highway 410.

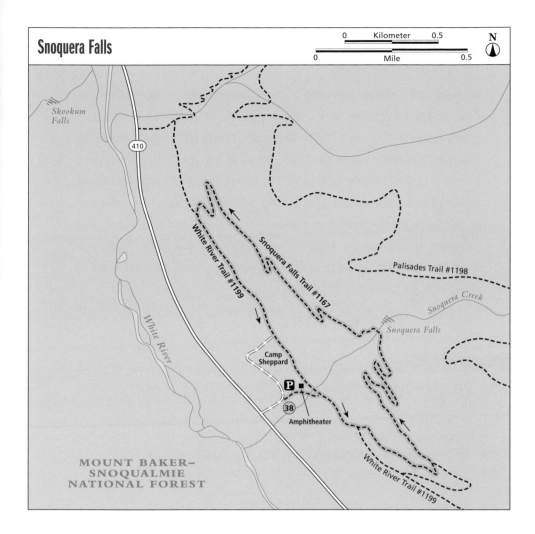

Snoquera Falls

Skookum Falls

410

White River Trail #1199

Snoquera Falls Trail #1167

Palisades Trail #1198

Snoquera Creek

Snoquera Falls

White River

Camp Sheppard

P ■

38

Amphitheater

White River Trail #1199

MOUNT BAKER–
SNOQUALMIE
NATIONAL FOREST

an impressive waterfall is so easily accessible—although the short route up to the base of the falls is a bit of a scramble. But that short climb to the falls' base somehow leads to an area that feels much more remote than it actually is. As an added bonus, you can hike this trail nearly year-round, with the falls putting on a different show depending on the season. While this is a popular destination for sledding in the winter and camping in the summer, you can maximize your solitude by trying this hike in the spring.

◀   *Snoquera Falls*

Historical Background

Snoquera Falls is situated near a Boy Scouts of America campground now known as Camp Sheppard. But before Harry J. Sheppard purchased the land from the federal government in 1947, it was a Civilian Conservation Corps (CCC) base camp, dating from the Great Depression in the 1930s. From this site the CCC built roads and structures in Mount Rainier National Park as well as the Mount Baker–Snoqualmie National Forest. The men serving in the camp dubbed it "Snoquera," a combination of Snoqualmie and the Employment Recovery Act (ERA) that paid their wages. Even before the Great Depression, beginning in the 1890s the area was a regular stop along the wagon road leading up to Starbo Copper Mine, which pulled metal out of Mount Rainier for more than fifty years.

Miles and Directions

0.0 Begin at the Camp Sheppard parking area. Follow the signs leading toward Snoquera Falls Trail.

0.1 Arrive at a small amphitheater, followed shortly thereafter by the trail junction with Moss Lake Nature Trail. Continue straight ahead.

0.2 Trail junction with White River Trail #1199. Begin the loop by heading right.

0.3 Trail junction with Snoquera Falls Trail #1167. Veer left and uphill on the Snoquera Falls Trail.

0.6 Turn left and continue uphill on Snoquera Falls Trail.

1.6 Reach Snoquera Falls. Cross the creek to and find a boot path 100 feet down the trail leading up to the base of the falls.

2.9 At the trail junction with White River Trail #1199, turn left and follow the route back to the start of the loop and eventually the parking area.

3.6 Turn right back down the trail to the amphitheater.

3.8 Arrive back at the parking area.

Take a trail-less-traveled up to views of the White River Valley on this 5.5-mile hike.

Start: Skookum Flats Trailhead #1194

Distance: 5.5-mile summit

Hiking time: About 3–4 hours

Elevation gain: 1,500 feet

High point: 3,900 feet

Difficulty: Moderate due to elevation gain

Best season: May–Oct

Traffic: Bike use; moderate foot traffic

Fees and permits: Northwest Forest Pass

Maps: USGS Sun Top; *Green Trails Map #238* (Greenwater)

Trail contacts: Snoqualmie Ranger District–Enumclaw Office, 450 Roosevelt Ave. E., Enumclaw, WA 98022; (360) 825-6585; fs.usda.gov/mbs

Finding the trailhead: From Seattle take I-5 south to SR 18 exit 142A. Follow SR 18 into Auburn and take the SR 164 exit. Head left on SR 164 through Enumclaw to Highway 410. Head left onto Highway 410 and continue to milepost 54 and the Buck Creek Recreation Area. Take a right over the bridge to find parking at Skookum Flats Trailhead #1194. Gear up and hike back out to 410, crossing the highway, either hiking straight up the hillside or a few hundred yards west to the junction with the White River Trail.

Douglas fir–lined trail

White River Valley from the summit

The Hike

The trail begins right off Highway 410, but road noise is soon replaced with the sound of the rushing waters of Ranger Creek. Within a few minutes you will find the Ranger Creek Trail junction leading up the mountainside and into stands of old growth. Occasional glimpses of the valley can be seen as you slowly climb up long and gentle switchbacks.

At just under 3 miles, the trail plateaus and a very short spur trail leads out to Little Ranger Peak. A quick scramble leads out to an open rocky area and commanding views of the White River Valley. As a word of caution, clambering all the way out to the viewpoint can be dangerous, especially if the rocks are slick with moisture. Use caution if you decide to risk the scramble. From here you can turn around and call it a day or continue onward for another 2 miles to the Ranger Creek Shelter, a three-sided log shelter built by Boy Scouts a number of years ago. Still want some more mileage? A little over 1 mile beyond the shelter, the trail connects with the Dalles Ridge Trail, an excellent ridge walk on a sunny day.

With its gentle grade and quick rewards, consider this little hike up to a rocky prominence if you're short on time. Be aware that you may be sharing the trail with mountain bikers, so be prepared to give them a little room.

39 Melmont Townsite

Wander down a former railroad grade to explore what remains of the once-booming community of Melmont.

Start: Fairfax Bridge
Distance: 2.5 miles out and back
Hiking time: About 2–3 hours
Elevation gain: 100 feet
High point: 1,360 feet
Difficulty: Easy, but be prepared for mud
Best season: Hikeable year-round; best June–Sept

Traffic: Off-highway vehicle (OHV) use; low foot traffic
Fees and permits: None
Maps: USGS Wilkeson
Trail contacts: Pierce County Parks and Recreation, 9112 Lakewood Dr. SW, Lakewood, WA 98499; (253) 798-4177; co.pierce.wa.us

Finding the trailhead: From Seattle take I-5 south to I-405. From I-405 take SR 167 south toward Auburn. In 20 miles take the Highway 410 exit toward Sumner/Yakima. Follow Highway 410 for 12 miles to SR 165. Take a right and continue on SR 165 for about 10 miles through Carbonado to the Fairfax Bridge. A small gravel turnout on the far side of the bridge provides parking. Hike back across the bridge and head toward the rock wall. Hop the guardrail to find a rough path down to the railroad grade. Trailhead GPS: N47 02.467' / W122 02.507'

The Hike

The trail begins on the north side of the bridge with a short scramble down to the Northern Pacific railroad grade. From here Melmont is an easy 1-mile stroll along the river, following a wide path under mossy alders and young hemlock. However, because OHV traffic churns up a lot of earth, during the wetter months a thick layer of mud can cover the trail. Although the mud can be a little messy, it is not so bad that it makes hiking more difficult.

Shortly after you leave the bridge behind, you'll pass a large rock retaining wall followed quickly by a structure most refer to as the "Dynamite Shack." As you push onward, the trail splits just above an open field that was once the residential area of town. Heading uphill leads to the crumbling foundation of one of Melmont's schoolhouses, while pushing onward will lead to the site of the hotel and the remains of Melmont's bridge. Either way you choose, enjoy wandering the area and finding traces of the hundred-year-old town.

If you're looking for a short stroll through Washington's history, Melmont is a good choice. Other than the short drop down to the railroad grade, which could be tricky for some very young hikers, the trip out to the townsite is very easy. At

▶ Much like parts of Olympic National Park, the Carbon River Valley is a temperate rain forest. Once known as the Upthascap River, it was changed to Carbon after coal was discovered nearby.

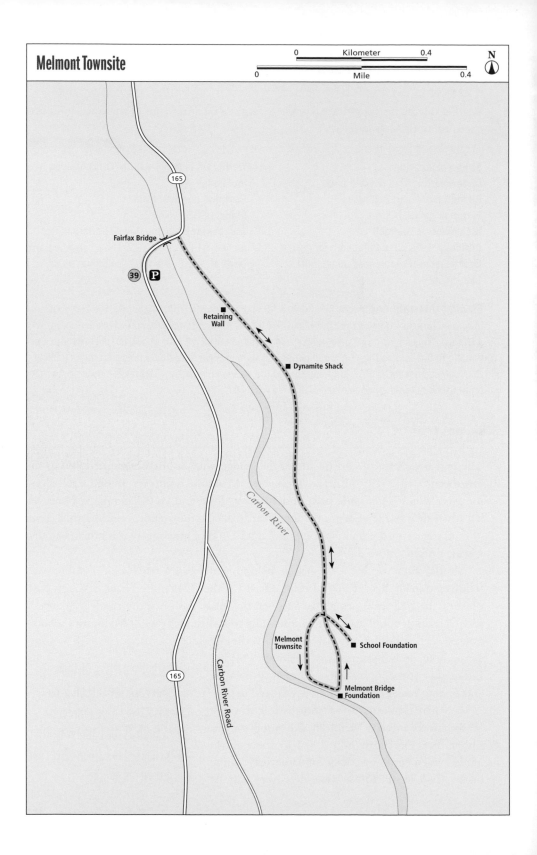

Melmont Townsite

0   Kilometer   0.4
0   Mile   0.4
N

165

Fairfax Bridge

39 P

Retaining
Wall

Dynamite Shack

Carbon River

165

Carbon River Road

Melmont
Townsite

School Foundation

Melmont Bridge
Foundation

Dynamite Shack

the same time there is not much in the way of serious hiking. You can extend your hike a bit by pushing down to the river, but other than that, we are not sure there is much more to see. We recommend this hike for those interested in ghost towns or who are looking for a quick all-season hike. The area tends to be snow-free most of the year.

Miles and Directions

0.0 Cross the Fairfax Bridge to find a small parking area on the left side of the road. Walk back across the bridge to begin the hike.

0.1 Step over the guardrail on the right-hand side of the road and follow the boot path down to the railroad grade.

0.3 Turn right on a boot path to find an old retaining wall.

0.5 Reach the Dynamite Shack.

Historical Background

Melmont was founded in 1900 around the Melmont Coal Mine, producing coal exclusively for the Northern Pacific Railway. For a few years the small town boomed, boasting a train depot, hotel, post office, and schoolhouse. Although the mine yielded upwards of 750 tons of coal per day, when the railroad shifted away from coal-driven trains to more-modern diesel models, the town crumbled. By 1915 the post office was shuttered, and by 1920 the mines were largely closed. A forest fire cleared out all but a few cement foundations around the same time. In 1921 the Fairfax Bridge opened above the Carbon River, bypassing Melmont's railroad bridge and connecting Fairfax to the state highway system. When it opened, the Fairfax Bridge was the tallest in Washington, and it was added to the National Register of Historic Places in 1982.

1.0 The road comes to a Y. Head left for a short side trip up to the old school. Going right leads to the fields of the old townsite.

1.1 Arrive at the old school foundations. Double back and take the other fork in the road toward the townsite.

1.3 Reach the Carbon River and scramble down the hillside to find what is left of the crumbling foundations of the Melmont Bridge.

2.5 Arrive back at the trailhead.

40 Pack Forest

Discover peaks, lakes, and waterfalls hidden within a 50-mile network of trails.

Start: Pack Forest Main Office
Distance: 7.0-mile loop
Hiking time: About 4–5 hours
Elevation gain: 1,300 feet
High point: 1,728 feet
Difficulty: Moderate due to some elevation and sections of rugged trail
Best season: Hikeable year-round; best Apr–Nov

Traffic: Equestrian and bike use; hunting allowed; moderate foot traffic
Fees and permits: None
Maps: USGS Eatonville; www.packforest.org/education/11x17_low2.pdf
Trail contacts: Pack Forest, 9010 453rd St. E., Eatonville, WA 98328; (206) 685-4485; packforest.org

Finding the trailhead: From Seattle take I-5 south to Tacoma, taking exit 127 for SR 512. In about 2 miles take the SR 7 exit toward Spanaway. Continue on SR 7 for roughly 22 miles to the signed entrance to the University of Washington Pack Forest on the left. Find visitor parking near the main office. Trailhead GPS: N46 50.627' / W122 18.710'

The Hike

The Hugo Peak Trail begins at the gatehouse and heads somewhat steeply up the mountainside. At just over 1,700 feet, Hugo Peak is not exactly imposing, but the rough and narrow trail is a little overgrown in places, making the ascent a little challenging. The route cuts across a few trails and roads along the way, including the 1000 Road, a large loop open to vehicle traffic during the week. If you choose, you can cut out the lower section of the Hugo Peak Trail and just pick up the trail along the 1000 Road.

Near the top the trail suddenly changes into the 1081 Road, and you are soon at a somewhat confusing intersection. Head uphill to find the small, grassy clearing that is Hugo Peak. Over the years trees have grown to block out most of the view. Currently the view is limited to a narrow opening in the trees looking north toward the surrounding valleys. Take in the view, sign the summit register, and head back down to the intersection.

▶ Hugo Peak, the highest point in Pack Forest, is named for former dean of the College of Forestry Hugo A. Winkenwerder.

From Hugo Peak the next big destination is the waterfalls along the Little Mashel River, which are in the northern section of the park. To get there, just head downhill on the 1080 Road toward Kirkland Pass, where most of the park's major roads meet. If you have some extra time, take a short stroll through the Trail of the Giants, a walk

through a section of Pack Forest's old growth. From Kirkland Pass the more direct route is to follow the 1000 Road east to connect with the 1070 Road and eventually the Falls Trail. However, if you are looking for more trail time, you can take the Reservoir Trail that heads north and eventually leads to the 1000 Road.

Whichever way you go, you will soon be walking down the 1070 Road to the Falls Trail, which leads down into a canyon carved by the Little Mashel River. There are three waterfalls to see, starting with Tom Tom Falls, then Little Mashel Falls (often referred to as Bridal Veil Falls), and finally Lower Little Mashel Falls. The Falls Trail skips Tom Tom Falls, though you can catch glimpses of it by wandering a bit off-trail. The wide path quickly descends toward the river, with side trails branching off for views of the falls.

Follow the first branch for Little Mashel Falls, the largest of the three waterfalls. You'll have a choice between exploring the upper falls or the lower; we recommend you start with the upper, which takes you to the wide, flat rocks above the falls. This is the perfect place to settle down for lunch or a snack. If you prefer a closer look at Little Mashel Falls, take the steep trail down to the river. The trail can be very slippery, so use caution as you approach the falls. During the summer when the river flow is a little lighter, you can easily climb over the rocks and walk behind the falls. Again, the rocks are often slick, so be careful when clambering around beneath the waterfall.

To reach the final waterfall, Lower Little Mashel Falls, head back to the main Falls Trail and continue downward to the next branch. This trail is very overgrown, rough, and often muddy. Expect to be climbing over blowdowns and fallen logs. The trail ends in an overlook of the multitiered Lower Mashel Falls. It is easily worth the extra effort to see them. After you've had your fill, head back out to the 1000 Road and follow it back to the gatehouse.

Pack Forest is always open and almost always free of snow in the winter. While some of the trails can be a little difficult to navigate, forest roads can take a hiker nearly anywhere in the park. With minimal elevation gain and easy access, this is a great pick for winter walks, hiking with youngsters, or bringing out the dog for an adventure. We suggest that you bring along a map, as the multiple roads and trails can be confusing, and maps are not always available from the gatehouse in the winter. If you make it out to Pack Forest, we highly recommend you take the time to head out to the waterfalls—they are well worth the trip.

Miles and Directions

0.0 Find visitor parking near the main office and head right, up 1000 Road.

0.1 Walk past the gate on 1000 Road.

0.4 At the trail junction with the Hugo Peak Trail, turn left.

1.5 At the trail junction with 1081 Road, turn left.

◀ *Old-growth Douglas fir on the Trail of the Giants*

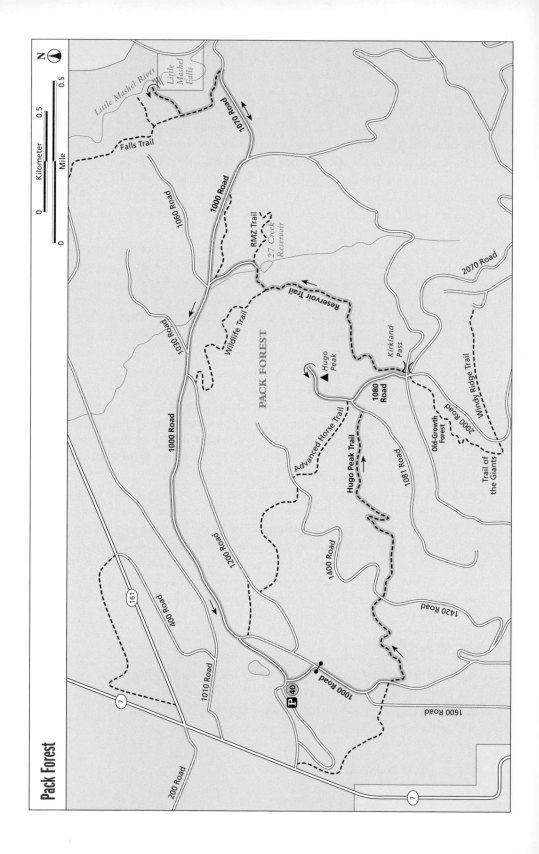

Pack Forest

Little Mashel River

Little Mashel Falls

Falls Trail

1070 Road

1060 Road

1000 Road

1030 Road

RMZ Trail

27 Creek Reservoir

Wildlife Trail

PACK FOREST

Reservoir Trail

Hugo Peak

Kirkland Pass

Old-Growth Forest

2000 Road

2070 Road

Windy Ridge Trail

Trail of the Giants

1080 Road

Advanced Horse Trail

Hugo Peak Trail

1081 Road

1200 Road

1400 Road

1420 Road

1600 Road

1010 Road

400 Road

200 Road

1000 Road

161

7

7

P 40

N

Kilometer

Mile

0.5

0.5

0

Historical Background

In the 1920s Charles Lathrop Pack was one of the richest men in the United States, with wealth built on timber and real estate. In 1926 he gave the University of Washington College of Forest Resources enough cash to purchase 334 acres of forestland, and the Charles L. Pack Experimental Forest was born. Today, Pack Forest has grown to a sprawling 4,300 acres, dedicated to forestry research, education, and recreation. With more than 50 miles of lowland trails, Pack Forest attracts hikers, bikers, equestrians, and hunters year-round.

1.6 Continue uphill past the Advanced Horse Trail toward the summit of Hugo Peak.

1.8 Reach the summit of 1,728-foot Hugo Peak. Retrace your steps back to 1081 Road.

2.0 Turn to the left, following 1080 Road downhill.

2.1 At the trail junction with the Reservoir Trail, turn left.

2.8 At the trail junction with RMZ Trail, turn left.

3.1 Turn right onto 1000 Road.

3.5 Turn left down 1070 Road.

3.8 Turn left onto the trail leading down to the falls.

4.0 At the trail junction, head right to Mashel Falls. Head downhill to the lower falls.

4.2 Reach Mashel Falls. Turn around and head back to 1000 Road.

4.8 Turn right onto 1000 Road and follow it back to the parking area.

7.0 Arrive back at the trailhead.

The Art of Hiking

For most of us, a hike into the "wild" means loading up the SUV with the latest hiking gear and driving to a toileted trailhead. We could mourn the loss of navigating mountain passes with only a map and compass or lament how much more accessible technology has made the great outdoors. Or we could consider how all these advances have changed our outlook. With survival now on the back burner, we've begun to understand that we have a responsibility to protect our wild places: that they, not we, are at risk. So please, do what you can. The following section will help you understand better what it means to "do what you can" while still making the most of your hiking experience. Anyone can take a hike, but hiking safely and well is an art requiring preparation and proper equipment.

Trail Etiquette

Leave no trace. Always leave an area just like you found it—if not better than you found it. Avoid camping in fragile alpine meadows and along the banks of streams and lakes. Use a camp stove versus building a wood fire. Pack up all of your trash and extra food. Bury human waste at least 100 feet from water sources under 6 to 8 inches of topsoil. Don't bathe with soap in a lake or stream—use prepackaged moistened towels to wipe off sweat and dirt, or bathe in the water without soap.

Stay on the trail. It's true, a path anywhere leads nowhere new, but purists will just have to get over it. Paths serve an important purpose: They limit impact on natural areas. Straying from a designated trail may seem innocent, but it can cause damage to sensitive areas—damage that may take years to recover, if it can recover at all. Even simple shortcuts can be destructive. So please, stay on the trail.

Leave no weeds. Noxious weeds tend to overtake other plants, which in turn affects animals and birds that depend on them for food. To minimize the spread of noxious weeds, hikers should regularly clean their boots, tents, packs, and hiking poles of mud and seeds. Also brush your dog to remove any weed seeds before heading off into a new area.

Keep your dog under control. You can buy a flexi-lead that allows your dog to go exploring along the trail while allowing you the ability to reel him in should another hiker approach or should he decide to chase a rabbit. Always obey leash laws and be sure to bury your dog's waste or pack it out in resealable plastic bags.

Respect other trail users. Often you're not the only one on the trail. With the rise in popularity of multiuse trails, you'll have to learn a new kind of respect, beyond the nod and "hello" approach you may be used to. When encountering other hikers, always yield to the person coming uphill. Be conscientious of other hikers or trail runners who may come from behind and wish to pass. Politely step aside. If you need to stop and take a break, find a spot where you won't block the trail. Keep in mind that others can easily hear you and you may be impacting their hiking experience even if they are nowhere in sight. Sound travels surprisingly far in the outdoors, particularly on the lakeshore and when switchbacking up a mountainside.

Investigate whether you're on a multiuse trail, and assume the appropriate precautions. When you encounter off-highway vehicles (OHVs), be alert. Though they should always yield to the hiker, often they're going too fast or are too lost in the buzz of their engine to react to your presence. If you hear activity ahead, step off the trail just to be safe. Note that you're not likely to hear a mountain biker coming, so be prepared and know ahead of time whether you share the trail with them. Cyclists should always yield to hikers, but that's little comfort to the hiker. Be aware. When you approach horses or pack animals on the trail, always step quietly off the trail, preferably on the downhill side, and let them pass. If you're wearing a large backpack, it's often a good idea to sit down. To some animals, a hiker wearing a large backpack might appear threatening. Many national forests allow domesticated grazing, usually for sheep and cattle. Make sure your dog doesn't harass these animals, and respect ranchers' rights while you're enjoying yours.

Getting into Shape

Unless you want to be sore—and possibly have to shorten your trip or vacation—be sure to get in shape before a big hike. If you're terribly out of shape, start a walking program early, preferably eight weeks in advance. Start with a 15-minute walk during your lunch hour or after work and gradually increase your walking time to an hour. You should also increase your elevation gain. Walking briskly up hills really strengthens your leg muscles and gets your heart rate up. If you work in a storied office building, take the stairs instead of the elevator. If you prefer going to a gym, walk the treadmill or use a stair machine. You can further increase your strength and endurance by walking with a loaded backpack. Stationary exercises you might consider are squats, leg lifts, sit-ups, and push-ups. Other good ways to get in shape include biking, running, aerobics, and, of course, short hikes. Stretching before and after a hike keeps muscles flexible and helps avoid injuries.

Preparedness

It's been said that failing to plan means planning to fail. So do take the necessary time to plan your trip. Whether going on a short day hike or an extended backpack trip, always prepare for the worst. Simply remembering to pack a copy of *The US Army Survival Manual* is not preparedness. Although it's not a bad idea if you plan on entering truly wild places, it's merely the tourniquet answer to a problem. You need to do your best to prevent the problem from arising in the first place. In order to survive— and to stay reasonably comfortable—you need to concern yourself with the basics: water, food, and shelter. Don't go on a hike without having these bases covered. And don't go on a hike expecting to find these items in the woods.

Water. Even in frigid conditions, you need at least two quarts of water a day to function efficiently. Add heat and taxing terrain and you can bump that figure up to one gallon. That's simply a base to work from—your metabolism and your level of

View from the summit of Beckler Peak (hike 20)

conditioning can raise or lower that amount. Unless you know your level, assume that you need one gallon of water a day. Now, where do you plan on getting the water?

Preferably not from natural water sources. These sources can be loaded with intestinal disturbers, such as bacteria, viruses, and fertilizers. *Giardia lamblia,* the most common of these disturbers, is a protozoan parasite that lives part of its life cycle as a cyst in water sources. The parasite spreads when mammals defecate in water sources. Once ingested, giardia can induce cramping, diarrhea, vomiting, and fatigue within two days to two weeks after ingestion. Giardiasis is treatable with prescription drugs. If you believe you've contracted giardiasis, see a doctor immediately.

Treating water. The best and easiest solution to avoid polluted water is to carry your water with you. Yet, depending on the nature of your hike and the duration, this may not be an option—one gallon of water weighs eight and a half pounds. In that case you'll need to look into treating water. Regardless of which method you choose, you should always carry some water with you in case of an emergency. Save this reserve until you absolutely need it.

There are three methods of treating water: boiling, chemical treatment, and filtering. If you boil water, it's recommended that you do so for 10 to 15 minutes. This is often impractical because you're forced to exhaust a great deal of your fuel supply. You

A marmot basks in the sun (hbike F).

can opt for chemical treatment, which will kill giardia but will not take care of other chemical pollutants. Another drawback to chemical treatments is the unpleasant taste of the water after it's treated. You can remedy this by adding powdered drink mix to the water. Filters are the preferred method for treating water. Many filters remove giardia and organic and inorganic contaminants, and don't leave an aftertaste. Water filters are far from perfect, as they can easily become clogged or leak if a gasket wears out. It's always a good idea to carry a backup supply of chemical treatment tablets in case your filter decides to quit on you.

Food. If we're talking about survival, you can go days without food as long as you have water. But we're also talking about comfort. Try to avoid foods that are high in sugar and fat like candy bars and potato chips. These food types are harder to digest and are low in nutritional value. Instead bring along foods that are easy to pack, nutritious, and high in energy (e.g., bagels, nutrition bars, dehydrated fruit, gorp, and jerky). If you are on an overnight trip, easy-to-fix dinners include rice mixes with dehydrated potatoes, corn, pasta with cheese sauce, and soup mixes. For a tasty breakfast, you can fix hot oatmeal with brown sugar and reconstituted milk powder topped off with banana chips. If you like a hot drink in the morning, bring along herbal tea bags or hot chocolate. If you are a coffee junkie, you can purchase coffee that is packaged like tea bags. You can prepackage all of your meals in heavy-duty resealable plastic bags to keep food from spilling in your pack. These bags can be reused to pack out trash.

Shelter. The type of shelter you choose depends less on the conditions than on your tolerance for discomfort. Shelter comes in many forms—tent, tarp, lean-to, bivy sack, cabin, cave, etc. If you're camping in the desert, a bivy sack may suffice, but if you're above the tree line and a storm is approaching, a better choice is a three- or four-season tent. Tents are the logical and most popular choice for most backpackers, as they're lightweight and packable—and you can rest assured that you always have shelter from the elements. Before you leave on your trip, anticipate what the weather and terrain will be like and plan for the type of shelter that will work best for your comfort level (see "Equipment" later in the appendix).

Finding a campsite. If there are established campsites, stick to those. If not, start looking for a campsite early—around 3:30 or 4:00 p.m. Stop at the first decent site you see. Depending on the area, it could be a long time before you find another suitable location. Pitch your camp in an area that's level. Make sure the area is at least 200 feet from fragile areas like lakeshores, meadows, and stream banks. And try to avoid areas thick in underbrush, as they can harbor insects and provide cover for approaching animals.

If you are camping in stormy, rainy weather, look for a rock outcrop or a shelter in the trees to keep the wind from blowing your tent all night. Be sure that you don't camp under trees with dead limbs that might break off on top of you. Also, try to find an area that has an absorbent surface, such as sandy soil or forest duff. This, in addition to camping on a surface with a slight angle, will provide better drainage. By all means, don't dig trenches to provide drainage around your tent—remember, you're practicing zero-impact camping.

If you're in bear country, steer clear of creek beds or animal paths. If you see any signs of a bear's presence (i.e., scat, footprints), relocate. You'll need to find a campsite near a tall tree where you can hang your food and other items that may attract bears, such as deodorant, toothpaste, or soap. Carry a lightweight nylon rope with which to hang your food. As a rule, you should hang your food at least 20 feet from the ground and 5 feet away from the tree trunk. You can put food and other items in a waterproof stuff sack and tie one end of the rope to the stuff sack. To get the other end of the rope over the tree branch, tie a good-size rock to it, and gently toss the rock over the tree branch. Pull the stuff sack up until it reaches the top of the branch, and tie it off securely. Don't hang your food near your tent! If possible, hang your food at least 100 feet away from your campsite. Alternatives to hanging your food are bear-proof plastic tubes and metal bear boxes.

Lastly, think of comfort. Lie down on the ground where you intend to sleep and see if it's a good fit. For morning warmth (and a nice view to wake up to), have your tent face east.

First Aid

I know you're tough, but get 10 miles into the woods and develop a blister and you'll wish you had carried that first-aid kit. Face it, it's just plain good sense. Many companies produce lightweight, compact first-aid kits. Just make sure yours contains at least the following:

- ❑ adhesive bandages
- ❑ moleskin or duct tape
- ❑ various sterile gauze pads and dressings
- ❑ white surgical tape
- ❑ an Ace bandage
- ❑ an antihistamine
- ❑ aspirin
- ❑ Betadine solution
- ❑ a first-aid manual
- ❑ antacid tablets
- ❑ tweezers
- ❑ scissors
- ❑ antibacterial wipes
- ❑ triple-antibiotic ointment
- ❑ plastic gloves
- ❑ sterile cotton-tip applicators
- ❑ syrup of ipecac (to induce vomiting)
- ❑ thermometer
- ❑ wire splint

Here are a few tips for dealing with and hopefully preventing certain ailments.

Sunburn. Take along sunscreen or sunblock, protective clothing, and a wide-brimmed hat. If you do get a sunburn, treat the area with aloe vera gel, and protect the area from further sun exposure. At higher elevations the sun's radiation can be particularly damaging to skin. Remember that your eyes are vulnerable to this radiation as well. Sunglasses can be a good way to prevent headaches and permanent eye damage from the sun, especially in places where light-colored rock or patches of snow reflect light up in your face.

Blisters. Be prepared to take care of these hike-spoilers by carrying moleskin (a lightly padded adhesive), gauze and tape, or adhesive bandages. An effective way to apply moleskin is to cut out a circle of moleskin and remove the center—like a doughnut—and place it over the blistered area. Cutting the center out will reduce the pressure applied to the sensitive skin. Other products can help you combat blisters. Some are applied to suspicious hot spots before a blister forms to help decrease friction to that area, while others are applied to the blister after it has popped to help prevent further irritation.

Insect bites and stings. You can treat most insect bites and stings by applying hydrocortisone 1 percent cream topically and taking a pain medication such as ibuprofen or acetaminophen to reduce swelling. If you forgot to pack these items, a cold compress or a paste of mud and ashes can sometimes assuage the itching and discomfort. Remove any stingers by using tweezers or scraping the area with your fingernail or a knife blade. Don't pinch the area, as you'll only spread the venom.

Some hikers are highly sensitive to bites and stings and may have a serious allergic reaction that can be life threatening. Symptoms of a serious allergic reaction can include wheezing, an asthmatic attack, and shock. The treatment for this severe type of reaction is epinephrine. If you know that you are sensitive to bites and stings, carry a prepackaged kit of epinephrine, which can be obtained only by prescription from your doctor.

Ticks. Ticks can carry diseases such as Rocky Mountain spotted fever and Lyme disease. The best defense is, of course, prevention. If you know you're going to be hiking through an area littered with ticks, wear long pants and a long-sleeved shirt. You can apply a permethrin repellent to your clothing and a deet repellent to exposed skin. At the end of your hike, do a spot-check for ticks (and insects in general). If you do find a tick, grab the head of the tick firmly—with a pair of tweezers if you have them—and gently pull it away from the skin with a twisting motion. Sometimes the mouth parts linger, embedded in your skin. If this happens, try to remove them with a disinfected needle. Clean the affected area with an antibacterial cleanser and then apply triple antibiotic ointment. Monitor the area for a few days. If irritation persists or a white spot develops, see a doctor for possible infection.

Poison ivy, oak, and sumac. These skin irritants can be found most anywhere in North America and come in the form of a bush or a vine, having leaflets in groups of three, five, seven, or nine. Learn how to spot the plants. The oil they secrete can cause an allergic reaction in the form of blisters, usually about 12 hours after exposure. The itchy rash can last from ten days to several weeks. The best defense against these irritants is to wear clothing that covers the arms, legs, and torso. For summer, zip-off cargo pants come in handy. There are also nonprescription lotions you can apply to exposed skin that guard against the effects of poison ivy/oak/sumac and can be washed off with soap and water. If you think you were in contact with the plants, after hiking (or even on the trail during longer hikes) wash with soap and water. Taking a hot shower with soap after you return home from your hike will also help to remove any lingering oil from your skin. Should you contract a rash from any of these plants, use an antihistamine to reduce the itching. If the rash is localized, create a light bleach/water wash to dry up the area. If the rash has spread, either tough it out or see your doctor about getting a dose of cortisone (available both orally and by injection).

Snakebites. Snakebites are rare in North America. Unless startled or provoked, the majority of snakes will not bite. If you are wise to their habitats and keep a careful eye on the trail, you should be just fine. When stepping over logs, first step on the log, making sure you can see what's on the other side before stepping down. Though your chances of being struck are slim, it's wise to know what to do in the event you are.

If a nonvenomous snake bites you, allow the wound to bleed a small amount and then cleanse the wounded area with a Betadine solution (10 percent povidone iodine). Rinse the wound with clean water (preferably) or fresh urine (it might sound ugly, but it's sterile). Once the area is clean, cover it with triple antibiotic ointment and a clean bandage. Remember, most residual damage from snakebites, venomous or otherwise, comes from infection, not the snake's venom. Keep the area as clean as possible, and get medical attention immediately.

If somebody in your party is bitten by a venomous snake, follow these steps:

1. Calm the patient.

2. Remove jewelry, watches, and restrictive clothing, and immobilize the affected limb. Do not elevate the injury. Medical opinions vary on whether the area should be lower or level with the heart, but the consensus is that it should not be above it.

3. Make a note of the circumference of the limb at the bite site and at various points above the site as well. This will help you monitor swelling.

4. Evacuate your victim. Ideally he or she should be carried out to minimize movement. If the victim appears to be doing OK, he or she can walk. Stop and rest frequently, and if the swelling appears to be spreading or the patient's symptoms increase, change your plan and find a way to get your patient transported.

5. If you are waiting for rescue, make sure to keep your patient comfortable and hydrated (unless he or she begins vomiting).

Snakebite treatment is rife with old-fashioned remedies: You used to be told to cut and suck the venom out of the bite site or to use a suction cup extractor for the same purpose; applying an electric shock to the area was even in vogue for a while. Do not do any of these things. Do not apply ice, do not give your patient painkillers, and do not apply a tourniquet. All you really want to do is keep your patient calm and get help. If you're alone and have to hike out, don't run—you'll only increase the flow of blood throughout your system. Instead, walk calmly.

Dehydration. Have you ever hiked in hot weather and had a roaring headache and felt fatigued after only a few miles? More than likely you were dehydrated. Symptoms of dehydration include fatigue, headache, and decreased coordination and judgment. When you are hiking, your body's rate of fluid loss depends on the outside temperature, humidity, altitude, and your activity level. On average a hiker walking in warm weather will lose four liters of fluid a day. That fluid loss is easily replaced by normal consumption of liquids and food. However, if a hiker is walking briskly in hot, dry weather and hauling a heavy pack, he or she can lose one to three liters of water an hour. It's important to always carry plenty of water and to stop often and drink fluids regularly, even if you aren't thirsty.

Heat exhaustion is the result of a loss of large amounts of electrolytes and often occurs if a hiker is dehydrated and has been under heavy exertion. Common symptoms of heat exhaustion include cramping, exhaustion, fatigue, lightheadedness, and nausea. You can treat heat exhaustion by getting out of the sun and drinking an electrolyte solution made up of one teaspoon of salt and one tablespoon of sugar dissolved in a liter of water. Drink this solution slowly over a period of 1 hour. Drinking plenty of fluids (preferably an electrolyte solution/sports drink) can prevent heat exhaustion. Avoid hiking during the hottest parts of the day, and wear breathable clothing, a wide-brimmed hat, and sunglasses.

Hypothermia is one of the biggest dangers in the backcountry, especially for day hikers in the summertime. That may sound strange, but imagine starting out on a hike in midsummer when it's sunny and 80°F out. You're clad in nylon shorts and a cotton T-shirt. About halfway through your hike, the sky begins to cloud up, and in the next hour a light drizzle begins to fall and the wind starts to pick up. Before you know it, you are soaking wet and shivering—the perfect recipe for hypothermia. More advanced signs include decreased coordination, slurred speech, and blurred vision. When a victim's temperature falls below 92°F, the blood pressure and pulse plummet, possibly leading to coma and death.

To avoid hypothermia, always bring a windproof/rainproof shell, a fleece jacket, long underwear made of a breathable, synthetic fiber, gloves, and a hat when you are hiking in the mountains. Learn to adjust your clothing layers based on the temperature. If you are climbing uphill at a moderate pace, you will stay warm, but when you stop for a break, you'll become cold quickly, unless you add more layers of clothing.

If a hiker is showing advanced signs of hypothermia, dress him or her in dry clothes and make sure he or she is wearing a hat and gloves. Place the person in a sleeping bag in a tent or shelter that will protect him or her from the wind and other elements. Give the person warm fluids to drink and keep him or her awake.

Frostbite. When the mercury dips below 32°F, your extremities begin to chill. If a persistent chill attacks a localized area, say, your hands or your toes, the circulatory system reacts by cutting off blood flow to the affected area—the idea being to protect and preserve the body's overall temperature. And so it's death by attrition for the affected area. Ice crystals start to form from the water in the cells of the neglected tissue. Deprived of heat, nourishment, and now water, the tissue literally starves. This is frostbite.

Prevention is your best defense against this situation. Most prone to frostbite are your face, hands, and feet, so protect these areas well. Wool is the traditional material of choice because it provides ample air space for insulation and draws moisture away from the skin. Synthetic fabrics, however, have made great strides in the cold-weather-clothing market. Do your research. A pair of light silk liners under your regular gloves is a good trick for keeping warm. They afford some additional warmth, but more importantly they'll allow you to remove your mitts for tedious work without exposing the skin.

If your feet or hands start to feel cold or numb due to the elements, warm them as quickly as possible. Place cold hands under your armpits or bury them in your crotch. If your feet are cold, change your socks. If there's plenty of room in your boots, add another pair of socks. Do remember, though, that constricting your feet in tight boots can restrict blood flow and actually make your feet colder more quickly. Your socks need to have breathing room if they're going to be effective. Dead air provides insulation. If your face is cold, place your warm hands over your face, or simply wear a head stocking.

Should your skin go numb and start to turn lighter in color—sometimes white —and waxy, chances are you've got or are developing frostbite. Don't try to thaw the area unless you can maintain the warmth. In other words, don't stop to warm up your frostbitten feet only to head back on the trail. You'll do more damage than good. Tests have shown that hikers who walked on thawed feet did more harm, and endured more pain, than hikers who left the affected areas alone. Do your best to get out of the cold entirely and seek medical attention—which usually consists of performing a rapid rewarming in water for 20 to 30 minutes.

The overall objective in preventing both hypothermia and frostbite is to keep the body's core warm. Protect key areas where heat escapes, like the top of the head, and maintain the proper nutrition level. Foods that are high in calories aid the body in producing heat. Never smoke or drink when you're in situations where the cold is threatening. By affecting blood flow, these activities ultimately cool the body's core temperature.

Altitude sickness (AMS). High, lofty peaks, clear alpine lakes, and vast mountain views beckon hikers to the high country. But those who like to venture high may become victims of altitude sickness (also known as acute mountain sickness—AMS). Altitude sickness is your body's reaction to insufficient oxygen in the blood due to decreased barometric pressure. While some hikers may feel lightheaded, nauseous, and experience shortness of breath at 7,000 feet, others may not experience these symptoms until they reach 10,000 feet or higher.

Slowing your ascent to high places and giving your body a chance to acclimatize to the higher elevations can prevent altitude sickness. For example, if you live at sea level and are planning a weeklong backpacking trip to elevations between 7,000 and 12,000 feet, start by staying below 7,000 feet for one night, then move to between 7,000 and 10,000 feet for another night or two. Avoid strenuous exertion and alcohol to give your body a chance to adjust to the new altitude. It's also important to eat light food and drink plenty of nonalcoholic fluids, preferably water. Loss of appetite at altitude is common, but you must eat!

Most hikers who experience mild to moderate AMS develop a headache and/or nausea, grow lethargic, and have problems sleeping. The treatment for AMS is simple: Stop heading uphill. Keep eating and drinking water, and take meds for the headache. You actually need to take more breaths at altitude than at sea level, so breathe a little faster without hyperventilating. If symptoms don't improve over 24 to 48 hours, descend. Once a victim descends about 2,000 to 3,000 feet, his or her symptoms will usually begin to diminish.

Severe AMS comes in two forms: **High Altitude Pulmonary Edema (HAPE) and High Altitude Cerebral Edema (HACE).** HAPE, an accumulation of fluid in the lungs, can occur above 8,000 feet. Symptoms include rapid heart rate, shortness of breath at rest, AMS symptoms, dry cough developing into a wet cough, gurgling sounds, flulike or bronchitis symptoms, and lack of muscle coordination. HAPE is life threatening, so descend immediately, at least 2,000 to 4,000 feet. HACE usually occurs above 12,000 feet but sometimes occurs above 10,000 feet. Symptoms are similar to HAPE but also include seizures, hallucinations, paralysis, and vision disturbances. Descend immediately—HACE is also life threatening.

Hantavirus pulmonary syndrome (HPS). Deer mice spread the virus that causes HPS, and humans contract it from breathing it in, usually when they've disturbed an area with dust and mice feces from nests or surfaces with mice droppings or urine. Exposure to large numbers of rodents and their feces or urine presents the greatest risk. As hikers, we sometimes enter old buildings, and often deer mice live in these places. We may not be around long enough to be exposed, but do be aware of this disease. About half the people who develop HPS die. Symptoms are flulike and appear about two to three weeks after exposure. After initial symptoms a dry cough and shortness of breath follow. Breathing is difficult. If you even think you might have HPS, see a doctor immediately!

Natural Hazards

Besides tripping over a rock or tree root on the trail, there are some real hazards to be aware of while hiking. Even if where you're hiking doesn't have the plethora of poisonous snakes and plants, insects, and grizzly bears found in other parts of the United States, there are a few weather conditions and predators you may need to take into account.

Lightning. Thunderstorms build over the mountains almost every day during the summer. Lightning is generated by thunderheads and can strike without warning, even several miles away from the nearest overhead cloud. The best rule of thumb is to start leaving exposed peaks, ridges, and canyon rims by about noon. This time can vary a little depending on storm buildup. Keep an eye on cloud formation, and don't underestimate how fast a storm can build. The bigger they get, the more likely a thunderstorm will happen. Lightning takes the path of least resistance, so if you're the high point, it might choose you. Ducking under a rock overhang is dangerous, as you form the shortest path between the rock and ground. If you dash below tree line, avoid standing under the only or the tallest tree. If you are caught above tree line, stay away from anything metal you might be carrying, Move down off the ridge slightly to a low, treeless point and squat until the storm passes. If you have an insulating pad, squat on it. Avoid having both your hands and feet touching the ground at once and never lay flat. If you hear a buzzing sound or feel your hair standing on end, move quickly, as an electrical charge is building up.

Fall leaves cover the trail (hike 16).

Flash floods. On July 31, 1976, a torrential downpour unleashed by a thunderstorm dumped tons of water into the Big Thompson watershed near Estes Park. Within hours a wall of water moved down the narrow canyon, killing 139 people and causing more than $30 million in property damage. The spooky thing about flash floods, especially in western canyons, is that they can appear out of nowhere from a storm many miles away. While hiking or driving in canyons, keep an eye on the weather. Always climb to safety if danger threatens. Flash floods usually subside quickly, so be patient, and don't cross a swollen stream.

Bears. Most of the United States (outside of the Pacific Northwest and parts of the Northern Rockies) does not have a grizzly bear population, although some rumors exist about sightings where there should be none. Black bears are plentiful, however. Here are some tips in case you and a bear scare each other. Most of all, avoid surprising a bear. Talk or sing where visibility or hearing are limited, such as along a rushing creek or in thick brush. In grizzly country especially, carry bear spray in a holster on your pack belt where you can quickly grab it. While hiking, watch for bear tracks (five toes), droppings (sizable with leaves, partly digested berries, seeds, and/or animal fur), or rocks and roots along the trail that show signs of being dug up (this could be a bear looking for bugs to eat). Keep a clean camp, hang food or use bear-proof storage containers, and don't sleep in the clothes you wore while cooking. Be especially careful to avoid getting between a mother and her cubs. In late summer and fall, bears are busy eating to fatten up for winter, so be extra careful around berry bushes and oak brush.

If you do encounter a bear, move away slowly while facing the bear, talk softly, and avoid direct eye contact. Give the bear room to escape. Since bears are very curious, it might stand upright to get a better whiff of you, and it may even charge you to try to intimidate you. Try to stay calm. If a black bear attacks you, fight back with anything you have handy. If a grizzly bear attacks you, your best option is to "play dead" by lying face down on the ground and covering the back of your neck and head with your hands. Unleashed dogs have been known to come running back to their owners with a bear close behind. Keep your dog on a leash or leave it at home.

Mountain lions appear to be getting more comfortable around humans as long as deer (their favorite prey) are in an area with adequate cover. Usually elusive and quiet, lions rarely attack people. If you meet a lion, give it a chance to escape. Stay calm and talk firmly to it. Back away slowly while facing the lion. If you run, you'll only encourage the cat to chase you. Make yourself look large by opening a jacket, if you have one, or waving your hiking poles. If the lion behaves aggressively, throw stones, sticks, or whatever you can while remaining tall. If a lion does attack, fight for your life with anything you can grab.

Moose. Because moose have very few natural predators, they don't fear humans like other animals. You might find moose in sagebrush and wetter areas of willow, aspen, and pine, or in beaver habitats. Mothers with calves, as well as bulls during mating season, can be particularly aggressive. If a moose threatens you, back away slowly and talk calmly to it. Keep your pets away from moose.

Other considerations. Hunting is a popular sport in the United States, especially during rifle season in October and November. Hiking is still enjoyable in those months in many areas, so just take a few precautions. First, learn when the different hunting seasons start and end in the area in which you'll be hiking. During this time frame be sure to wear at least a blaze orange hat, and possibly put an orange vest over your pack. Don't be surprised to see hunters in camo outfits carrying bows or rifles around during their season. If you would feel more comfortable without hunters around, hike in national parks and monuments or state and local parks where hunting is not allowed.

Navigation

Whether you are going on a short hike in a familiar area or planning a weeklong backpack trip, you should always be equipped with the proper navigational equipment—at the very least a detailed map and a sturdy compass.

Maps. There are many different types of maps available to help you find your way on the trail. Easiest to find are USDA Forest Service maps and BLM (Bureau of Land Management) maps. These maps tend to cover large areas, so be sure they are detailed enough for your particular trip. You can also obtain national-park maps as well as high-quality maps from private companies and trail groups. These maps can be obtained either from outdoor stores or ranger stations.

US Geological Survey topographic maps are particularly popular with hikers—especially serious backcountry hikers. These maps contain the standard map symbols such as roads, lakes, and rivers, as well as contour lines that show the details of the trail terrain like ridges, valleys, passes, and mountain peaks. The 7.5-minute series (1 inch on the map equals approximately 0.4 mile on the ground) provides the closest inspection available. USGS maps are available by mail (US Geological Survey, Map Distribution Branch, PO Box 25286, Denver, CO 80225), or at store.usgs.gov.

If you want to check out the high-tech world of maps, you can purchase topographic maps on CD-ROM. These software mapping programs let you select a route on your computer, print it out, then take it with you on the trail. Some software mapping programs let you insert symbols and labels, download waypoints from a GPS unit, and export the maps to other software programs.

The art of map reading is a skill that you can develop by first practicing in an area you are familiar with. To begin, orient the map so the map is lined up in the correct direction (i.e., north on the map is lined up with true north). Next, familiarize yourself with the map symbols and try to match them up with terrain features around you such as a high ridge, mountain peak, river, or lake. If you are practicing with a USGS map, notice the contour lines. On gentler terrain these contour lines are spaced farther apart, and on steeper terrain they are closer together. Pick a short loop trail, and stop frequently to check your position on the map. As you practice map reading, you'll learn how to anticipate a steep section on the trail or a good place to take a rest break, and so on.

Compasses. First off, the sun is not a substitute for a compass. So, what kind of compass should you have? Here are some characteristics you should look for: a rectangular base with detailed scales, a liquid-filled housing, protective housing, a sighting line on the mirror, luminous alignment and back-bearing arrows, a luminous north-seeking arrow, and a well-defined bezel ring.

You can learn compass basics by reading the detailed instructions included with your compass. If you want to fine-tune your compass skills, sign up for an orienteering class or purchase a book on compass reading. Once you've learned the basic skills of using a compass, remember to practice these skills before you head into the backcountry.

If you are a klutz at using a compass, you may be interested in checking out the technical wizardry of the GPS (Global Positioning System) device. The GPS was developed by the Pentagon and works off twenty-four NAVSTAR satellites, which were designed to guide missiles to their targets. A GPS device is a handheld unit that calculates your latitude and longitude with the simple press of a button. The Department of Defense used to scramble the satellite signals a bit to prevent civilians (and spies!) from getting extremely accurate readings, but that practice was discontinued in May 2000, and GPS units now provide nearly pinpoint accuracy (within 30 to 60 feet).

There are many different types of GPS units available, and they range in price from $100 to $400. In general, all GPS units have a display screen and keypad where you input information. In addition to acting as a compass, the unit allows you to plot your route, easily retrace your path, track your traveling speed, find the mileage between waypoints, and calculate the total mileage of your route.

Before you purchase a GPS unit, keep in mind that these devices don't pick up signals indoors, in heavily wooded areas, on mountain peaks, or in deep valleys. Also, batteries can wear out or other technical problems can develop. A GPS unit should be used in conjunction with a map and compass, not in place of those items.

Pedometers. A pedometer is a small, clip-on unit with a digital display that calculates your hiking distance in miles or kilometers based on your walking stride. Some units also calculate the calories you burn and your total hiking time. Pedometers are available at most large outdoor stores and range in price from $20 to $40.

Trip Planning

Planning your hiking adventure begins with letting a friend or relative know your trip itinerary so they can call for help if you don't return at your scheduled time. Your next task is to make sure you are outfitted to experience the risks and rewards of the trail. This section highlights gear and clothing you may want to take with you to get the most out of your hike.

Day Hikes

- ❑ bear repellent spray (if hiking in grizzly country)
- ❑ camera
- ❑ compass/GPS unit
- ❑ pedometer
- ❑ daypack
- ❑ first-aid kit
- ❑ food
- ❑ guidebook
- ❑ headlamp/flashlight with extra batteries and bulbs
- ❑ hat
- ❑ insect repellent
- ❑ knife/multipurpose tool
- ❑ map
- ❑ matches in waterproof container and fire starter
- ❑ fleece jacket
- ❑ rain gear
- ❑ space blanket
- ❑ sunglasses
- ❑ sunscreen

- ❑ swimsuit and/or fishing gear (if hiking to a lake)
- ❑ watch
- ❑ water
- ❑ water bottles/water hydration system

Overnight Trip

- ❑ backpack and waterproof rain cover
- ❑ backpacker's trowel
- ❑ bandanna
- ❑ bear repellent spray (if hiking in grizzly country)
- ❑ bear bell
- ❑ biodegradable soap
- ❑ pot scrubber
- ❑ collapsible water container (two- to three-gallon capacity)
- ❑ clothing—extra wool socks, shirt, and shorts
- ❑ cook set/utensils
- ❑ ditty bags to store gear
- ❑ extra plastic resealable bags
- ❑ gaiters
- ❑ garbage bag
- ❑ ground cloth
- ❑ journal/pen
- ❑ nylon rope to hang food
- ❑ long underwear
- ❑ permit (if required)
- ❑ rain jacket and pants
- ❑ sandals to wear around camp and to ford streams
- ❑ sleeping bag
- ❑ waterproof stuff sack
- ❑ sleeping pad
- ❑ small bath towel
- ❑ stove and fuel
- ❑ tent
- ❑ toiletry items
- ❑ water filter
- ❑ whistle

Experimental tunnel entrance and campsite (hike 18)

Equipment

With the outdoor market currently flooded with products—many of which are pure gimmickry—it seems impossible to both differentiate and choose. Do I really need a tropical-fish-lined collapsible shower? (No, you don't.) The only defense against the maddening quantity of items thrust in your face is to think practically—and to do so before you go shopping. The worst buys are impulsive buys. Since most name brands will differ only slightly in quality, it's best to know what you're looking for in terms of function. Buy only what you need. You will, don't forget, be carrying what you've bought on your back. Here are some things to keep in mind before you go shopping.

Clothes. Clothing is your armor against Mother Nature's little surprises. Hikers should be prepared for any possibility, especially when hiking in mountainous areas. Adequate rain protection and extra layers of clothing are a good idea. In summer a wide-brimmed hat can help keep the sun at bay. In the winter months the first layer you'll want to wear is a "wicking" layer of long underwear that keeps perspiration away from your skin. Wear long underwear made from synthetic fibers that wick moisture away from the skin and draw it toward the next layer of clothing, where it then evaporates. Avoid wearing long underwear made of cotton, as it is slow to dry and keeps moisture next to your skin.

The second layer you'll wear is the "insulating" layer. Aside from keeping you warm, this layer needs to "breathe" so you stay dry while hiking. A fabric that provides insulation and dries quickly is fleece. It's interesting to note that this one-of-a-kind fabric is made out of recycled plastic. Purchasing a zip-up jacket made of this material is highly recommended.

The last line of layering defense is the "shell" layer. You'll need some type of waterproof, windproof, breathable jacket that will fit over all of your other layers. It should have a large hood that fits over a hat. You'll also need a good pair of rain pants made from a similar waterproof, breathable fabric. Some Gore-Tex jackets cost as much as $500, but you should know that there are more affordable fabrics out there that work just as well.

Now that you've learned the basics of layering, you can't forget to protect your hands and face. In cold, windy, or rainy weather, you'll need a hat made of wool or fleece and insulated, waterproof gloves that will keep your hands warm and toasty. As mentioned earlier, buying an additional pair of light silk liners to wear under your regular gloves is a good idea.

Footwear. If you have any extra money to spend on your trip, put that money into boots or trail shoes. Poor shoes will bring a hike to a halt faster than anything else. To avoid this annoyance, buy shoes that provide support and are lightweight and flexible. A lightweight hiking boot is better than a heavy, leather mountaineering boot for most day hikes and backpacking. Trail running shoes provide a little extra cushion and are made in a high-top style that many people wear for hiking. These running shoes are lighter, more flexible, and more breathable than hiking boots. If you know you'll be hiking in wet weather often, purchase boots or shoes with a Gore-Tex liner, which will help keep your feet dry.

When buying your boots be sure to wear the same type of socks you'll be wearing on the trail. If the boots you're buying are for cold-weather hiking, try the boots on while wearing two pairs of socks. Speaking of socks, a good cold-weather sock combination is to wear a thinner sock made of wool or polypropylene covered by a heavier outer sock made of wool or a synthetic/wool mix. The inner sock protects the foot from the rubbing effects of the outer sock and prevents blisters. Many outdoor stores have some type of ramp to simulate hiking uphill and downhill. Be sure to take advantage of this test, as toe-jamming boot fronts can be very painful and debilitating on the downhill trek.

Once you've purchased your footwear, be sure to break them in before you hit the trail. New footwear is often stiff and needs to be stretched and molded to your feet.

Hiking poles. Hiking poles help with balance and more importantly take pressure off your knees. The ones with shock absorbers are easier on your elbows and knees. Some poles even come with a camera attachment to be used as a monopod. And heaven forbid you meet a mountain lion, bear, or unfriendly dog, the poles can make you look a lot bigger.

Backpacks. No matter what type of hiking you do, you'll need a pack of some sort to carry the basic trail essentials. There are a variety of backpacks on the market, but let's first discuss what you intend to use it for. Day hikes or overnight trips?

If you plan on doing a day hike, a daypack should have some of the following characteristics: a padded hip belt that's at least 2 inches in diameter (avoid packs with only a small nylon piece of webbing for a hip belt); a chest strap (the chest strap helps stabilize the pack against your body); external pockets to carry water and other items that you want easy access to; an internal pocket to hold keys, a knife, a wallet, and other miscellaneous items; an external lashing system to hold a jacket; and, if you so desire, a hydration pocket for carrying a hydration system (which consists of a water bladder with an attachable drinking hose).

For short hikes, some hikers like to use a fanny pack to store just a camera, food, a compass, a map, and other trail essentials. Most fanny packs have pockets for two water bottles and a padded hip belt.

If you intend to do an extended, overnight trip, there are multiple considerations. First off, you need to decide what kind of framed pack you want. There are two backpack types for backpacking: the internal frame and the external frame. An internal frame pack rests closer to your body, making it more stable and easier to balance when hiking over rough terrain. An external frame pack is just that, an aluminum frame attached to the exterior of the pack. Some hikers consider an external frame pack to be better for long backpack trips because it distributes the pack weight better and allows you to carry heavier loads. It's often easier to pack, and your gear is more accessible. It also offers better back ventilation in hot weather.

The most critical measurement for fitting a pack is torso length. The pack needs to rest evenly on your hips without sagging. A good pack will come in two or three sizes and have straps and hip belts that are adjustable according to your body size and characteristics.

When you purchase a backpack, go to an outdoor store with salespeople who are knowledgeable in how to properly fit a pack. Once the pack is fitted for you, load the pack with the amount of weight you plan on taking on the trail. The weight of the pack should be distributed evenly and you should be able to swing your arms and walk briskly without feeling out of balance. Another good technique for evaluating a pack is to walk up and down stairs and make quick turns to the right and to the left to be sure the pack doesn't feel out of balance. Other features that are nice to have on a backpack include a removable daypack or fanny pack, external pockets for extra water, and extra lash points to attach a jacket or other items.

Sleeping bags and pads. Sleeping bags are rated by temperature. You can purchase a bag made with synthetic insulation, or you can buy a goose-down bag. Goose-down bags are more expensive, but they have a higher insulating capacity by weight and will keep their loft longer. You'll want to purchase a bag with a temperature rating that fits the time of year and conditions you are most likely to camp in. One caveat: The techno-standard for temperature ratings is far from perfect. Ratings vary from manufacturer to manufacturer, so to protect yourself, you should purchase a bag rated 10° to 15°F below the temperature you expect to be camping in. Synthetic bags are more resistant to water than down bags, but many down bags are now made with a

Gore-Tex shell that helps to repel water. Down bags are also more compressible than synthetic bags and take up less room in your pack, which is an important consideration if you are planning a multiday backpack trip. Features to look for in a sleeping bag include a mummy-style bag, a hood you can cinch down around your head in cold weather, and draft tubes along the zippers that help keep heat in and drafts out.

You'll also want a sleeping pad to provide insulation and padding from the cold ground. There are different types of sleeping pads available, from the more expensive self-inflating air mattresses to the less expensive closed-cell foam pads. Self-inflating air mattresses are usually heavier than closed-cell foam mattresses and are prone to punctures.

Tents. The tent is your home away from home while on the trail. It provides protection from wind, rain, snow, and insects. A three-season tent is a good choice for backpacking and can range in price from $100 to $500. These lightweight and versatile tents provide protection in all types of weather, except heavy snowstorms or high winds, and range in weight from four to eight pounds. Look for a tent that's easy to set up and will easily fit two people with gear. Dome-type tents usually offer more headroom and places to store gear. Other handy tent features include a vestibule where you can store wet boots and backpacks. Some nice-to-have items in a tent include interior pockets to store small items and lashing points to hang a clothesline. Most three-season tents also come with stakes so you can secure the tent in high winds. Before you purchase a tent, set it up and take it down a few times to be sure it is easy to handle. Also, sit inside the tent and make sure it has enough room for you and your gear.

Cell phones. Many hikers are carrying their cell phones into the backcountry these days in case of emergency. That's fine and good, but please know that cell phone coverage is often poor to nonexistent in valleys, canyons, and thick forest. More importantly, people have started to call for help because they're tired or lost. Let's go back to being prepared. You are responsible for yourself in the backcountry. Use your brain to avoid problems, and if you do encounter one, first use your brain to try to correct the situation. Only use your cell phone, if it works, in true emergencies. If it doesn't work down low in a valley, try hiking to a high point where you might get reception.

Hiking with Children

Hiking with children isn't a matter of how many miles you can cover or how much elevation gain you make in a day; it's about seeing and experiencing nature through their eyes.

Kids like to explore and have fun. They like to stop and point out bugs and plants, look under rocks, jump in puddles, and throw sticks. If you're taking a toddler or young child on a hike, start with a trail that you're familiar with. Trails that have interesting things for kids, like piles of leaves to play in or a small stream to wade through during the summer, will make the hike much more enjoyable for them and will keep them from getting bored.

You can keep your child's attention if you have a strategy before starting on the trail. Using games is not only an effective way to keep a child's attention, it's also a great way to teach him or her about nature. Quiz children on the names of plants and animals. Pick up a family-friendly outdoor hobby like geocaching (geocaching .com) or letterboxing (atlasquest.com), both of which combine the outdoors, clue solving, and treasure hunting. If your children are old enough, let them carry their own daypack filled with snacks and water. So that you are sure to go at their pace and not yours, let them lead the way. Playing follow-the-leader works particularly well when you have a group of children. Have each child take a turn at being the leader.

With children, a lot of clothing is key. The only thing predictable about weather is that it will change. Especially in mountainous areas, weather can change dramatically in a very short time. Always bring extra clothing for children, regardless of the season. In winter have your children wear wool socks and warm layers such as long underwear, a fleece jacket and hat, wool mittens, and good rain gear. It's not a bad idea to have these along in late fall and early spring as well. Good footwear is also important. A sturdy pair of high-top tennis shoes or lightweight hiking boots are the best bet for little ones. If you're hiking in the summer near a lake or stream, bring along a pair of old sneakers that your child can put on when he wants to go exploring in the water. Remember when you're near any type of water, always watch your child at all times. Also, keep a close eye on teething toddlers who may decide a rock or leaf of poison oak is an interesting item to put in their mouth.

From spring through fall you'll want your kids to wear a wide-brimmed hat to keep their face, head, and ears protected from the hot sun. Also, make sure your children wear sunscreen at all times. Choose a brand without PABA—children have sensitive skin and may have an allergic reaction to sunscreen that contains PABA. If you are hiking with a child younger than 6 months old, don't use sunscreen or insect repellent. Instead, be sure that his or her head, face, neck, and ears are protected from the sun with a wide-brimmed hat, and that all other skin exposed to the sun is protected with the appropriate clothing.

Remember that food is fun. Kids like snacks, so it's important to bring a lot of munchies for the trail. Stopping often for snack breaks is a fun way to keep the trail interesting. Raisins, apples, granola bars, crackers and cheese, cereal, and trail mix all make great snacks. Also, a few of their favorite candy treats can go a long way toward heading off a fit of fussing. If your child is old enough to carry his or her own backpack, let him or her fill it with some lightweight "comfort" items such as a doll, a small stuffed animal, or a little toy (you'll have to draw the line at bringing the ten-pound Tonka truck). If your kids don't like drinking water, you can bring some powdered drink mix or a juice box.

Avoid poorly designed child-carrying packs—you don't want to break your back carrying your child. Most child-carrying backpacks designed to hold a forty-pound child will contain a large carrying pocket to hold diapers and other items. Some have an optional rain/sun hood.

Beargrass and lupine by the trail (hike 37)

Hiking with Your Dog

Bringing your furry friend with you is always more fun than leaving him behind. Our canine pals make great trail buddies because they never complain and always make good company. Hiking with your dog can be a rewarding experience, especially if you plan ahead.

Getting your dog in shape. Before you plan outdoor adventures with your dog, make sure he's in shape for the trail. Getting your dog into shape takes the same discipline as getting yourself into shape, but luckily, your dog can get in shape with you. Take your dog with you on your daily runs or walks. If there is a park near your house, hit a tennis ball or play Frisbee with your dog.

Swimming is also an excellent way to get your dog into shape. If there is a lake or river near where you live and your dog likes the water, have him retrieve a tennis ball or stick. Gradually build your dog's stamina up over a two- to three-month period. A good rule of thumb is to assume that your dog will travel twice as far as you will on the trail. If you plan on doing a 5-mile hike, be sure your dog is in shape for a 10-mile hike.

Training your dog for the trail. Before you go on your first hiking adventure with your dog, be sure he has a firm grasp of the basics of canine etiquette and behavior. Make sure he can sit, lie down, stay, and come. One of the most important commands you can teach your canine pal is to "come" under any situation. It's easy for your friend's nose to lead him astray or to possibly get lost. Another helpful command is the "get behind" command. When you're on a hiking trail that's narrow, you can have your dog follow behind you when other trail users approach. Nothing is more bothersome than an enthusiastic dog that runs back and forth on the trail and disrupts the peace of the trail for others—or, worse, jumps up on other hikers and gets them muddy. When you see other trail users approaching you on the trail, give them the right-of-way by quietly stepping off the trail and making your dog lie down and stay until they pass.

Equipment. The most critical pieces of equipment you can invest in for your dog are proper identification and a sturdy leash. Flexi-leads work well for hiking because they give your dog more freedom to explore but still leave you in control. Make sure your dog has identification that includes your name and address and a number for your veterinarian. Other forms of identification for your dog include a tattoo or a microchip. You should consult your veterinarian for more information on these last two options.

The next piece of equipment you'll want to consider is a pack for your dog. By no means should you hold all of your dog's essentials in your pack—let him carry his own gear! Dogs that are in good shape can carry 30 to 40 percent of their own weight.

Most packs are fitted by a dog's weight and girth measurement. Companies that make dog packs generally include guidelines to help you pick out the size that's right for your dog. Some characteristics to look for when purchasing a pack for your dog include a harness that contains two padded girth straps, a padded chest strap, leash attachments, removable saddle bags, internal water bladders, and external gear cords.

You can introduce your dog to the pack by first placing the empty pack on his back and letting him wear it around the yard. Keep an eye on him during this first introduction. He may decide to chew through the straps if you aren't watching him closely. Once he learns to treat the pack as an object of fun and not a foreign enemy, fill the pack evenly on both sides with a few ounces of dog food in resealable plastic bags. Have your dog wear his pack on your daily walks for a period of two to three weeks. Each week add a little more weight to the pack until your dog will accept carrying the maximum amount of weight he can carry.

You can also purchase collapsible water and dog food bowls for your dog. These bowls are lightweight and can easily be stashed into your pack or your dog's. If you are hiking on rocky terrain or in the snow, you can purchase footwear for your dog that will protect his feet from cuts and bruises.

Always carry plastic bags to remove feces from the trail. It is a courtesy to other trail users and helps protect local wildlife.

The following is a list of items to bring when you take your dog hiking: collapsible water bowls, a comb, a collar and a leash, dog food, plastic bags for feces, a dog pack, flea/tick powder, paw protection, water, and a first-aid kit that contains eye ointment, tweezers, scissors, stretchy foot wrap, gauze, antibacterial wash, sterile cotton tip applicators, antibiotic ointment, and cotton wrap.

First aid for your dog. Your dog is just as prone—if not more prone—to getting in trouble on the trail as you are, so be prepared. Here's a rundown of the more likely misfortunes that might befall your little friend.

Bees and wasps. If a bee or wasp stings your dog, remove the stinger with a pair of tweezers and place a mudpack or a cloth dipped in cold water over the affected area.

Porcupines. One good reason to keep your dog on a leash is to prevent him from getting a nose full of porcupine quills. You may be able to remove the quills with pliers, but a veterinarian is the best person to do this nasty job because most dogs need to be sedated.

Heatstroke. Avoid hiking with your dog in really hot weather. Dogs with heatstroke will pant excessively, lie down and refuse to get up, and become lethargic and disoriented. If your dog shows any of these signs on the trail, have him lie down in the shade. If you are near a stream, pour cool water over your dog's entire body to help bring his body temperature back to normal.

Heartworm. Dogs get heartworms from mosquitoes, which carry the disease in the prime mosquito months of July and August. Giving your dog a monthly pill prescribed by your veterinarian easily prevents this condition.

Plant pitfalls. One of the biggest plant hazards for dogs on the trail are foxtails. Foxtails are pointed grass seed heads that bury themselves in your friend's fur, between his toes, and even in his ear canal. If left unattended, these nasty seeds can work their way under the skin and cause abscesses and other problems. If you have a long-haired dog, consider trimming the hair between his toes and giving him a summer haircut to help prevent foxtails from attaching to his fur. After every hike always look your dog over for these seeds—especially between his toes and in his ears.

Other plant hazards include burrs, thorns, thistles, and poison oak. If you find any burrs or thistles on your dog, remove them as soon as possible before they become an unmanageable mat. Thorns can pierce a dog's foot and cause a great deal of pain. If you see that your dog is lame, stop and check his feet for thorns. Dogs are immune to poison oak, but they can pick up the sticky, oily substance from the plant and transfer it to you.

Protect those paws. Be sure to keep your dog's nails trimmed so he avoids getting soft-tissue or joint injuries. If your dog slows and refuses to go on, check to see that his paws aren't torn or worn. You can protect your dog's paws from trail hazards such as sharp gravel, foxtails, lava scree, and thorns by purchasing dog boots.

Sunburn. If your dog has light skin, he is an easy target for sunburn on his nose and other exposed skin areas. You can apply a nontoxic sunscreen to exposed skin areas that will help protect him from overexposure to the sun.

Ticks and fleas. Ticks can easily give your dog Lyme disease as well as other diseases. Before you hit the trail, treat your dog with a flea and tick spray or powder. You can also ask your veterinarian about a once-a-month pour-on treatment that repels fleas and ticks.

Fairfax bridge (hike 39)

Mosquitoes and deer flies. These little flying machines can do a job on your dog's snout and ears. Best bet is to spray your dog with fly repellent for horses to discourage both pests.

Giardia. Dogs can get giardia, which results in diarrhea. It is usually not debilitating, but it's definitely messy. A vaccine against giardia is available.

Mushrooms. Make sure your dog doesn't sample mushrooms along the trail. They could be poisonous to him, but he doesn't know that.

When you are finally ready to hit the trail with your dog, keep in mind that national parks and many wilderness areas do not allow dogs on trails. Your best bet is to hike in national forests, BLM lands, and state parks. Always call ahead to see what the restrictions are.

Clubs and Trail Groups

The Mountaineers
7700 Sand Point Way NE
Seattle, WA 98115
(206) 521-6000
Fax: (206) 523-6763
info@mountaineers.org
mountaineers.org
Founded in 1906, the Mountaineers have been exploring Washington's outdoors for more than one hundred years. Local chapters of the organization offer opportunities to take classes, join group hikes, and volunteer.

Washington Trails Association
705 2nd Ave., Suite 300
Seattle, WA 98104
(206) 625-1367
wta.org
The Washington Trails Association has been promoting and supporting hiking in Washington since 1966 through advocacy, education, and volunteer activities. A large community utilizes their website to post trip reports that often give a good impression of current trail conditions.

Index

About the Authors

Born and raised in the Pacific Northwest, the Barnes brothers' enthusiasm for the outdoors was cultivated at a young age by trips to the Columbia River Gorge, Bend, Mount Rainier, Mount St. Helens, and countless hikes though the region's forests. A few years after college, they needed a new challenge and decided to tackle Mount Rainier. After months of training they reached their goal and attained Columbia Crest on September 7, 2008.

In the weeks that followed, Nathan and Jeremy resolved to keep up their training regimen of weekly hikes to stay in shape. Before long, they decided it would be fun to track their progress, and hikingwithmybrother.com was born. Nathan researches the background on their hikes and writes most of the content, while Jeremy takes almost all of the photographs, creates the maps, and manages most of the technical aspects of the website.

Jeremy and Nathan have learned a lot about how to present their hikes over the years. Their reviews focus on recommending hikes *they* like, detailing the pitfalls, capturing the essence of each hike in pictures, and striving to give a little extra background to the hikes they do.

Authors: Jeremy on the left, Nathan on the right

Long ago they moved beyond the confines of Snoqualmie Pass, and they continue to add more hikes to the website from around the state. The Barneses hope to continue to broaden their coverage across the state in years to come.

Along the way Nathan and Jeremy have met a lot of hikers and outdoors lovers, as well as partnered with *Backpacker Magazine,* the *Seattle Times,* Washington State Parks, and the Washington Trails Association. Today they continue to hike almost every week, but they no longer do it simply for the exercise. They also do it for everyone who follows hikingwithmybrother.com and enjoys up-to-date trail reports, out-of-the-way destinations, and adventuresome hikes.

Feel free to drop them a line at hikingwithmybrother@gmail.com.

◀ *Kyes Peak above the trail (hike 19)*

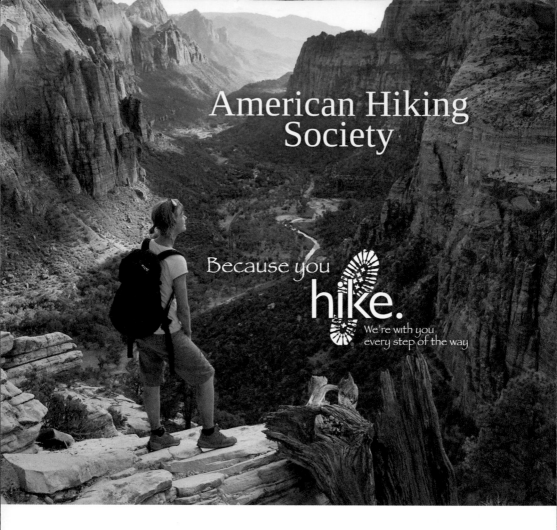

American Hiking Society

Because you **hike.**
We're with you every step of the way

As a national voice for hikers, **American Hiking Society** works every day:

- Building and maintaining hiking trails
- Educating and supporting hikers by providing information and resources
- Supporting hiking and trail organizations nationwide
- Speaking for hikers in the halls of Congress and with federal land managers

Whether you're a casual hiker or a seasoned backpacker, become a member of American Hiking Society and join the national hiking community! You'll enjoy great member benefits and help preserve the nation's hiking trails, so tomorrow's hike is even better than today's. We invite you to join us now!

American Hiking Society

www.AmericanHiking.org • info@AmericanHiking.org